Children as
Consumers

Children as Consumers

Insights and Implications

James U. McNeal
Texas A&M University

87

Lexington Books
D.C. Heath and Company/Lexington, Massachusetts/Toronto

Library of Congress Cataloging-in-Publication Data

McNeal, James U.
    Children as consumers.

    Includes index.
    1. Youth as consumers.   2. Television advertising and children.   I. Title.
HC79.C6M39 1987   658.8'348'   86-45052
ISBN 0-669-13087-7 (alk. paper)

Published simultaneously in Canada
Printed in the United States of America
International Standard Book Number: 0-669-13087-7
Library of Congress Catalog Card Number: 86-45052

The paper used in this publication meets the minimum requirements of American National Standard for Information Sciences—Permanence of Paper for Printed Library Materials, ANSI Z39.48-1984.
  ⊚ ™

88 89 90 8 7 6 5 4 3

To Chad
A marketer's prize
A father's treasure

Contents

Figures

Tables

Preface

T here is presently no book or monograph available that describes the many research findings about the child as a consumer or discusses the issues and concepts in this area. The nearest approximation is the 1977 work by Ward, Wackman and Wartella in which they primarily describe their own work. Yet many different audiences have a strong interest in the subject. Academicians in the fields of consumer behavior, consumer affairs, consumer education, psychology, sociology, and marketing certainly have demonstrated a concern for the topic of children as consumers by their research and publications in the area. Likewise, a wide range of practitioners are involved seriously in the consumer behavior of children; these include manufacturers of products for children, marketing researchers, advertisers, retailers, package designers, broadcast and print journalists, consumer affairs officials, and various individuals in government. This book is intended to serve all these audiences by organizing a variety of research and thought on the consumer behavior of children and presenting it in an easy-to-read fashion.

The topic of children as consumers is both easy and difficult to write about. It is easy because children are a delight to study; they can be hard to manage in a research setting, perhaps, but they are so refreshing. They are remarkably innocent even in their fantasies and exaggerations. They are difficult to write about, however, at least from a consumer behavior perspective, because analyzing something pure is such a contradiction. Writing about the consumer behavior of any market conjures up such notions as profit, sales, and share of the market—concepts that usually are not considered in the same breath with little children. When I published my second major paper on the consumer behavior of children in 1969, I actually received some hate mail. Several people, including a marketing professor's wife, were upset with the idea of children being termed a market. This feeling to some extent is still around; I harbor it myself, to an even greater degree than I did in the 1960s. Nonetheless, reality says that children are consumers. They make up a market or a portion of a market for a variety of goods and services. Many manufacturers and retailers court them, and parents generally encourage them to be consumers at as early an age as possible. I accept these facts, but I report them with gentleness, even with some caution, much as I would if I were writing of rare gems.

I have been speaking and writing about children as consumers since 1964, the year I completed my doctoral dissertation on the topic. I found myself exploring the topic of penny-candy purchasers in 1962 in a retailing course I took from Dr. Aaron Chute. The subject truly intrigued me, so I decided to pursue it as a dissertation topic. Here was a chance to study consumers in embryonic form. Hardly anyone had written about the topic at the time; there were only some minor notes and research on children's allowances and money matters in home economics journals. It was difficult to get my dissertation topic approved, but Dr. Tom Tucker finally accepted the responsibility and eventually became as wrapped up in the topic as I was. The dissertation was published in 1964 by the University of Texas; years later it was reported to have had the largest sale among the Bureau of Business Research publications. Thus, it was a topic whose time had come.

Many people have now written about children's consumer behavior. The reference list at the end of this book attempts to enumerate most of these publications. An examination of the list, however, will show that only a handful of people have written on the subject frequently. The references will also indicate that research in the field has generally been unorganized and sporadic. Probably one-half of the research has been on one topic, that of advertising in relationship to children. Reasons for this are discussed in the chapter on this topic. Needless to say, this lopsided research approach has produced a lot of good information on this topic, but it has advanced the general topic very little. It is hoped that this book will give some balance and organization to the entirety of this important subject.

I wish to acknowledge the extensive assistance provided to me in the research and development of this project by Nanette (Julliard) Jamieson, Louise Maynard, and Sally Suh. These three very special individuals made the impossible look normal, and I greatly appreciate them.

Part I
Confirming Children as a Market

1
An Overview

A recent cartoon in the *New Yorker* shows two business tycoons leaning back in their overstuffed chairs, cigars in their mouths, and one saying to the other: "Kids today don't care about anything except money— thank God." This book reflects that sentiment to some extent because it is about kids spending money as consumers while being pushed by their parents and pulled by marketers. The child as a consumer is a relatively new phenomenon that is receiving much attention from the business community. Just consider the following recent remarks by marketers about children consumers.

"The children's market has come of age. Offspring of the 25- to 39-year-old baby boomers have captured the attention of the advertising world because of their numbers and influence on the purchasing power of the family." (*Marketing News*, January 3, 1986)

"Manufacturers, retailers and observers of the children's market all agree that children in 1985 are far more sophisticated and demanding than children were in 1975 or even 1980. In fact, retailing to children is becoming more and more stratified, paralleling recent trends in adult retailing." (*Advertising Age*, February 14, 1985)

"Bowling believes its competition for youngsters lies not only in the traditional sports but also with the relatively new health and fitness club boom and with such endeavors as eating out at Mac's. . . . So the National Bowling Council . . . is striking out with a $3 million network TV campaign [to 7-12 year-olds]. (*Advertising Age*, March 11, 1985)

"Video cassettes may increasingly become part of youngsters' playing environment. . . . Matchbox has video gift sets for its Robotech line. . . . Girls can buy a Robotech girl fashion doll and a 60-minute video on its life history; boys can get a video of two half-hour, off-TV episodes and a fighter spacecraft." (*Advertising Age*, February 10, 1986)

"Pre-teens now have a full-time radio network dedicated to their educational and entertainment needs . . . Children's Radio Network. . . . So far, advertising support has been enthusiastic . . . including discount department stores, learning centers and banks. . . . (*Advertising Age*, April 12, 1985)

"For the second year in a row, kidvid shapes up as the hottest syndication trend after game shows. . . . Specials, films, and toy line tie-ins have become the key to finding space on tv stations' competitive kidvid program schedules." (*Advertising Age*, January 16, 1986)

"Kids know what they like. And they aren't shy about telling their parents. Plus they have their own income or allowance to spend. Every day, in every part of the country, kids are a major buying force." (from an advertisement by Marvel Comics Group in *Advertising Age* to potential advertisers, August 1, 1983)

There was a time—in fact, only 30 or 40 years ago—when children were not spoken of as spenders or consumers or customers but as savers and future consumers. Sure, they bought penny candy and an occasional soft drink, but retailers did not think of them as customers per se. They were more often perceived as "a customer's kids" or "Mrs. Bohuslov's kids" who just happened to buy something while they were in the store. Children had money, but it was for saving, not spending. They were always saving up for something, according to them, but they actually never seemed to buy very much. They would, for example, save up for a football or bicycle, or even a college education, but usually these items and almost anything else they saved up for were bought by their parents or perhaps their grandparents.

Children received allowances then perhaps as frequently as they do today. Their allowances were relatively smaller, however, and parents usually dictated the amount or percent that could be spent—and this also was often small. Parents would justify this strict guidance with such sayings as, "A penny saved is a penny earned" and "Save for a rainy day." They used to say that a lot.

The youngest population segment that was of concern to retailers was the teens. Accounting for teen's expenditures by marketers did not begin to take place seriously until the late 1950s. In fact, in-depth analysis of the consumer behavior of teens was not forthcoming until the early 1960s. In general, teens were viewed as tomorrow's consumers, whereas kids were characterized only as future consumers.

All that changed with a phenomenon that we still talk about and write about, the baby boom. The number of children under age five in the United States just prior to World War II was actually less than it was shortly after the turn of the century (10,541,000 compared to 10,631,000). When World War II ended, however, families started having babies as if they were making up for all the lost war years. By 1950 the under-five population was 16,163,000—an unheard of 60 percent increase in ten years! As these baby boomers reached ages five to twelve their small amount of spending became very noticeable because of their substantially increased number. Moreover, these were prosperous years, and the amount that each child spent also increased; we do not know by how much because no one kept track. It was not considered important.

Today it is. Today, children are viewed as a viable market by many manufacturers and retailers. Saturday morning television with its $100 million of child-focused advertising is a moving monument to this new market.

Saying that children constitute a market requires some clarification. This is one of the purposes of this overview. Marketers react to children as not one market but three, although any particular marketer at a particular time may perceive them as one or more of these markets. The three markets, in brief, are as follows.

Current Market. Children are seen by many producers and retailers as a ready market for a variety of goods and services. In this sense children are viewed as having needs, having money to spend on items that satisfy their needs, and having a willingness to spend money. Producers of candy, gum, frozen desserts, soft drinks, toys, comic books, records, and cassettes are good examples of entire industries that treat children as a current market. At the retail level, such outlets as video game parlors, movie houses, and convenience stores also treat children as a ready market. Chapter 3 will justify children as a current market.

Future Market. It should be obvious to all except the most myopic marketers that today's children are tomorrow's customers. Therefore, many manufacturers and retailers respond to children as future consumers who are to be cultivated now. After all, most businesses are in business for the long haul. They have to plan for their markets five, ten, even twenty years from now. It is logical, then, for many of them to practice "growing" customers. Thus, in addition to viewing children as current consumers, soft drink and candy bar producers, for example, may be equally interested in children as future consumers among whom brand awareness and preferences can be created now so that they will be consumers of these products when they become teenagers and adults. As another example of the marketers who have an eye on children as a future market, some department stores have special promotional programs for children—a sci-fi Saturday, for example—in order to get youngsters accustomed to the store's environment so that they will seek them when they start buying their own clothes.

Influential Market. Children are commonly considered by many marketers to have substantial influence on the purchases of their parents. These marketers, to oversimplify, believe that informing children of their offerings and persuading them that they are desirable will lead the children to pressure their parents to purchase the offerings. Probably best known of these marketers are cereal firms that intensively advertise to children on Saturday morning television and directly or indirectly encourage the children to persuade their parents to buy certain brands of cereal. In the spring of 1986, General Mills introduced a new presweetened cereal to children as an influential market via television advertising. "General Mills promised grocery store buyers that 95% of all children ages 2 through 11 will see the Circus Fun TV spot an average of 107 times during the cereal's first year" (Franz, 1986, p. 104). Some supermarkets, department stores, and specialty stores attempt in various ways to win favor with children so that the children will influence their parents toward these stores and their offerings. Of the three types of markets—current, future, and influential—children as influentials are probably researched most and talked about most in the popular press.

This book recognizes and discusses children as all three of these market segments but attempts to focus primarily on one of them—*children as current consumers*. Within these pages we will describe, discuss, and debate the concept and practicality of children as a current market for goods and services. We will prove the market viability of this market segment through descriptions of children's income and expenditures, through profiles of their ongoing consumer behavior patterns, and through first-hand reports of marketing efforts aimed at them for the purpose of stimulating actual purchase. Finally, we will discuss how children respond to a variety of marketing efforts.

Casting children as customers is not done without recognizing that there are many moral questions concerning this position. Almost an entire chapter is devoted to a discussion of these issues, and they are also discussed at appropriate times throughout the book. There are major groups of consumer advocates or protectionists who devote most of their resources and energies to this matter. We will give consideration to their viewpoints. Because children are the ultimate in innocence in our society, studying them and treating them as objects of profit is, at least, a very serious matter, and we will dwell specifically on this issue, particularly as it pertains to conducting research among children.

As the discussion of children as bona fide consumers unfolds in this book, questions about their similarities and differences in terms of adults will surely arise. If children are in fact a market for various goods and services, does this mean we should consider them as adults to a greater extent than we do? Alternatively, from the standpoint of the consumer role, are children mini-consumers? Should we use a child model or an adult model to explain their consumer behavior?

The answers to these questions are difficult for two reasons: (1) there are no consumer behavior models of children per se to guide analysis of children as consumers; and (2) analysis of the consumer behavior of children on a child-to-adult scale tends to produce varying results depending on the assessor's background as parent, consumer advocate, or marketer. For example, consider the analysis of children's consumer behavior on the three dimensions of mobility, motivation, and mentality.

Mobility. It is a fact that children can not get around as well as adults; neither do they have the adult's knowledge of where to go in order to obtain various products and services. As consumers, children are limited mainly to nearby stores, often convenience stores, that are within walking or bicycling distance of home. For more complex shopping trips, children usually must rely on parents for mobility. Consequently, children often must shop at stores and shopping centers chosen by parents. Once inside the stores and shopping centers, children usually find it more difficult than adults to locate departments, goods, salespeople, and checkout counters, often having to traverse the same path twice and often having to obtain directions. Moreover, complex shopping areas such as multifloor department stores and superstores with hundreds of fixtures each twice the height of the average child are often intimidating. Finally, reaching up to many of these fixtures is often difficult or impossible. Most store fixtures were not designed with children in mind, although there are some changes taking place. Today, there are more fixtures appearing at children's eye level, including shelving and single-purpose shelving.

In spite of children's limited mobility, it appears in general that parents want their children to have easy and continuing access to marketplace facilities. Retailers, on the other hand, have mixed reactions; some are very responsive to youngsters, while others discourage them. Consumer advocates would probably defend the children's ready access to stores as sources of information to be used in the children's consumer socialization process, but would be doubtful about their ability to function in the shopping setting.

Motivation. The reasons why children want certain products and services and not others and want to shop and buy in some stores and not others are theoretically the same as those of adults: to satisfy needs. However, for some reason it simply does not sound right to say that children have unsatisfied needs, and the same needs as adults, even though motivational theorists tell us this is so. Marketing researchers nonetheless seem to have no trouble recognizing the desire among children for need expression through consumer behavior and providing advertisers with appropriate information about children's needs. Consequently, a McDonald's advertisement, to illustrate, may suggest that children can satisfy their needs for affiliation, nutrition, and play by eating at a McDonald's restaurant. Many parents, on the other hand, seem to view children's consumer wants as being practically nonexistent if it were not for such ads. Advertising, according to many parents, teaches children materialism, which is to want things for the sake of having them, not because they satisfy a variety of needs. Consumer protectionists, who are usually parents themselves, also tend to fault marketing for creating wants among children. While they speak of materialism, they more often protest about children wanting things they don't need as a result of perceived heavy-handed efforts by marketers, mainly through advertising.

Mentality. There are many questions about the child's ability to process, organize, and store information and to assign appropriate meaning to information emanating from the marketplace. These questions arise about children's abilities as compared to adults. Answers to the questions vary considerably depending upon the respondent and the kind of information that is the focus of the questions, but also because we simply do not yet know much about the cognitive processes of children. Cognitive state theorists suggest that what children can do with information is a function of their cognitive structures at a certain time in their development. These developmental stages, which are roughly equivalent to age levels, suggest that the older a child gets the more he can do in terms of information processing. Another group of theorists would argue with the term *more*; they would say that as time passes not only the *quantity* of processing ability but also the *quality* or style changes. In simple terms, they would say that kids are not just mini-adults when it comes to consumer behavior, but that they differ from adults in the way they think. Parents and consumer advocates alike argue against using an adult model to explain children's consumer behavior. Many marketers, however, probably do not see the difference, particularly after age seven or eight.

Since this book is not intended to explore substantial new areas of thought regarding the consumer behavior of children, but mainly to summarize existing thoughts and findings and draw conclusions, resolution to the above issues will not be attempted. The book does contain a number of new findings as well as most of the notable past findings about the consumer behavior of children, but it does not develop theories or select one as being most appropriate for describing and discussing the various data. However, neither is the book intended to be a totally unbiased account of children's consumer behavior. The various current viewpoints about the findings are discussed, and a position is taken on practical as opposed to theoretical matters. The book also attempts some answers to persistent questions about children as consumers and marketers' responses to them.

This book is organized into three parts. Part I consists of three chapters. Chapter 1 gives an overview of the subject matter and the book. Chapter 2 discusses children's learning of consumer behavior. This slightly theoretical treatment is an "in the beginning" description. It discusses how children become consumers, the environmental inputs to this socialization, and other socialization issues. Chapter 3 uses new data to establish children as consumers by describing their income, expenditures, and objects of expenditures. Thus, it is more of an economic view of children.

Part II covers the interaction of children with marketing. Chapter 4 describes the interaction of children with stores using new, unpublished findings. It is at the retail store that children and business come face to face to consummate the exchange of goods and services for money. Chapter 5 discusses research and theorization about advertising in relation to children. Emphasis is on television advertising and its impact. In Chapter 6, the topic of products that children buy is discussed, along with the concepts of brand and price. Here we see the dearness of money in children's pockets competing with the desirability of products on retailers' shelves. The last chapter of this section, Chapter 7, treats the topic of packaging and premiums. Metaphorically speaking, the only thing that stands between children and the products they want is the package. As we will see, it sometimes stands between them impervious to the children's efforts to remove it.

Part III treats very important issues about the consumer behavior of children. Chapter 8 discusses the research of children in the consumer role. Focus is principally on problems. Educating the child in the consumer role is the topic of Chapter 9; both a historical and descriptive examination is presented. Chapter 10 covers the ethical issues involved in viewing children as consumers. In this chapter, some business behaviors are examined closely.

Because it is hoped that the book will encourage more research into this exciting subject, an effort has been made to provide the most extensive references available about children as consumers. Although this is a rather exhaustive bibliography on the topic of consumer behavior of children, it is selective on such topics as consumer education and money management.

A final note about the character of the book is necessary. It is not an attempt to act in judgement of the research efforts in the field. It does not get wrapped up in sample sizes, tests of significance, and methodology in general. Neither does it attempt to describe all studies in the topical area regardless of their quality. The research in the field of children's consumer behavior is overwhelmingly biased toward advertising and its relationship to children; there is little information in other equally important areas. The book attempts a balanced approach to the topic, however. It opts for broad coverage of all aspects of children as consumers rather than focusing chiefly on advertising. Additionally, it treats these various topics from not one but from several points of view.

In sum, this book is about the consumer behavior of children with a primary focus on children as a current market for goods and services. Whether as a current market, a future market, or a market of influentials, children encounter all kinds of marketing stimuli; this book will document their reactions to them. Within the discussions of these major topics, and with some attempt at balance, the viewpoints of five concerned parties will be observed—those of marketers, parents, consumer advocates, public policy makers, and, most important, children.

2
Learning To Be Consumers

At-school interviews among third-grade and fourth-grade students were conducted by a university professor to ascertain the extent to which children participate in the consumer role. Following is part of an interview with Chad, a third grader who has an income of approximately $30 per month in the form of an allowance and earnings from odd jobs.

INTERVIEWER: Approximately how much of your own money do you spend each week?

CHAD: I'd say around $5.00.

INTERVIEWER: What do you mainly spend it on?

CHAD: Anything I want to. Lots of things.

INTERVIEWER: Do you buy clothes?

CHAD: No, my mom picks those out. I bought these Adidas.

INTERVIEWER: Really? Tell me about that.

CHAD: They're Adidas. I saved my money and bought 'em at the Sport Shop in Culpepper Plaza. They cost $22.95.

INTERVIEWER: That sounds like a high price.

CHAD: It's not. They were on sale. They usually would cost you $30.00.

INTERVIEWER: That's what I pay for my shoes. That's quite a bit of money.

CHAD: Boy's shoes and men's shoes cost the same, I think.

INTERVIEWER: I guess they do. Tell me what else you spend your money on.

CHAD: I buy a lot of things at the 7-11.

INTERVIEWER: What, for example?

CHAD: Candy, Cokes, a lot of things. I bought a kite there.

INTERVIEWER: You bought a kite?

CHAD: Yeah, they're the only ones that have Humming Birds.

INTERVIEWER: I didn't know that.

CHAD: Well, it's true. Just about everybody I know bought one there.

INTERVIEWER: Do you save your money?

CHAD: All that I don't spend.

A close examination of Chad's comments reveals the following facts: He spends money of his own ("I'd say around $5.00."), for many items just for himself ("Anything I want to. Lots of things."), and he also saves some of his money for future purchases ("I saved my money and bought 'em at the Sport Shop in Culpepper Plaza."). He has brand knowledge (Adidas, Humming Birds), store knowledge (Sport Shop, 7-11), even some brand preference (". . . they're the only one that have Humming Birds."). He has price knowledge ("They cost $22.95."), he is bargain conscious ("They were on sale. They usually would cost you $30.00."), and he even makes price comparisons ("Boy's shoes and men's shoes cost the same, I think.") He is aware of consumer role responsibility ("No, my mom picks those out.") and of other consumers like him ("Just about everybody I know bought one there."). From about any point of view, then, including an adult's view, Chad is a consumer. He just also happens to be a child.

Chad, and 30 million other children aged four to twelve, can offer ample attestation of their consumership. They can point to all the stores that display goods at their eye level and reach-level, goods that range from nickel jaw breakers at the 7-11 store to designer clothes at Saks. They can describe advertisements in large numbers that shout at them during Saturday morning television, ads such as those for Mattel toys and McDonald's hamburgers. They can even lay claim to a television cable channel just for children—Nicklelodeon. For a clincher, they can boast about having *Penny Power,* their own magazine from Consumer's Union that evaluates products for children much as *Consumer Reports* does for adults.

That children are consumers is no accident. Parents train and shape them for the consumer role. All twelve years of their schooling are sprinkled with consumer education, which is compulsory in many states. Manufacturers spend millions of dollars on advertising to them—$100 million a year on television alone—pushing and pulling them to the stores to buy thousands of different products made just for them. Many retailers who handle those thousands of products are appropriately prepared to show children how to buy, how to count their money, even how to return the goods if they are defective. Being a child consumer isn't an accident in our society; it's a requirement. All the skills, knowledge, and behavior patterns that together we call consumer behavior are purposely taught to our children right along with toilet training, toddling, and talking.

Consumer Socialization of Children

"The process by which individuals acquire the knowledge, skills and dispositions that enable them to participate as more or less effective members of groups and the society" is termed socialization (Brim, 1966, p. 3). For each role that people perform in a society, there is a socialization process, albeit often ill-defined, that determines what a person does in that role. Thus, there is a generally defined procedure for becoming a consumer. This procedure begins in childhood in our society and continues, to some extent, throughout life.

It should be noted that consumer socialization did not always begin in childhood. A hundred years ago, 75 percent of the population lived in rural areas. Children were perceived by parents as producers, not consumers. Consumer socialization tended not to begin until the teen years and then was given emphasis as marriage approached. With the maturity of industrialization, most families were no longer self-sufficient; their labor was spent for the benefit of others in factories, offices, and stores. Thus, it became necessary to purchase rather than produce for needs; consequently, consumer behavior became a wide spread standard role for everybody. Children had to learn it in order to become effective members of society.

Children learn consumer behavior through observation and participation (that is, incidental learning) and through intentional instruction by socialization agents. Thus, the process of consumer socialization is not a formalized system, because incidental learning is a major part of it. Neither is it random however; there is a considerable amount of intentional instructions involved. Furthermore, the child is not just a passive learner, as he might be in a classroom. He often initiates the socialization process, for example, by helping parents during a shopping trip. Let us look more closely at the consumer socialization process and particularly at the input of socialization agents. Perhaps then we can appreciate the complexity, and often the trauma, of becoming a consumer.

The Consumer Socialization Process

The consumer socialization process through which children learn consumer behavior consists minimally of a socialization agent, a method of learning/teaching, a medium through which learning/teaching takes place, the outcomes of the process, and of course, the child. The process could be pictured like this in the case of intentional instruction;

Socialization Agent → Method of Teaching → Medium for Teaching → Outcomes → Child Consumer

and like this in the case of incidental learning (observation and participation).

Child Consumer → Method of Learning → Medium for Learning → Socialization Agent → Outcomes

The difference in the two models is a function of the method of learning/teaching and the actors. In the intentional instruction model, a socialization agent is purposively teaching the child some aspect of consumer behavior, whereas in the incidental learning model the child initiates the process by observing or participating. Let us give an example of the process of consumer socialization utilizing each of the two models.

In the case of the intentional instruction model, let us assume the *socialization agent* is a third-grade teacher. She chooses two *methods* of teaching, classroom instructions and a field trip. She utilizes the classroom as a *medium* in the case of instructions and utilizes the supermarket as the *medium* for the field trip. In the classroom, the teacher explains why supermarkets carry several brands of most goods and uses cereals, milk, and cookies as examples. She arranges a field trip to a supermarket during which she requires her students to count the number of brands of cereals, milk, and cookies and to write the names of each in their notebooks. The *outcomes* of this may be several: Brand knowledge, choice opportunities in products, knowledge of product offerings in supermarkets, and perhaps the concept of brand preference. Because of this single consumer socialization experience, the child consumer will add to his effectiveness in the performance of the consumer role.

The second model of the consumer socialization process, that of incidental learning, focuses on the learner. As an example, let us assume a ten-year-old asks and receives parental permission to go to a nearby convenience store to buy a soft drink. The *method* of learning is mainly participation. The youngster rides her bicycle to the store, selects a soft drink, pays for it, and returns home. The *medium* of learning is the store, although the package (can or bottle) could be considered an additional medium. The *socialization agent* is the retailer, who is the person with whom the child interacts in the store. The *outcomes* include learning to make the trip to the store and the product selection and payment process. Additionally, the youngster learns store layout, location of products in the store, and perhaps forms some attitudes about the store or its personnel.

Both of these examples are oversimplified in order to explain the models of socialization. In the case of the field trip to the supermarket, for example, the supermarket personnel who escorted the children were additional socialization agents. Also, the children surely experienced incidental learning through both observation and participation while in the store. In the incidental learning model, there could have been intentional instructions on the part of the store person, and surely the learning method of observation was also present.

The fact is that the consumer socialization process is very complex, and we still know relatively little about it. In order to shed more light on this process, let us consider it from the standpoint of various socialization agents.

Parents as Consumer Socialization Agents

Parents are what sociologists call primary agents of socialization (Berger and Berger, 1976) and are surely the most important agents involved in the consumer socialization of children. By age four or five, when consumer behavior begins to have some significance for children, the parents are already established as the most important influences in the lives of their youngsters (McNeal, 1964). By this time, parents have taught children how to satisfy their viscerogenic and psychogenic needs and have established themselves as the children's primary source of need satisfiers. Thus it is logical that children look to their parents for guidance in their quest for familiarization with the marketplace and its elements.

It is the parents, while the children are still in their arms, who introduce their children to the retail store, the store personnel, the shelves of products, and the procedures of shopping and buying. It is the parents who initiate the youngster in the use of money by permitting the children to give money to the "store man" and put coins in vending machines. It is the parents who encourage the youngster to make his earthshaking solo shopping effort to the nearby convenience store.

As consumer trainees of their parents, children have numerous observational opportunities. At their vantage point high in the seat of a shopping cart, they can see their parents intensely choosing between what appear to be two similar heads of lettuce, giving the squeeze test to a loaf of bread, and scrutinizing from all angles a package of bacon. The children, at this point in their consumer training, may not know why parents do these things, but, based on incidental learning theory such as that by Albert Bandura (1962), it is likely that the children will be reproducing precisely these behaviors a few years later in life.

During the child's consumer training period, parents permit various degrees of participation in the consumer role. Parents may solicit the advice of the children about what to buy for a meal, may permit the children to choose between two brands of peanut butter, and may send them to the cereal aisle to select a box of cereal independently. While in a store, parents can take advantage of the opportunity to show their children the subtle differences in brands of luncheon meats, the different expiration dates on perishable goods such as canned biscuits, and other tricks in the art of consumership. To what extent these teachable moments are utilized by parents for the consumer socialization of their children is not known, but the various types of stores do provide a convenient laboratory for actual training exercises in consumer behavior for children.

In addition to the marketplace, and probably more credible, the home environment is another training ground for children's consumer behavior.

"Within the family environment, children have the opportunity to learn both effective and ineffective consumer behaviors by observing their parents' consumer practices, (and) by interacting with their parents about products and other consumption activities . . ." (Ward, Wackman, and Wartella, 1977A, p. 143). Within the home, parents talk with children about products for the home and products specifically for children. These discussions provide the children with some evaluative criteria that they may store and use later for product choices of their own, such as toys, snacks, and clothing. Children and parents talk about television advertisements, and again evaluative criteria are provided that help the children decide about the honesty and intent of the ads. Children also have the opportunity to see parents using products in the home and hear them verbally judging the products. There is opportunity to overhear conversations between mother and father about consumer purchases or even to participate in the decision-making process (Davis, 1976).

Perhaps a word of warning is in order here. We do not want to imply that parents in general are conscientiously training children in all the activities and nuances of consumer behavior. We simply do not have the research evidence to say this. One study related to this topic indicates that parents are seriously involved in the consumer training of their children (McNeal, 1964), while another group of researchers report being "struck by mother's lack of attention to socialization" (Ward, Wackman, and Wartella, 1977A). It is probably true, as Professors Grossbart and Crosby (1984) suggest, that parental influence is mediated by parental concern and involvement.

We know that the spare bedroom is rarely turned into a classroom for teaching marketplace behavior, or medicine, or marriage. We know that the children are not graded on the bargains they bring home or the money they save by comparison shopping, and we know that there are not pop quizzes on Saturday morning television advertisements. However, as former children and present parents, we know that successful consumer behavior on the part of our children is a major concern long before we become concerned with teaching children about sexual matters or getting their first job. Of course, parents expect their children to pick up some aspects of consumer behavior simply by observing the parents' consuming activities (Ward, Wackman and Wartella, 1977). Perhaps consumer behavior so permeates our lives that it masks the real concern of parents for the consumership of their children and makes much organized teaching of it unnecessary. As a leading sociologist observed in the 1950s, "Today there is no fast line that separates the consumption patterns of the adult world from those of the child except the consumption objects themselves" (Riesman, Glazer and Denney, 1953, p. 118). Overall, our intuition and some research suggest that parents are teaching their children a great deal of consumer behavior; in fact, we might worry that parents who are ineffective consumers also are teaching their children ineffective consumer behavior (Ward, 1974).

Peers as Consumer Socialization Agents

Every parent who has ever reared children is aware of the enormity of peer influence. It seems to begin in early elementary school and increases each year; by adolescence this influence often appears greater than that of parents. Research confirms this trend (Ward, 1974).

The influence of peers seemingly pervades all aspects of children's consumer behavior. Peer influence on consumer behavior has been noted among five-year-olds in the case of choosing flavors of soft drinks and types of candy (McNeal, 1964). The effect of peers on seven-year-old consumers has also been recorded in regard to the selection of clothing and games (McNeal, 1964). Among nine-year-olds, peer influence was also strong, even extending into children's desires for automobiles (McNeal, 1964). Caron and Ward (1975) found peer influence among third graders to be stronger than the influence of advertising, retailing, and catalogs in the gift requests of children to Santa Claus. Contrary to most findings, however, these researchers found relative peer influence to decline among older children. In an interesting experiment, Hawkins and Coney (1974) found that it was peer influence that determined the selection of cookies by children when there was little to distinguish the cookies except color of wrapper.

Peer influence among children, like parental influence, is to be expected. Since the turn of the century, theorists such as Veblen (1899) have focused on the influence of others on consumer behavior. By the 1950s, theorists were speaking of an "other-directed" generation (Riesman, Glazer and Denney, 1953). Explanations for the influence of others on consumer behavior are numerous but can be summarized under two headings: conformity and satisfaction of needs. In the case of conformity, children are expected to conform to group norms; perhaps more important, children normally want to fit in with a group, usually their age group, in order to gain acceptance. It is apparently easier to fit in when you wear the same brand of running shoes, have the same symbols on your shirt, and wear your hair the same way. Child development experts show that by age nine or ten the child is "detaching himself from apron strings" and is intensifying his group feelings (Gesell and Ilg 1954, p. 15). To firmly weld himself to groups, which will confirm independence from the family, conformity is necessary, and conspicuous products such as clothing conveniently permit this conformity.

Peer influence is not one-way, passive behavior. That is, peers do not as a rule command that their friends consume certain products in a certain manner. Rather, a child accepts the influence of other children in order to satisfy a variety of needs. It has been suggested that the following needs can be satisfied by accepting the influence of others (McNeal, 1982).

1. Need to understand. By accepting directions from others, a child can gain an understanding of certain products and certain aspects of his environment.

For example, children often play doctor and through such games learn what others know about medicine, about body functions, and about various products. For example, a Milton-Bradley game, that is simply called Operation is designed to be played by a group and potentially teaches children about body parts and about the concept of performing a medical operation while encouraging a good deal of fun.

2. Need for affiliation. In order to have good relationships with others, there must be some give-and-take. By accepting the influence of others, children obtain cooperative relationships with others that in turn permit development of independence from the family. For example, children who wear T-shirts with the same messages on them may further their fraternity. Trading comic books, baseball cards, and video games also promotes affiliation.

3. Need for infavoidance. Henry Murray (1938), the famous psychologist, coined the term *infavoidance* to refer to the need to avoid humiliation and embarrassment. Children are embarrassed frequently because their limited knowledge causes them to make mistakes. Their peers can help them to prevent these mistakes through recommendations or even subtle signals about consumer behavior. Peers, for example, can confirm what clothing is in fashion, what brand of shoes is the most popular, and what stores have the best prices on certain items.

4. Need for achievement. Children in our society are usually encouraged to achieve—to achieve recognition, win awards, make high grades, gain friends. Their friends can help them by recommending various products that help obtain certain achievements and by suggesting products for those that have achieved. For instance, a youngster may find, if he inquires, that Nikes' help him run faster, an Apple computer helps him make higher grades, and Michael Jackson tapes and records help him obtain friends. If this youngster is successful, he may find he can demonstrate it by wearing Izod shirts.

In general, the consumer socialization effects of peers on children are probably not intentional but incidental. Children usually learn consumer behavior from friends as a result of observing them—seeing and hearing them—and by participating in the consumption process with them. Although peer influence is received mainly through incidental learning methods, the results appear no less dramatic than the intentional teaching of parents. In fact, in regard to influencing children's consumer behavior, one consumer socialization authority concluded that "parents become less important as children enter adolescence, and peers become more important" (Ward, 1974, p. 9). Precisely at what age peer influence on consumer behavior becomes more important than parental influence is not known, but its significance is apparent as early as ages five or six (McNeal, 1964).

There is an important caveat that should be made about the actual impact of any group of socialization agents such as peers on the consumer behavior of children. The results of this influence usually cannot be delineated. That is, it is practically impossible to examine the consumer behavior repertoire of a child and declare that a particular set of behaviors, skills, attitudes, or knowledge is the result of the influence of a particular set of agents. Even where we can comfortably say that Johnny learned a certain consumer behavior in school from Ms. Jablonski, his third-grade teacher, its real impact, in terms of Johnny's use of that behavior, is unlikely to be known. There are numerous scientific reasons for this, but most of them are related to the mysteries of the mind. When a child makes a consumer decision, the mental operations that may go into it can be awesomely complex. Usually, the operations are at both conscious and subconscious levels; consequently, even the child does not know all the aspects of his decision (Tucker, 1964). It is unlikely, then, that he can verbalize who specifically influenced his decision and to what extent. Thus, when a child selects a model airplane as a birthday gift for a friend, he knows that it will be one that excites him, pleases his friend, and is viewed as silly by another, frivolous by his brother, expensive by his dad, and appropriate by his third-grade teacher. To empirically delineate the influence on his decision of each of these people is simply not possible. Yet we know that without their influence Johnny may not make a satisfactory consumer decision.

Teachers as Consumer Socialization Agents

The influence of school teachers on the development of the child cannot be overestimated. Every adult can surely recall one specific elementary school teacher or more who had a major impact on his or her childhood. Perhaps one useful influence consisted of tips on how to spend money wisely. "Economic competence is widely accepted as one of the goals of elementary school education" (Gavian and Nanassy, 1955). Economic competence, or economic literacy as educators often like to term it (Kourilsky, 1977), is a broad term that usually embraces consumer behavior. A narrower term, *consumer education,* is also a popular concept that refers to "the skills and knowledge that enable an individual to utilize available economic and personal resources for the satisfaction of personal wants and needs" (Richardson, 1977). Consumer education as presented in elementary school embraces such topical units as understanding the marketplace, understanding one's motives, and understanding the purchase transaction. One group of consumer education experts lists eleven building blocks with many more subtopics that might make up the contents of consumer education (Stampfl, Moschis, and Lawton, 1978). Teachers who teach such topics to children certainly must be recognized as important agents in the consumer socialization process of children; they are important because of what they teach and important because of their central role in the child's life.

In a few states, such as Florida, consumer education is required by law; in some others, such as Texas, it is encouraged by legislative resolution. As a philosophy, it is encouraged by most adults. Thus, we can be sure that consumer education is, to some degree, taught in all elementary schools. Often the teaching of consumer education is not apparent to an observer. This is due to the lack of classes specifically labelled consumer education. Closer examination, however, will reveal consumer education being taught in such classes as math, reading, and government. Also, it is taught under a number of other titles. In a recent study of consumer education in Texas high schools, for example, it was discovered that consumer education was formally taught under the following titles: Consumer Education, Consumer Economics, Consumer Math, Consumer Problems, Personal Money Management, Home and Family Living, and Distributive Education (McNeal, 1981).

In spite of the large amount of consumer education that is taught to elementary school-age children and in spite of the fact it has been going on for a long time, we do not know much about its specific results. Although consumer education is more formal than that taught by parents or peers, we do not know that it is more or less effective than the consumer behavior taught by other socialization agents. We do not know, either, whether Florida children who are required by law to be taught consumer education are more effective consumers than those educated in states where consumer education is not mandated. Even though we have not formally assessed the effectiveness of school teachers in the consumer socialization of children, however, we would be naive to assume it to be insignificant. As we observed earlier, the elementary school teacher surely has a major impact on the general development of the child. It should not be less obvious that the elementary school teacher who teaches consumer education to children in various ways has major impact on their consumer socialization.

Business as Consumer Socialization Agents

Much of this book is about the relationship of business to children as consumers; therefore, what we say here is only introductory in nature. It is important that we include business as a socialization agent along with parents, peers, and teachers because its role in the development of consumer behavior among children is vital and unique. In fact, if the number of published studies related to a particular consumer socialization agent is an indication of the significance of that agent in the lives of children, then business is definitely number one.

Let us review the significant elements of business that influence the development of consumer behavior patterns and thoughts among children.

Extensive treatments of each of these as well as other influential business elements will be presented in later chapters.

Advertising

The primary vehicle used by manufacturers to influence children's consumer behavior is advertising, especially television advertising. Its potential power over children is attested to by the Federal Trade Commission's attempted ban on television advertising to children during the 1970s (*Advertising Age,* 1978A). Many parents also fear the socialization effects of advertising, principally because the effects may conflict with their own goals and desires for their children (Grossbart and Crosby, 1984).

The potential influence of television advertising on children's consumer behavior patterns is due to its situation and nature. Most of the advertising is presented in the context of children's programming that contains endless fun and happiness. (Noticeably, it is not usually presented to parents during adult-oriented programming, which would permit parents to mediate its influence.) Children's advertisements are then attached to these appealing programs; the advertisements, in turn, contain additional equally exciting and funny circumstances. The advertisements go a step further. They specify exactly how the children can obtain this fun and excitement, which obviously interests the children; in fact, it may hold them spellbound.

There is little question, then, that some advertising is able to persuade children to persuade their parents to buy things. In Quebec and England, this is not the case, because advertising to children is not permitted by law. There is a choice for parents, albeit a difficult choice. If parents permit advertising to entertain their children, they have, in effect, invited a salesperson to be their babysitter. That salesperson will participate in the consumer socialization of the children.

Stores

A very important socialization agent that practically goes unnoticed in the literature is the retailer. In our self-service society, this socialization agent, like advertising, is mainly impersonal. Although research reports overlook this generalized person and his influence is often impersonal, the retailer's influence on children's learning of consumer behavior is potentially great because of his central role in the purchase process. At an early age, perhaps four or five, children begin to recognize that it is the retailer, rather than the parents, who owns the goods and services that give them so much pleasure and satisfaction (McNeal, 1964). From this point on, store visits and interactions take on much more significance to the children. This viewpoint provides opportunities for retailers to influence the children's learning of consumer behavior.

A recent study delineated five general activities practiced by retailers that are intended to influence the consumer behavior of children (McNeal, 1985). All of these activities have potential socialization effects and therefore are examined in some detail in chapter 4.

1. Provide shopping/buying facilitators for children, such as eye-level displays in convenience stores and special credit cards in department stores.
2. Provide consumer education to elementary school classes, such as field trips to a restaurant to see how food is prepared or printed materials that describe how to make the best buy in shoes.
3. Undertake promotion efforts such as advertising on Saturday morning television or window displays oriented to children.
4. Train store personnel to be responsive to children, such as helping youngsters to count their change or checking on their satisfaction with the food served in a restaurant.
5. Cooperate in ethical practices such as removing potentially harmful glues from a store or hiding sexually oriented magazines.

Because it is at the store that children and business come face to face to consummate the exchange of goods and services for money, the chances of the retail store influencing children's consumer behavior is great. Moreover, it is unlikely that parents can mediate this influence to the extent they can that of advertising. Therefore, the retail person and the retail store environment are likely to play a major role in the consumer socialization of children. This role will become even more significant as children spend more money in stores. This point will be discussed more fully in chapter 3.

Products

The focal point of all consumer behavior of children is the product. Consequently, the product is so intermingled with all consumption activities (prepurchase, purchase, and postpurchase) that it is difficult to delineate the product's role in the consumer socialization of children. For example, in a study of children's beliefs, attitudes, and behavior toward medicines, researchers were not "particularly successful in explaining the child's beliefs toward medicines" (Robertson, Rossiter, and Gleason, 1979A, p. 254). That is, did their beliefs result from parents, from advertising, or from experience with medicines? Consider another example. In a case study, the investigator found that the package played a major role in determining the meanings of products among children (McNeal, 1976). There is little doubt about the important role of the package in product's images, but what about the influence of product usage on the meanings of the product? How is this to be separated from the meanings obtained from the package?

The point to be made here is that the product, in terms of its taste, appearance, results, and so on, causes a great amount of consumer learning among children. The children may learn what products are good and bad, what products are expensive, and even that certain products symbolize attributes about people (McNeal, 1964). Some products appear to be designed for the purpose of teaching children consumer behavior. Consider, for example, the game by Milton Bradley called Bargain Hunter. Its package declares in big print that it is "The Smart-Shopping Game with Lots of Fun in Store for You." This game's goal, as stated on the package is, "Be the first player to complete your shopping list and owe nothing on your charge account." Surely such a product teaches some consumer behavior to its users.

It is possible that some reported research that gives so much credit to parental consumer socialization of children may actually discredit the contribution of products. Consider how many opportunities a day a preschool child has to observe the use of hundreds of products by his parents. Actual socialization effects may be a function of the products and their results, at least as much as the responses to the products by the parents.

Besides the intrinsic aspects of the product and the uses of the product, which are determined culturally, there is the product's brand to be accounted for in the product's consumer socialization role. The brand is the marketer's most powerful tool. Through the brand, he imbues the product with many additional meanings beyond those inherent in the product. For example, the child soon learns that beverages are useful for socializing with others, and that children socialize with soft drinks while adults socialize with coffee and alcoholic beverages. In more detail, however, the presence of certain brands in his or her household, the use of certain brands by peers, and the frequent advertising of certain brands confirm that certain brands are for more specific affiliative activities. Just for example, the youngster may soon learn that adults socialize at special times with Lowenbrau beer, whereas summertime backyard socializing by children is facilitated by Kool-Aid.

In sum, the product, along with its brand, package, and other attributes, is deeply involved in the consumer socialization process of children. However, because its influence is intertwined with that of other socialization agents and other activities of business, and because the product is so basic to the consumption process, we may not be fully conscious of the product's important role in children learning to be consumers. The product's impact should become more apparent when it is discussed in greater detail in a later chapter.

Outcomes of the Consumer Socialization Process

The logical outcome of the consumer socialization process is a consumer. There is a tendency, however, for people to associate the term *consumer* with adults, not children. The plain fact of the matter is that there is no precise definition of a consumer that will permit us to conclude from it that some people are consumers and some are not or that children are not consumers until some mystical age. We recognize, however, that it would be ludicrous to refer to a two-year-old as a consumer simply because she has been taught to put a coin in a gumball machine and receive a piece of gum. Likewise, it does not make much sense to classify a child as a consumer just because he has learned to take a box of cereal from the supermarket shelf and drop it in Mommy's shopping cart. An act, per se, does not make a consumer.

We acknowledge that there are some minimum prerequisites to being a consumer. A person must have money, a willingness to spend it, and unsatisfied wants or needs. Most children possess these prerequisites. Beyond these, however, we are not sure what constitutes a bona fide consumer. We do know that being a consumer involves both mental and motor behavior, and when we refer to a child as a consumer we infer both. What we can do is itemize some findings from the first major published study that classified children as consumers. This study was conducted two decades ago. Not only have the study's conclusions about children being consumers never been challenged, but its findings have been utilized widely as a springboard for other studies. In very brief form, table 2-1 lists a set of cognitions (attitudes and knowledge) and a set of behaviors that were revealed in a study of children under the age of ten.

Table 2-1
Consumer Cognitions and Behaviors Found
Among a Sample of Children in 1964

Cognitions
Brand knowledge
Brand preference
Store knowledge
Store preference
Product knowledge
Product preference
Understanding of the purposes of advertising
Understanding of the goals of retailers
Understanding of money
Understanding of price and competitive prices
Plans for purchases
Purchase decisions
Feelings of purchase satisfaction/dissatisfaction

Behaviors
Making independent shopping trips
Shopping (comparative) for products
Seeking personal information about product purchases
Accepting personal influence related to product purchases
Choosing products in stores
Performing the purchase act
Using purchased products
Demonstrating purchased products to others

Source: McNeal, James U. (1964), *Children as Consumers*, Austin: University of Texas Bureau of Business Research.

It is assumed that all of these initially resulted from consumer socialization via the various socialization agents described earlier.

Although this list of cognitive and behavioral outcomes does not encompass the entire study and actually is in very brief form, it should be easy to agree that the children in this study are consumers. The children in this study were not unusual; they were middle class children living in Austin, Texas, whose parents were office workers, maintenance employees, retail clerks, and college students. All of the outcomes of consumer socialization have not been defined by research; therefore, some are simply unknown. The list in table 2-1, however, is at least representative of consumer socialization outcomes among children and is indicative of the complexity and importance of this process.

Final Note

This entire book is devoted to the position that children are consumers. Its title emphasizes this. Here we simply want to establish this fact as simply as possible and to point out that children learn to be consumers through the socialization process just as they learn many other roles. Subsequent chapters will demonstrate in detail that children are consumers and that they constitute a viable market for many businesses. Serious consideration will also be given to the wide range of implications of these two realities.

3
Income and Expenditures of Children

An exploratory study using in-depth interviews was conducted among parents to determine the amount of income, expenditures, and savings of their children. Following is an excerpt from a recorded interview with the mother of two girls, Jennifer, age six, and Becky, age eleven. Their father is a production supervisor at a plant that produces electronic components.

INTERVIEWER: What is your viewpoint about children having their own money to spend?

MOTHER: I think that kids need to learn money responsibilities as early as possible. That will probably be the greatest problem they have in life.

INTERVIEWER: I see. At what age do you think they should have their own money to spend?

MOTHER: It depends on the kid. We started giving Becky an allowance when she started to school. We will do the same thing with Jenny this fall. So, I would say around seven years old.

INTERVIEWER: I see. You mentioned that Becky receives an allowance. How much is that?

MOTHER: We give her five dollars a week and we plan on increasing that soon to probably seven or eight. We will also start Jenny on one.

INTERVIEWER: What other sources of money do the children have besides their allowance?

MOTHER: As I said, Jenny does not receive an allowance. Becky does. We give Jenny money when she asks for it if it makes sense. She also gets money for helping clean up her room and for helping me do a lot of little things.

INTERVIEWER: Good. Any other ways they get money?

MOTHER: Becky is always selling something. She sells greeting cards, she sells mistletoe at Christmas. She does some baby-sitting on weekends.

INTERVIEWER: Fine. Any other people give them money for any reasons?

MOTHER: No, just us. Well, they do sometimes receive money from their grandparents. And some of the neighbors give them money for doing little things for them.

INTERVIEWER: Do the children spend all the money they receive?

MOTHER: Lands, yes. Becky goes through her allowance by midweek. She's always asking for more. On the other hand, Jenny saves some of her money. She has a piggy bank that's crammed full.

INTERVIEWER: Do they get to spend their money on anything they wish, or do you as parents determine that?

MOTHER: Like I said a while ago, spending money is a responsibility that has to be learned. So they can pretty much spend it any way they want to.

These two children, Becky and Jenny, are probably good examples of today's typical young consumers; they have several sources of funds, can spend their money on objects of their choice, and are encouraged by their parents to become economically responsible as soon as possible. Notice, too, that this mother does not demonstrate any concern about the notion of her children becoming consumers. Rather, she apparently sees it, as most parents do, as a natural role to be assumed by children. This appears to be the prevalent viewpoint among parents regarding consumer behavior in childhood. The idea of parent-blessed mini-consumers appears to be a post-World War II phenomenon. Sociologists at the University of Chicago observed in 1953 that "American middle class children have allowances of their own at four or five" and that "the allowances are expected to be spent, whereas in an earlier era they were often used as cudgels of thrift" (Riesman et al., 1953, p. 120).

Financing Consumer Behavior in Childhood

Theoretically, children do not require money because the products and services that they may purchase are ordinarily provided by parents. Then how is it that by age six or seven children have money to spend and are spending it? There are several social forces that produce this activity, but ultimately the parents determine it through their desire to *please* their children and their desire to *prepare* their children. Regarding the first, it is really unnecessary to elaborate on the extent to which we go to please our children. Items in the national press about child abuse notwithstanding, we usually pamper our children from day one by giving to them an unending range of things obtained from the marketplace. As soon as they develop some money awareness, probably at around age four or five, we begin giving them money in a desire to please them more, so that they may independently obtain some of the things we have been giving them. By this time many of these items, particularly sweets such as candy, gum, and cookies, have become important to the child as rewards from parents for good behavior. It is only natural that when the kids receive the means to enter the marketplace, they particularly seek out these items. Consequently, it is easy for the youngsters to find a lot of consumer pleasure, even in a convenience store, and this in turn pleases the parents as much as when they provided the children with these store-bought items.

Parents strongly desire to prepare their children for adulthood or at least for self-sufficiency. This may be a carry-over from our nineteenth-century agrarian society, but in any case this desire takes the form of providing skills to the youngsters so that they may cope without the assistance of parents. These skills, like things, come in an endless range, but include at least those that prepare the child for education, work, and marriage. Being a consumer is one of these skills, so parents provide their children with money that pays for the practice of them. So much the better that the process also provides the youngster with those pleasures referred to earlier. The consumer socialization of the child that was discussed in chapter 2 does not come without a price tag. By giving the children money to make both household and personal purchases, but mainly the latter, the parents are facilitating the consumer socialization process and giving pleasure to the youngsters.

Financing the consumer socialization process, so to speak, is primarily the responsibility of the parents, but usually receives a boost from grandparents, other relatives, and neighbors. Whether these donors are deliberately trying to aid the consumer socialization of the children or simply please the children with money that will be exchanged for pleasurable things is not apparent from our research. In the case of neighbors who pay the children for odd jobs, socialization often appears to be a major motive, while gratification probably is the main focus of grandparents.

Children as a Consumer Market Segment

It seems clear, then, that children are turned into consumers at a very early age in our society through the desires and encouragement of parents, who also provide the youngsters with the necessary financial support. The net result of this is that the children become a relatively big market segment for such items as sweets, snacks, soft drinks, and toys as they pursue self-gratification and self-sufficiency. From a marketer's standpoint, however, should children be referred to as a market? In addition to being offensive to some parents, referring to them as a market may not be technically correct. Most marketing textbooks tell us what is required in order for a group of people to be described as a market. According to a recent edition of the best-selling principles of marketing textbook, "for an aggregate of people to be a market, it must meet four requirements" (Pride and Ferrell, 1985, p. 34). These can be summarized as follows:

1. The people must need the product. That is, if children are referred to as a market for candy, for example, there must be a definable need for this product by this group.
2. Individuals in the group must have the authority to buy the specific product. This requirement addresses the concept of the child being permitted by social custom or by those in charge to buy things.
3. The people in the group must have the ability to purchase the products. This, of course, refers to the child having money and having control of it.
4. The people in the aggregate must be willing to use their buying power. This simply means that having money is not enough; there must be a willingness to part with it.

As we look closely at each of these requirements, children appear to be a bona fide market. The first requirement, need for the product, might be in question in the sense that children may not really need such items as bubble gum or candy bars. It is true that these products are not necessary for sustaining a person; needs, however, are not only for *being,* but also *becoming* (McNeal, 1982). That is, there are needs that sustain a person, such as food, and there are needs that, if met, permit the child to develop socially and personally. In the latter sense, then, children need such items as bubble gum and ice cream bars. These and many other items that children buy are used to facilitate socialization with others and to express achievement, role performance, and, of course, gender.

The second requirement, authority to buy, does not seem to be difficult to meet. Children get their authority to make typical purchases from society and specifically from parents. This authority is more apparent if we realize that children usually are not permitted to buy some things such as firearms and alcoholic beverages. This also hints of another authority that permits children to make purchases—the retail store. We rarely think of this, but the retailer implicitly grants permission for children to enter and make purchases. This permission is not given by all retailers (for example, alcoholic beverage stores) and, as we will discover in chapter 4, it is given reluctantly by some.

The third and fourth requirements are the major concern of this chapter. These requirements state that children must have both money and the willingness to spend it. We have already pointed out that parents are programmed to give their children money, and children do spend it and want to spend it. The requirement does not state how much money the children must have; interestingly, there is not much current information about this. Many years ago, a substantial amount was written about children receiving allowances, but it has become a much less important topic, perhaps because it is such a common practice. It is also significant to note that the older literature on the subject of giving money to children tended to assume that the money was to be saved until the child had needs and the wisdom to spend it. In a paper written almost a century ago on this topic, the author noted that "the money sense of the young child, as a primitive man, is feeble and nascent" (Monroe, 1899, p. 152), and he goes on to emphasize the value of thrift and to suggest that parental giving of money to children is to teach saving, not spending. Today, in our market-driven society, the purpose of giving money to children is spending; saving is secondary.

In the case of children, it might be appropriate to add a fifth requirement for an aggregate of people to be a market. The fifth requirement is that individuals in the group must have knowledge and understanding of the marketplace. It is one thing to have money and the willingness to spend it; it is quite another to understand how, where, and when to spend it and what to spend it on. Understanding these things requires some understanding of the marketplace in which the money is spent. There are groups of people, such as consumer educators, consumer advocates, and some Federal Trade Commissioners, who disagree with the notion that children have adequate knowledge and understanding of the forces that operate in the marketplace. For example, it was concluded by members of these groups that children, at least those under eight, did not understand the intent of advertising, and therefore advertising to them should be banned. This has not yet occurred as it has in some other nations, but the possibility underlines the question of the child's understanding of the marketplace. In later chapters, we will discuss and elaborate on this particular issue at length. For the present, the position will be taken that children do constitute a market, just as in chapter 1 it was argued that children are legitimate consumers. This position is based partially on the common practice of parents giving their children money and encouraging them to spend it. This common earning/spending behavior of children, with the blessing and support of parents, is indicative of market behavior. In subsequent chapters, other behaviors of children that further support the position of children as a market will be described.

In order to establish early in this book that children constitute a bona fide market for a variety of products, a description of their earning, saving, and spending behavior will be presented. A study at Texas A&M University provides us with the most up-to-date information. Let us present the essential findings of this study and identify some of the points of significances to marketers and to those interested in the consumer socialization aspects of children.

A Study of the Economic Behavior of Children

A probability sample of households with children in a southwestern metropolitan area was studied during 1984 to determine children's average weekly

Table 3-1
Average Income, Expenditures, and Savings of Children

	Sample Results (N = 585)		National Estimates
	Weekly	*Annually*	*Annually*
Income	$3.03	$157.56	$4,729,793,640
Expenditures	$2.72	$141.44	$4,245,887,360
Savings	$0.31	$16.12	$ 483,906,280

Table 3-2
Average Weekly Income, Expenditures, and
Savings of Children According to Age

Age	Income	Expenditures	Savings
4	$1.08	$0.49	$.59
5	1.12	0.90	.22
6	1.28	1.25	.03
7	1.85	1.80	.05
8	2.50	2.31	.19
9	3.52	3.19	.33
10	4.05	3.39	.66
11	4.79	4.33	.46
12	5.49	5.26	.23

income, sources of income, amount of weekly spending by each child, objects of expenditure, and extent of savings. A total of 585 children, ranging in age from four through twelve, within 321 households were studied through interviews of approximately 25 minutes in length with one or both parents. The characteristics of the sampled households, when compared with a summary of 1980 U.S. census data, suggest that the results of the study are generalizable to the U.S. population of children. The findings, therefore, where appropriate are cautiously extended to the national level.

Table 3-1 presents an overview of the findings. It shows that indeed children are earners and spenders, and their willingness to spend is revealed by the fact that they spend most of what they receive. It was determined that approximately one-half (49.05 percent) of all the children's income is derived from allowances; the remainder comes chiefly from gifts from parents and relatives and payment for household chores and odd jobs. Their average weekly income amounts to $3.03; they spend $2.72 a week and save the rest. On a national basis, these data suggest that the 30,019,000 children in the United States aged four to twelve have $4,729,793,640 in annual income, spend $4,245,887,360, and save the difference of $483,906,280. Although $4.2 billion in expenditures is relatively small, bear in mind that the entire amount is discretionary and can be spent on anything the child chooses. For example, it does not include expenditures on school lunches or required school supplies. About one-half of the children's savings is placed in a savings account of some sort, including bonds; the remainder is located in piggy banks and similar home depositories.

Table 3-2 provides more detail on the child's income, spending, and saving by viewing each from the standpoint of the child's age. It reveals that the incomes for ages four, five, and six do not vary much, ranging from $1.08 to $1.28 a week, but expenditures increase and savings decrease dramatically during these years. Probably these latter figures reflect the discovery of many new wants among children at ages five and six, and most likely they are a function of being permitted to go to the store on their own. (Chapter 4 will discuss independent shopping in detail.) Beginning at age nine, children are spending well over $3 a week, and by age twelve their expenditures go above $5 a week. Savings appear to be the highest per child at age 10; then they begin to decline, indicating that the youngster is again spending almost all that he earns. Thus, it does not appear that the tradition of "saving for a rainy day" is common among today's children. Four- and five-year-old children save 55 percent and 20 percent of the incomes, respectively, but this appears to be more a function of inability to spend rather than a savings ethic.

A serviceable index of social class was calculated using family occupation in order to determine if children's economic behavior varied according to the household's social class. The children were divided into upper (23 percent), middle (52 percent), and lower (25 percent) class, and the mean weekly income and expenditures of each class were calculated according to the age. The results are depicted in figures 3-1 and 3-2. What appears significant in this analysis of the data are the relationships among classes. In figure 3-1, we see that among children ages four, five, and six, those in the lower social class receive slightly more income. This is also true for children ages nine, ten, and eleven. In fact, the average weekly income of children of all ages in the lower social class is just slightly less than that of all children in the middle class ($3.05 and $3.16 per week, respectively), and both are higher than the average of $2.72 a week for upper class children. Reasons for the greatest incomes being among lower and middle class children are not clear. Ward, Wackman, and Wartella (1977A) produced similar findings in their well-known study. Perhaps lower class parents give a relatively large amount of money to their children in order to provide them the instant gratification they seek, whereas middle class parents give freely to their children so that they can keep up with the times (Coleman, 1983). The relatively lower income of the upper class may be a function of the fact that for most upper class Americans, "income is not sufficient to afford all their dreams simultaneously," so giving to children is slighted (Coleman, 1983, p. 271). Although the data do not indicate it, the difference in incomes may be a function of resourcefulness; that is, lower and middle class children may seek and find more ways to earn more money (selling aluminum cans, for example) than upper class children. Interestingly, by age 12 upper class children have the highest weekly income, possibly reflecting the time in these children's lives when parents feel the children need more money in order to afford those things representative of good taste.

Looking at figure 3-2, which depicts the average weekly expenditures of children within the three social classes, we see about the same relationships

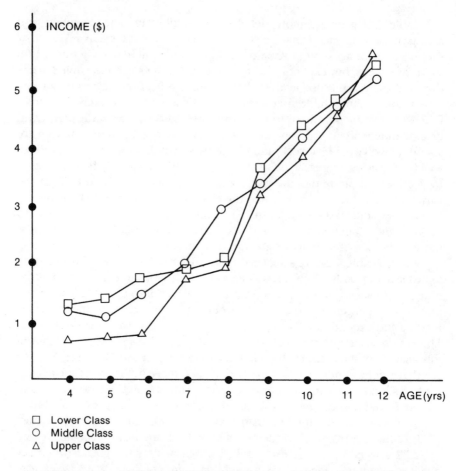

Figure 3-1. **Children's Mean Weekly Income by Social Class**

as were shown for income. In general, lower- and middle-class children are spending about the same, $2.80 and $2.89, respectively, which is higher than the $2.54 per week of upper-class children. These expenditures are obviously limited by income, but it does appear that children of all three classes save about the same amount. An exception appears to be at age 12, where the data show that upper-class children spend a little less and thus save a little more. Perhaps upper-class parents begin enforcing responsible money management at around age 12 more than do parents in lower and middle classes.

The principal items children buy with their money are summarized in table 3-3. It describes the projected annual amounts spent nationally on five product/service categories by children, using the findings of this study as a base. Not unexpectedly, the largest category of purchases consists of snacks and sweets and amounts to approximately $1.4 billion annually. The items in

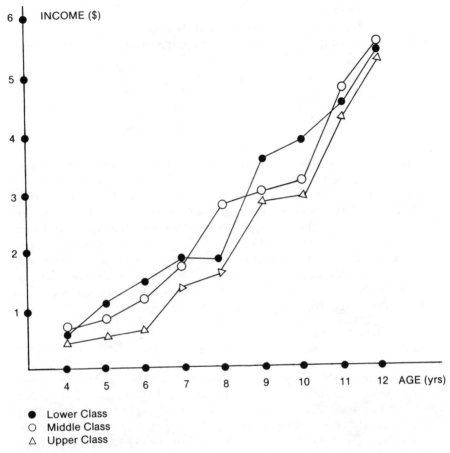

Figure 3-2. Children's Mean Weekly Expenditures by Social Class

this category are many, but mainly include candy, gum, soft drinks, frozen desserts, ice cream, and chips. The second largest category of children's expenditures is broadly termed toys/games/crafts and is made up of models (airplanes, autos, weapons, and so on), mechanical toys, puzzles, games, and video game cartridges. Children spend over $771 million a year on movies and sports entertainment. The sports include swimming, skating, bowling, and a variety of others found in small parks or entertainment centers. Table 3-3 shows further that children spend approximately $766 million on video games. These games, usually costing a quarter, are played mainly in video-games parlors, but also are found in many retail outlets, particularly convenience stores. Finally, the table indicates that youngsters devote a small portion of their expenditures to gifts. This category, amounting to over $164 million a year, consists mainly of birthday and holiday gifts for parents, friends, siblings, and other relatives.

Table 3-3
Estimated Annual Expenditures of Children
among Five Product/Service Categories

Product/Service	Annual Expenditure
Snacks/sweets	$1,440,600,000
Toys/games/crafts	1,104,100,000
Fun machines	765,900,000
Movies/sports	771,200,000
Gifts	162,300,000

Although the standard categories of food, clothing, and shelter are conspicuously missing from the descriptions of children's expenditures, there is still a wide range of items here. The study, in fact, produced an even wider range, but many items were omitted from table 3-3 beacause expenditures on them were small. The largest category omitted was clothing, which amounted to roughly $40 million a year. For the record, let us list some of the other items not specifically noted but subsumed within the five categories: tools; books; magazines; bicycle parts; flower and vegetable seeds; telephones; television sets; radios ("jam boxes"); hobby items such as stamps, coins, and rocks; and fast food items including hamburgers and french fries.

Discussion

Whether or not children ages four to twelve constitute a market per se does not appear very debatable when their income and expenditures as described above are examined. They have needs and money to spend on items to meet those needs. They have authority, given to them by their parents, to buy a wide range of items, and they buy them. They spend over $4 billion annually, up from an estimate of $2 billion in 1969 (McNeal, 1969).

The items that children buy are limited when compared to adults, but that is only because parents are still providing the standard package. Because the food/clothing/shelter package is taken care of by parents, children spend their income mostly on items for immediate self-gratification. For the manufacturers and sellers of these products and services, the youngster is a market; the child probably is not the main market in most cases, but nevertheless a market. For example, in the case of video games, the child is probably viewed as a major market by video game parlors. Likewise, children are probably targeted as a major market for bubble gum and many types of candies by their manufacturers. Most likely, the candy and gum that are often displayed near the floor in convenience stores is a response to this product market. On the other hand, probably neither the manufacturer nor the retailer of chips or ice cream sees children as a major purchaser, although both items are frequently bought by youngsters.

The study reported here indicates that parents perceive their children as a market. They give their children most of the money the children spend with the expectation that it will be spent. The parents have knowledge of what the children buy and where they buy, and in interviews the parents describe their children's consumer behavior in a matter-of-fact manner. The parents do not demonstrate concern for any inability of their children to perform adequately in the marketplace. They seem to see the situation as a training time during which some mistakes will be made. This calmness is in noticeable contrast to the Federal Trade Commission, which wanted to ban television advertisements for children because they were not mature enough to deal with them (*Advertising Age,* 1978A).

Many members of the business community also seem to view children as a market. There are several types of retailers, described in the next chapter, that respond to children as consumers; examples are some chains of convenience stores, discount houses, and supermarkets. Manufacturers of such items as toys and bubble gum are directing at least $100 million a year in television advertising to children (Jennings, 1984). There are at least two cable television networks, Nickelodeon and Walt Disney, that have children targeted as their main audience. Many magazines have as their primary market children, such as *Highlights for Children* and *Humpty Dumpty.* There are almost 3,000 books published annually for children (Duke, 1979). There are around 225 comic book titles published each year (Duke, 1979), and most of these contain advertisements aimed at children. One comic book publisher, Marvel Comics, recently ran an ad in *Advertising Age,* a magazine aimed at marketers, that shows a youngster's backside with a comic book in his pocket, and states in the copy that if you advertise in Marvel Comics, you can "have kids in your hip pocket" (*Advertising Age,* 1985, p. 73). The ad then goes on to tell us that such companies as Nabisco, General Mills, Life Savers, and Mattel advertise in Marvel Comics. In this case the notion that children constitute a market is apparent, and in fact, the children's market is large enough so that Marvel Comics can appeal to a large number and range of potential advertisers for its various comic books.

Recently, a franchised radio network, Children's Radio Network, was formed for the "educational and entertainment needs" of children (Reiling, 1985, p. 14). It signed station WEXI in Jacksonville, Florida, as its first licensee; it has already received enthusiastic support from local advertisers. The bowling industry has announced a $3 million network campaign to attract seven- to twelve-year old children to bowling alleys. This advertising effort is funded by 8,000 bowling alleys (Meyers, 1985). On a long-range basis, the industry expects to spend $32 million on advertising to youths, which is a large amount for an industry made up almost solely of small businesses. Such a large dollar amount certainly supports the concept of children as a market, in this case for a service rather than a product.

In another dimension, the Young Model Builders Club is sending a mailing to children in which it encourages children to begin membership in the club. The children are offered five free gifts to join, one being a model kit of the space shuttle, after which the children will receive two new model kits a month for around $4 each plus postage and handling. Thus, some direct mail marketers also apparently perceive children as a potential market.

The preceding material has documented the status of children as a market for both manufacturers and retailers of products and services, but what can be said about this market in the future? Will it increase or decrease in size? Will its spending behavior change? These are important questions to marketers of such products as candy bars and soft drinks and of such services as bowling and movies. By the year 2000, the population of children ages four to twelve will increase approximately 10 percent according to the Bureau of Census. This is a modest increase of around 3 million children and is not the kind of increase that excites the economic nerve endings of marketers. Still, if there are marketers today who are seeking business from this group of consumers (and there are, as will be demonstrated more fully in subsequent chapters), then it may be comforting to them to know that the group will remain stable in size and increase slightly each year.

Economic theory also tells us that the more scarce a resource is, the more it is treasured. As the number of children per household declines, as it has for many years, it may be that the children will be blessed with more and more material wealth including, of course, money. This appears to be the case over the past decade, although reliable figures on children's income are not available. It is probable, then, that while the children's market will grow only modestly in number, it will gain substantially in buying power.

There are no indications that the nation's parents are going to do anything to reduce the consumption efforts of their children. In fact, parents in general seem more determined than ever that their children will become consumers at an early age or, more fundamentally, become adult at an earlier age. Kids are marching toward adulthood at a much brisker pace than they used to and are wanting more mature things to go with this accelerated growth (Keyes, 1985). Already marketers are obliging this market segment with such adult items as peel-off nail polish and personalized stationery (Keyes, 1985). The children seem to enjoy these efforts by both parents and markets and are in fact responding by wanting a home computer and a video cassette recorder and showing more brand consciousness in formerly unimportant areas such as clothes. One writer noted that "as early as the third grade youngsters are as conscious of the importance of an Izod alligator or a Calvin Klein label as are adults" (Sloan, 1982).

In sum, there is a children's market out there with many wants and the money to support them. Parents concur, and marketers do, too, in growing numbers.

Questions and Implications

The findings in this chapter about children's earning and spending behavior combined with the examples of various businesses responding to this group adequately support the notion that children constitute a market for many goods and services of producers and retailers. Later chapters will offer more evidence of this post-war phenomenon. Ethical, economic, and social questions arise in regard to this finding for which answers are not easily constructed. Efforts to provide these answers, or at least partial answers, will be made in each of the subsequent chapters and particularly in the last three chapters. At this point it seems appropriate to raise some of these questions, so that they may be in the back of the mind when the other chapters are considered.

1. Are parents aware that giving their children money to spend gives the children market power? While the money that one child receives is minor, the combined amount for all children causes children to have buying power and to be recognized as a market by some producers and retailers.

2. Why do parents really need to give their children money, particularly during preschool years? The parents meet the children's needs already and do it better than the children can.

3. Are parents cognizant of retailers' feelings about children being given money to spend and being encouraged to spend it? Regardless of what motives the parents have for giving their children money, by virtue of giving it to them they set in motion certain activities at the retail level, such as stocking and displaying goods. Yet parents may not know the viewpoint of retailers.

4. Are parents giving their children money, encouraging them to spend it, but relying principally on business and elementary school to teach the children appropriate consumer behavior? There is not much evidence that parents deliberately teach their children consumer behavior, yet they encourage them to be consumers. Because knowing how to be a consumer is not a genetic matter, someone must or should teach them both prior to and during consumer activities.

5. If parents insist on their children being consumers by giving them money and encouraging them to spend it, are they also giving approval to marketers to court their children as potential customers? We hear a lot of condemnation of marketers, particularly advertisers, for pursuing children as consumers, but from a theory of business standpoint, it would be more surprising if they did not.

Although children as consumers have become a normal part of our socioeconomic fabric, it seems that parents are creating many problems for themselves, for their children, and for marketers by giving their children money and the encouragement to spend it. It certainly places a heavy responsibility on all three parties. There are not any formal ground rules for children being consumers except those for adults. Therefore, parents must be concerned with teaching their children consumer knowledge and skills, while marketers must be concerned with interacting properly with children in what is mainly an adult setting. The children probably should be most concerned, however, for they must satisfy some of their needs in the marketplace and concurrently please their parents and behave in an adult-like manner with marketers.

Part II
Children's Interaction with Marketing

4
Children and Their Stores

During the spring of 1983, a study was conducted among 105 fifth-grade students in the Houston, Texas, area to determine their store preferences and store patronage habits. Excerpts from one of these in-depth personal interviews with an eleven-year old boy follows.

INTERVIEWER: What is your favorite store?

TRAVIS: I'd say Triangle Sporting Goods.

INTERVIEWER: What is it about that store that makes it your favorite?

TRAVIS: It handles all kinds of sporting goods like crossbows and things, and every kind of fishing tackle.

INTERVIEWER: Any other reasons?

TRAVIS: Their prices are good, and they help you if you don't understand how something works.

INTERVIEWER: Good. How often do you go to Triangle Sporting Goods?

TRAVIS: Whenever my mom will take me. Quite a bit.

INTERVIEWER: How often do you buy things at Triangle?

TRAVIS: Real often. I just bought an arrow there that cost $4. I've bought fishing tackle there before.

INTERVIEWER: Let me ask you, Travis, how many things have you bought there within the past month?

TRAVIS: None in the past month. I looked at their bows, but they cost a lot. I did buy some things there at Christmas, but that was a couple of months ago.

INTERVIEWER: What other stores do you like? Do you have some other favorites?

TRAVIS: Let's see. I like Wright's Sporting Goods store. They have a lot of good things. And Wal-Mart. That's a good store. And I guess Sears.

INTERVIEWER: Of all of the stores you go to, Travis, which one do you go to the most?

TRAVIS: I'd say the 7-11. I go there sometimes every day.

INTERVIEWER: What do you buy at the 7-11 store?

TRAVIS: Everything. Ice cream bars, Cokes, bubble gum, and I buy things there for Mom, sometimes, too.

INTERVIEWER: What do you like best about the 7-11 store?

TRAVIS: All the things you can buy there. And they have a Spy Hunter game and some others.

INTERVIEWER: Anything else?

TRAVIS: The guy who works there is real friendly. His name is Lewis. He doesn't mind giving you change.

INTERVIEWER: Let me ask you this, Travis. Which store do you like the best: Triangle or 7-11?

TRAVIS: Triangle like I told you.

The scenario revealed in this interview centers around a Houston, Texas, youngster, but it could have occurred in Cleveland, Boston, Sacramento, or any other city or town and with many children even younger than Travis. There are several points in this one interview that give us clues about children's preferences and activities related to stores. (1) Travis easily talks about stores, (2) he can name several, (3) he has some store preferences that vary according to product offering, (4) he buys a variety of items in these stores, (5) he buys frequently in one or more of them, and (6) he has knowledge of the product offerings of the stores and even the store personnel in the case of one.

It was only 20 years ago that a study of children's consumer behavior first documented in published form the fact that children, as early as age five or six, interact independently with retailers for purchase purposes (McNeal, 1964). However, ten years earlier, a study of children's store behavior was conducted by the Kroger Food Foundation (1954); although never published, it demonstrated that children ages six to ten easily understand how to shop for typical supermarket items. A couple of years prior to the Kroger study, sociologists at the University of Chicago had declared that very young children were being turned into "consumer trainees" by their parents (Riesman, Glazer and Denney 1950). As a consequence, for 35 years we have known that children commonly make purchases at stores, but published studies about this specific activity are rare.

It was demonstrated in chapter 3 that children have money to spend and do spend it. In this chapter, we want to follow the children to the stores where they spend their money and to describe their interactions with retailers, including their frequency and purpose. We also will attempt to assay children's knowledge about stores and any store preferences they may have. To complete the report, we then take a look at children as consumers from the standpoint of the retailers and attempt to answer two major questions. To what extent do retailers seek the patronage of children? What special efforts, if any, do retailers make to attract children as customers?

Frequency and Purpose of Children's Store Visits

Probably by the time the typical kid makes his first solo trip to a store, he has been in most types of stores several times and in a few types hundreds of times. Parents normally take their children with them to shop. These visits, which start during infancy, probably provide the foundation for children's consumer education, yet we know so little about them. In McNeal's 1964 study, five year olds could not refer to any training in consumer behavior per se received from their parents, but all of them could give extensive descriptions of their mother's buying activities on a typical shopping trip, thus indicating that much learning takes place through observation during store visits with parents. Whatever is learned through observation probably is sharpened when children make some selections on their own and offer purchase suggestions to parents, as all of the five year olds reported doing. One-half of the children also reported that their mothers gave explanations when the children's suggestions were rejected. This exercise probably produces useful learning among the consumer trainees, although many reported their mothers giving them stereotypical refusals, such as "We can't afford it" and "It's not good for you." According to Ward and Wackman (1972), parents yield to children's requests and suggestions as children increase with age. A study by Berey and Pollay (1968) revealed that mothers who were child-centered tended not to honor children's requests for cereals. These researchers explained that child-centered mothers probably purchase the cereals they believe are best for their youngsters and not necessarily the ones their children want. Atkin (1978), in a well-known study of children's purchase requests while accompanying parents, concluded that children who demand products, compared to requesting them, received them most of the time. Apparently, according to Atkin, the parents are trying to avoid trouble. Wells and Lo Sciuto (1966) suggested that parental yielding to children's requests or suggestions seems to vary depending on whether the families are urban or suburban, with the latter yielding more. The amount of suggestions or requests do vary somewhat among children for many reasons; more assertive children may simply make more requests (Berey and Pollay, 1968), or children who zero in on television commercials a lot may tend to make more purchase influence efforts (Galst and White, 1976).

It appears that those teachable moments that children and parents have together in retail stores are useful in the development of consumer behavior patterns among children. Even though the behavior of parent and child may not be programmed in the sense that parents carefully plan to use these times to teach the children specific consumer behavior patterns, much learning appears to take place through children's participation and observation. In fact, it appears that much of what is learned is a result of the children's initiative, at least as much as that of the parents. It is almost as if children are genetically determined consumers. Probably much of what we see as consumer behavior in children was learned much earlier than we realize, perhaps at age two or three rather than suddenly at age four or five. Possibly it is a result of observing parents as consumers, making many store visits with parents, watching much parent-blessed television including, of course, advertising, interacting with many products in the household as well as many packages that encourage consumer behavior, and imitating of parents' consumer behavior in their play. Additionally, there are many toys, as will be described in chapter 6, the purpose of which appears to be to teach consumer behavior to children. These, of course, are purchased by parents and other caring adults such as grandparents. Although we do not have empirical support for these suppositions now, we will probably discover one of these days that children's consumer behavior patterns start developing in the cradle as a result of the unconscious behavior of their consumption-driven parents.

In the McNeal (1964) study, 50 percent of the children made their first solo shopping trip at age five, with boys being permitted this independence more often than girls. Usually this anxiety-filled effort was made at a nearby convenience store. By age seven, all of the youngsters reported going to the store on their own and, in fact, often replied with a confident "of course" when asked if they did go to the store alone. These first trips to the store were usually for parental purposes—to get bread and milk, for example—but were relished by the children as symbols of adulthood. They were quickly followed by more store visits the purposes of which were principally those of the children.

The extent to which children independently interact with retailers is demonstrated in a 1984 study of 585 children within 321 households. In this random sample of households taken from a city of 100,000, parents were asked (1) how many times a week their children go to a store for themselves and which stores; (2) how many times a week their children accompany them on shopping trips during which the children spend their own money; and (3) in which stores, while shopping with their parents, the children perform as independent consumers. Let us consider these findings in two parts. First, let us examine the independent shopping trips made by children; then we will take a look at the independent purchases made by children while shopping with parents.

Independent Shopping Trips Made by Children

Table 4-1 reveals a small degree of independent shopping by children as early as age four and a still small amount at age five, but then a rapid growth during the sixth year. Although it is surprising to see some four year olds going to the

Table 4-1
Children's Independent Shopping Trips
to Stores

Age	Children (%)	Average Number of Trips/Week	Average Number of Different Stores
4	6.1	1.0	1.0
5	9.1	1.0	1.0
6	52.1	1.2	1.4
7	80.1	1.6	2.1
8	87.5	1.7	2.2
9	98.1	2.2	2.2
10	100.0	2.3	2.3
11	100.0	2.7	2.2
12	100.0	2.8	2.3

store alone, in general these findings suggest that independent shopping starts a little later, at age six rather than age five, than shown in the 1964 study. Also different from the 1964 data, this study indicates that all of the children do not shop independently until they reach age nine. Whether these differences are real or are a function of the research procedures is not clear. The 20-year time difference might have been expected to produce opposite results, that is, that children would be operating independently at even an earlier age, if we can accept the current thinking that children are prepared for life earlier, as is espoused in such books as *Children Without Childhood* by Marie Winn and *The Disappearance of Childhood* by Neil Postman.

The average number of shopping trips per week, as shown in table 4-1, that children make to the store increases with age, as might be expected. Through age five, the few children who go to the stores alone rarely make more than one visit a week. There is a slight increase in the number of store visits at age six, but the number of children who make unassisted store visits increases dramatically. During the seventh and eighth years, the average number of trips increases substantially, and by age nine children are going to the store, on an average, more than twice a week. By age twelve, their average number of store visits is approximately three.

The increases in the average number of different stores visited by children parallel the increases in the average number of trips made until age eight, and then the former flattens out. Thus, the older the child becomes, the more times he goes to the store alone and to some extent the more different stores he visits. Determining the exact number of stores that the child visits alone was difficult in this study because the interviewing procedures permitted responding parents to use the terms *shopping center and shopping mall* without designating which stores in the shopping complexes were actually patronized by the youngsters. As one example, one mother reported that her eleven-year-old son visited a 7-11 convenience store twice a week and a nearby shopping center twice a week. In this case, the total number of stores visited was recorded as four. Thus, the average number of different stores visited, as shown in table 4-1, is probably understated. As a rule, the youngster visits two to three stores a week, most commonly two. The most popular store visited, according to this study, is the convenience store, with all parents reporting that their children shopped in one. Supermarkets and discount houses were also commonly visited by children, and this was true, too, for shopping centers and malls. Specialty stores were mentioned quite a bit as places that children made purchases. These included sporting goods stores, toy stores, video game parlors, barber/hairstyling shops, and fast food restaurants. Although children do not visit shopping malls as frequently as they do the corner convenience store, according to the parents the children love the malls most because they meet so many needs in addition to those met by the products and services purchased there. Parents reported that children like the enclosed malls because they "can spend hours there," presumably in play of various forms, they can "see lots of their friends there," and they "don't have to worry about the weather or the dark." The tone of these remarks suggested that the parents were equally pleased with the malls as a shopping setting for their children.

A partial explanation for the relatively large number of store visits and different stores visited is the fact that many of the children go to stores and shopping complexes after school, many on a daily basis. These visits are normally for the purpose of obtaining snacks and playing video games. Sometimes the youngsters' after-school store visits are for haircuts and school supplies. Some of the parents' remarks suggested that the after-school store visits were a combination of reward and entertainment for the children. One father said of his ten-year-old son, "Sometimes he and some buddies will stop off at the Circle-K store for a break after school. They have some fun playing video games and have a Coke or something."

Independent Purchases Made with Parents

In addition to going to the store alone, children make a large number of unassisted purchases while accompanying parents on shopping trips. Because the trips are often parent-initiated, the children may visit a range of stores that is beyond that ordinarily in the children's choice sets.

Table 4-2 reveals that more children make independent purchases earlier in life when shopping with parents than when shopping alone. There are several possible reasons for this. The parents are present to encourage the consumer trainee to participate in the exchange process, and they are there to provide money on the spot. From the child's point of view, it is a chance for

Table 4-2
Children's Independent Purchases While
Shopping with Parents

Age	Children (%)	Average Number of Trips/Week	Average Number of Different Stores
4	16.3	1.8	1.5
5	58.2	2.0	1.6
6	60.4	2.0	2.5
7	100.0	2.7	2.5
8	100.0	2.6	2.8
9	100.0	2.8	2.8
10	100.0	3.1	2.9
11	100.0	2.8	2.7
12	100.0	2.4	2.3

him to demonstrate his "adultness" to his parents while being assured by the fact that his parents are nearby for potential support. According to table 4-2, over one-half of the children make unassisted purchases while with parents as early as age five, and all of them become co-shoppers by age seven. From age seven on, all the children may make purchases independently when they go to the store with their parents. In contrast, it is not until age nine that all the children are going shopping on their own.

Children generally make more purchases a week when shopping with parents than they do when shopping alone, regardless of age. Again, feeling comfortable in the presence of parents helps to explain this difference in consumer behavior. Probably, though, the mere fact that parents take children to the stores frequently and to a greater variety of stores accounts for much of the independent purchases of their children. Table 4-2 shows that children make purchases on an average of around three trips a week with parents as compared to approximately two trips a week on their own. It appears that by age 12 the number of store visits a week with parents declines, whereas the number of visits without parents increases, suggesting that independent shopping is another way that children demonstrate growing away from their parents. There is a greater average number of different stores visited by children when accompanying parents than when shopping alone, although like the number of shopping trips with parents, this number declines at age twelve. The greater number of different stores is primarily a function of the shopping desires of the parents. The decline at age twelve in the number of different stores visited when shopping with parents may also reflect the beginning of adolescent rebellion.

The total of the average number of independent shopping trips together with those made with parents amounts to a large number, perhaps as many as made by adults. For example, after age nine the youngster is interacting with retailers around five times a week. The average number of different retailers with whom the child interacts consists of around five beginning at age seven. (There is a possible discrepancy in the total number of different stores visited because some of the stores visited when shopping with parents may be the same as those patronized on an independent basis.) This large number of store visits is to some extent a function of after-school behavior. Just as youngsters may visit stores after school for snacks and play, many parents also report taking their children shopping with them after school. One mother stated, "Since it is on the way, I often stop by the shopping mall after I pick up the kids at school." Thus, the total number of different stores visited a week is influenced a great deal by the shopping goals of the parents.

Visiting an average of five different stores a week and making purchases in them, be it a soft drink or a birthday gift for a friend, provides the youngster with a great deal of consumer behavior experience. This amounts to at least 250 store visits a year and a similar number of purchases. This means 250 opportunities to see retailers in action, to see other customers in action, to see and perhaps handle hundreds of products including new ones, and to learn the layout and product offerings of many stores. It also means much opportunity to form store loyalties, to become acquainted with various store personnel, and to develop dislikes of some stores. It is also 250 opportunities for retailers to influence the consumer learning and behavior of a child. This influence on children's consumer socialization is potentially much greater than that of advertising, which parents and policy makers seem so concerned about, because the influence is physical rather than mental and real rather than imaginary and it is unlikely to be buffered by parents.

Children's Store Knowledge and Preferences

As revealed in the preceding discussion, children frequently interact with retail stores independently of their parents. Although parents generally encourage this behavior, it is mainly a result of the children's own motives, knowledge, and store preferences. At around age five, children tend to start seeing the marketplace, rather than parents, as a source of satisfiers such as sweets and snacks, and to view the parents more as a source of funds for the purchase of these items (McNeal, 1964). By age seven, children consider shopping "necessary and exciting," and by age nine they see it as simply a "necessary part of life" (McNeal, 1964, p. 20). Thus, through observation of parents' consumer behavior and by actual participation in the shopping process at stores, children soon learn that buying things at stores is a normal way to satisfy many of their needs and, in fact, is a necessary thing to do.

Because children are motivated to go to stores, they quickly learn a lot about them in terms of their purposes, styles of operation, product offerings,

Table 4-3
Children's Preferences for Four Types of Stores

	Age 5-7	*Age 8-9*	*Age 10-12*
Convenience stores	1[a]	1	3
Supermarkets	2		
Discount houses	3	2	2
Specialty stores			
(toys, sporting goods)		3	1

[a]1, first preference; 2, second preference; 3, third preference.

and prices. Naturally, some of the information about retailers comes to the children through parents, peers, and consumer education in their schools, but it appears that much of it is learned or confirmed through participation in the stores. To demonstrate, research indicates that the purpose of stores is essentially vague to five-year-old children, even though they sense that the stores are owned by somebody. In effect, the stores just exist like trees or houses. By age nine, however, most children know that stores are owned by people and that their basic purpose is to sell goods at a profit (McNeal, 1964). These nine year olds also are aware that a large amount of retail goods have their origins on farms and in factories.

Children have some knowledge of price variations in stores. In a study of children's perceptions of retail store/price relationships, 90 percent or more of the children ages five to nine reported differences in prices of the same products at different stores (McNeal and McDaniel, 1981). The children in this study also always understood the term, discount, when someone referred to a discount house.

Children have store preferences. In the McNeal and McDaniel (1981) study, children referred to certain stores as their favorite stores depending on the specific product offerings of the stores. Like adults, they had a favorite store in which to buy candy and sweets, whereas another store was preferred for its selection of toys.

By combining three studies (McNeal, 1964; Anderson and McNeal, 1978; McNeal and McDaniel, 1981), general preferences for kinds of stores can be discerned among children. Table 4-3 shows these preferences by age groups. The convenience store is usually the preferred store among children up to around age 10. The convenience store, such as 7-11 and Circle-K, is nearby, has a good assortment of sweets, snack foods, and beverages, and usually has some video games to play. Although among the older children, the convenience store loses its top ranking to specialty stores, it still is an important kind of store to them. There is no clear second or third choice, but the discount house, such as K-Mart, is popular among all age groups mainly for its wide assortment. As one child said about her favorite discount house, "It's got everything." Finally, it should be noted that specialty stores, particularly toy and sporting goods stores, become important to the older child. Apparently, their significance is due to their depth of assortment of a relatively few items desired by children. It should be noted, too, that in the case of specialty stores, and particularly convenience stores, the relative prevalence of store personnel, usually sales clerks, plays a positive role in children's store preferences. Children often are acquainted with store personnel in convenience stores (McNeal, 1979). This interpersonal relationship, which is uncommon in large self-service stores such as discount houses and supermarkets, seems to provide an important bond for the youngster who is just getting acquainted with the marketplace.

Retailers' Responsiveness to Children as Consumers

The impact of retailers' influence on the consumer behavior of children is determined in great part by retailers' attitudes and behaviors toward children as consumers. However, we know very little about retailers' responsiveness to children, even though we know, as shown in the previous discussion, that children frequently patronize a variety of stores and their parents generally encourage them. Practically all marketing-focused studies about the consumer behavior of children involve children's interactions with advertising, rather than selling, even though nothing really happens until retailers offer the advertised goods for sale.

Recently an exploratory study was conducted of retailers' responsiveness to children as consumers (McNeal, 1984). Its purpose primarily was to answer three questions. (1) Do retailers recognize children as bona fide consumers? (2) Do retailers actively seek children as consumers? (3) What specific policies and practices, if any, are aimed at children? These three questions were essentially threaded into a letter to the chief executive officer (CEO) of 124 large retail chains and, in the case of two department chains with autonomous stores, to CEOs in several stores. All retail chains were included in the sample that handled any products of interest to children. The letter, which promised anonymity, went to 157 executives in total, and after a follow-up mailing, 92 (59 percent) replied. This represented over $220 billion in annual sales.

Based on the belief that retailers who were most concerned about children as consumers also would be very influential in their socialization, the ninety-two responding retail operations were first classified according to whether or not they were children-oriented. A retail chain was judged to be children-oriented if it reported any continuous policy or practice that gave recognition to children as current or potential consumers. Of the ninety-two retailers who answered the inquiry, thirty-four (37 percent) were classified as being children-oriented. These thirty-four are shown according to

Table 4-4
Types of Retailing Firms Sampled and Classified as
Children Oriented

Type	Contacted	Responded		Classified as Children Oriented	
		Number	(%)	Number	(%)
General merchandise					
Department stores	40[a]	22[b]	55.0	10	45.5
Variety stores	9	4	44.4	1	25.0
Discount houses	11	5	45.4	4	80.0
Food stores					
Supermarkets	25	19	76.0	6	31.6
Convenience stores	5	4	80.0	2	50.0
Eating and drinking places	32	18	56.3	7	38.9
Drug and proprietary stores	6	3	50.0	0	0.0
Apparel and accessory stores	7	4	57.1	1	25.0
Hotels/motels	9	4	44.4	1	25.0
Other (book, sporting goods, electronics, jewelry, gifts)	13	9	69.2	2	22.2
Total	157	92	58.6	34	37.0

[a]Consists of representatives from seven chains.
[b]Consists of representatives from five chains.

types in table 4-4. None of the retailers who were classified as children-oriented appeared to consider children as their main market, but ten of the thirty-four retail chains voluntarily stated that they counted children as an important part of their current customer profiles. For instance, one grocer stated that "while they are not big spenders, they are regular spenders." The remaining twenty-four retailers, while concerned with children as current consumers, saw children as mainly future consumers that were to be cultivated now. One department store executive said, "Because of our location children do make purchases with us, and we look forward to having them when they are grown." All thirty-four of the firms that reported a responsiveness to children also reported that they viewed children as very important consumer influentials, that is, as consumers who might influence parental purchases. As consumer influentials, the youngsters were regarded by these retailers as meriting courtship. "Children indirectly are responsible for a significant amount of household purchases. We hope we will receive a part of that business as a result of treating them with courtesy and respect," one soft-goods merchandiser stated.

Five general continuous activities were identified as indicators of an orientation to children among the responding retail chains. These five categories and the number of retailing units practicing each are displayed in table 4-5. The largest class of children-oriented activities consisted of

Table 4-5
Children's-Oriented Activities Practiced by Retailers

Activity	Number of Retailers	Children-Oriented Retailers (%)	Total Sample %
Shopping/buying facilitators	29	85.3	31.5
Consumer education	28	82.4	30.4
Promotion	18	52.9	19.6
Store personnel training	17	50.0	18.5
Ethical practices	14	41.2	15.2

shopping/buying facilitators. This category included such things as a children's menu in a restaurant, eye-level displays in a convenience store, and the children's own credit card in a department store. These items recognize that children require or merit special shopping/buying environments. A department store executive, for instance, reported that, "A youngster with his or her own credit card (with the parent's name below) feels more at ease in the adult world of shopping."

The next most prevalent children-oriented activity consisted of various consumer education efforts. Examples of consumer education activities were a tour through the food preparation area of a fast food restaurant, distribution to elementary schools by a department store of printed materials on how to buy clothing, and a brochure along with a free demonstration of proper shoe fit for children by a shoe store.

Eighteen of the retailers reported periodically conducting various promotion efforts aimed at children. For instance, one specialty store chain said it routinely advertises on Saturday morning television, three department stores described children-focused special events that combined advertising with major in-store promotionals, and four supermarket chains noted the use of "credit cards" for free cookies. One-half of the children-oriented stores said they provide formal training for store personnel in serving children. One restaurant's operating manual, for example, describes how its personnel are to deploy high chairs for the very young, furnish children with children's menus, and check back later on the children's satisfaction with the food. Finally, fourteen stores reported various ethical practices aimed at the welfare of children. These included not handling potential harmful glues and keeping sexually oriented magazines out of children's reach.

Of the ninety-two responding retail chains, fifty-eight (63 percent) reported that they were *not* oriented to children as consumers, neither as current nor as future consumers. Most of the respondents volunteered a reason for not placing any focus on children. Essentially, there were two general reasons given.

1. We treat everyone equally. Just over two-thirds of the retailers who reported not being oriented to children said they give equal treatment to

every customer and that children do not receive special treatment. One specialty retailer, for instance, said, "We could not imagine giving children preferential treatment at the expense of other customers." A department store executive said it more tactfully with this statement, "We try to make shopping for all members of the family as pleasant as possible." One legalistic sounding statement by a hotel/motel chain was, "Since fair treatment is our byword, we do not allow discriminatory policies or practices based on a customer's age."

2. Our offering is aimed at adults. One third of the retailers that reported not being oriented to children said, in general, that their product offerings were not aimed at children. Some examples of this kind of statement were:

"Our market is mainly the 18–49 age group" (fast food chain).

"Our focus is on the parent and grandparents, not the child" (discount house).

"There is no need . . . Our products are purchased strictly by adults" (family shoe store).

One retail chain executive, who might be more appropriately classified as anti-children, stated, "To us, the customer is the customer, except when he/she is playing video games or reading magazines from our magazine section. He/she is then a boisterous change-seeker or a page-smearer."

Discussion

Just over one-third of the retailers in this study were classified as children-oriented, although some retail categories were more involved with children than others. Among these retailers, five children-related ongoing activities were identified. Almost all of the children-oriented retailers provided shopping/buying facilitators. This type of activity encourages children to participate in the consumer role, makes the participation easier, and is more likely to effect successful participation by the youngsters. The department store, for example, that provides children with credit cards or permits them to use their parents' credit cards and then displays clothing at children's eye level is more likely to move a youngster to the completion of a successful clothing purchase than a store that treats all customers equally. In the latter case, more trial and error is likely because of the lack of purchase facilitators.

One-half of the children-oriented retailers reported that they train their store personnel in children-centered behavior. This type of activity, being personal in nature, should be even more significant in the consumer socialization of children than physical activities. It not only facilitates participation in the consumer role but also has educational potential. One supermarket chain executive, for instance, said that the checkout personnel in his stores were "trained to be more sensitive to children's needs," and would help children count their money and help them understand the amount of sales tax.

Over one-half of the children-oriented retailers reported promotional efforts targeted specifically at children. These efforts were mainly to encourage participation in the consumer role at those stores generating the promotion, although some advertising contained educational messages. One department store's summer promotion program to children consisted of advertising on Saturday morning television, lavish window displays employing science-fiction characters from the popular *Star Wars* movie enjoyed by children, and point-of-purchase use of these characters, as well as point-of-purchase children's music emanating from a free jukebox. The store's president reported good acceptance of this promotion effort by both children and parents. This parental response most likely would have a reinforcing effect on the children's learning of consumer behavior.

Over 80 percent of the retailers classified as children-oriented provided some type of consumer education for children. All of them made some consumer education materials available to schools, and one-half of these also provided in-store consumer education in various forms. One fast food restaurant chain, for example, offered tours through its restaurants to elementary school classes and provided similar information periodically in advertisements targeted to youngsters. There is some disagreement about who should perform the consumer education function among children—parents, schools, or business—but there is little disagreement that children in our society need such education. Much product information, however, such as the nutritional contents of fast foods, is so company-specific that the businesses themselves can provide it most efficiently (McNeal, 1978). Still, there are those who strongly disagree with much of the consumer education materials provided by business to schools (Harty, 1979).

Fourteen of the children-oriented retail chains reported ethical practices aimed at protecting the welfare of children. These practices, such as not handling products potentially harmful to children, have at least subtle educational benefits to them, but more importantly, they should direct the youngsters to purchases more satisfying for both children and parents.

As for the stores that are not children-oriented, which amounted to almost two-thirds of those studied, what can be said about the nature of their input into the consumer socialization of children as revealed in this study is only speculation. There were essentially two classes of stores unresponsive to children: those that "treat everyone equally," that is, they do not give children any special treatment, and those whose offerings are targeted for adults. Neither of these types of stores is likely to make a young consumer-in-training feel welcome or comfortable, and therefore the learning experience may be unsatisfying. If this be the case, learning theory tells us that the youngster probably will not return to that store. Perhaps it was one of these types of stores that caused children consumers in an earlier study to feel "ripped off" or to feel, "It's sometimes hard to get people to sell you things" (Anderson and McNeal, 1981). The main contribution of stores that are unresponsive to the consumer socialization of children may be to teach children the notion of market segmentation—that some stores do not seek their patronage, but rather that of older groups. This is a harsh reality, perhaps, but theoretically useful to the full development of the child in the consumer role.

Implications for Consumer Advocates

When one steps back from these findings about children/retailer interactions and cautiously views them in a general perspective, there appear to be several substantial reasons why consumer advocates should be concerned with retailers' influence on the consumer behavior of children, perhaps even more than with that of advertising. Let us highlight these reasons.

1. The influence that retailers can have on children's learning of consumer behavior appears to be potentially more elaborate and more forceful than the typical instructional type of influence of advertising. Children learn from advertising via a one-way communication system that inherently requires a somewhat passive audience. In contrast, children learn from retailers in two ways, through observation and participation, both of which require active audiences, and research tells us that active learning is more effective than passive learning (DeLozier, 1976). Through observation, with or without their parents, the youngsters may learn, for example, the exchange procedure in service and self-service stores, the general product offering of various types of stores, and the consumer behavior of contemporaries at the point of purchase. Deliberately designing parts of the store environment to encourage observations by children, such as is done by some retailers according to the above study, can have "powerful effects" on consumer behavior (Nord and Peter, 1980, p. 41).

Learning through participation might be compared to on-the-job training. The mere fact of doing something rather than imagining it, of being actively involved rather than passively involved, should cause learning to leave relatively major traces in the mind (Allport, 1961). For example, actually handling a particular brand of toy car, observing other comparable cars, selecting one, paying for it, and leaving the store with it is likely to have more impact on the mind's printing system and its future output than just seeing the toy car advertised on television. If, in fact, the car was advertised on television before the youngster bought it, this purchase activity probably amplifies and reinforces the advertised message by confirming and embellishing it. Also, the fact the stores offer children a wide variety of rewards, as compared to advertisements, causes stores to become powerful "generalized reinforcers" that are "effective under a variety of motivational conditions and extremely resistant to extinction" (Berelson and Steiner, 1964, p. 143).

2. Children are being pursued by many retailers, not for one reason, but for three. The retailers mentioned earlier indicated that they may view children as a current market for a wide range of items, a future market that is to be cultivated now, and an influential market that if courted could pay off in patronage from parents. This suggests that the influence of retailers on children will take a variety of forms, will be frequent, and, in total, will be substantial.

3. Interactions between children and retailers are large in number. For example, current data show that a ten-year-old child makes an average of 2.3 trips to a store per week and performs an average of 3.1 independent purchase efforts a week while shopping with parents. On an annual basis, this amounts to over 280 independent purchase transactions, thus permitting substantial opportunity for influence by retailers on the youngster's consumer behavior. What percentage of children's purchase transactions could be considered truly interpersonal is not known from present findings. Children do make a significant number of purchases in convenience stores, which they apparently consider a personable environment (Anderson and McNeal, 1981). On the other hand, purchases made at a supermarket or discount house are probably less interpersonal, although several supermarket chains use secondary reinforcers (Rothschild and Gaidis, 1981), namely cookie credit cards to personalize the child's store visit. Whether interpersonal or not, each purchase effort at a store is influenced by the store's atmosphere, such as music and color schemes (Kotler, 1973) that can be very persuasive to a youngster. For instance, a major west-coast department store gave display windows and certain selling areas a science fiction motif the purpose of which was to make the children feel welcome and to stimulate purchases among them. One successful strategy for many department stores has been to create a boutique for licensed items such as the Cabbage Patch line, bringing together clothes, accessories, and toys in one location. "These arrangements attract children," reports Helen Boehm, a consultant to the toy industry (Cleaver, 1985, p. 29).

4. On a scale of low to high involvement, it might be expected that the retail setting induces high involvement learning, as compared to advertising, for example. Factors such as high cost of goods (relative to the youngster's income), high interest (because the child in the store attends mainly to those products of value to him), and the novel situation (the store is still mainly an adult object) contribute to a high involvement activity (Robertson, Zielinski, and Ward, 1984). Also, the reality of the store setting is likely to be more anxiety-arousing than an advertisement. The store has live people in it who are buying things; it has products waiting to be bought that can be handled; and it has displays, aisles, and fixtures that encourage purchase. Finally, in the case of service stores such as department stores, there are store personnel seeking

the child's purchase. It may be, in fact, as one study reported (Anderson and McNeal, 1981), that some store settings create almost too much anxiety for the inexperienced child consumer, causing the child to feel uneasy or even scared.

5. Parents are practically partners with the retailers in the consumer training of children in the sense that parents provide children with much of their income (one-half or more according to the study reported here) and then encourage the children to make independent purchase efforts at stores (Riesman, Glazer and Denney, 1950; McNeal, 1964). Further, parents give retail stores legitimacy by visiting them often, themselves, and also by taking the children with them. According to research described earlier, over a period of time children make more independent purchases in a greater variety of stores when with parents than without them. Thus, the retail store, in general, is parent-blessed. This seems much less true of the advertising that concerns parents so much (for example, see Cosmas and Yannopoulos, 1981). Also, parents can buffer much of the influence of advertising to their children that occurs in the home, but it seems much more difficult to buffer the influence of retailers when the children are engaged in an independent purchase act with them. Thus, what children learn in their interactions with retailers is probably determined more by the retailers than by the parents, but it has at least tacit approval of the parents.

6. When a person or organization, such as the retailer, is a major source of reward and punishment, he plays a central role in the children's learning of consumer behavior (Moschis, 1978A). The retailer possesses all the products that children have seen advertised, all the products that parents use as rewards for children's good behavior, and all the products that are rewards for the youngster's own purchasing efforts. The retailer also can dispense punishments such as showing reluctance to serve the child, ignoring him, or being generally unfriendly to him. Any of these negative behaviors certainly may occur in the majority of stores that, as shown in the 1984 study, either do not want children's business or desire to treat them as adults.

7. Finally, all the products that are not advertised to children because rules of good taste forbid it, all the products assessed as being of poor quality by rating services such as Consumer Union, and all the products that are forbidden by parents are offered for sale in retail stores. Some stores in the present study did report attempts to control the sale or display of certain products not for children, such as harmful glues or sexually oriented magazines. Although a few local laws regulate some of these activities, society must rely on the moral values of retail managers to protect children from many undesirable products. For example, currently there are serious questions being posed about possibly unhealthy effects of smokeless tobacco, such as snuff and chewing tobacco, yet these items can easily be purchased in many retail outlets by children.

Recommendations

Parents encourage children to be consumers, and many retailers seek their patronage. A large number of retailers, however, do not want their business. Children are consumer trainees and often cannot distinguish the children-oriented from the adult-oriented store. Further, as trainees, children often need some special considerations from retailers. Assurances of fair treatment certainly are needed.

There are already some protective legislative models available, for example, minimum age limits for purchasing alcoholic beverages or requiring the accompaniment of a parent to certain movies. Such models, however, are aimed mainly at products rather than sellers of products, and, too, these are legal models rather than voluntary ones, which are more desirable.

What seems to be needed is some mechanism introduced into the child/retailer interaction that will assure that the youngster develops properly from the experience and that both parties receive satisfaction from it. The buffer should not discourage the retailer from welcoming and serving the youngster. It, in fact, should encourage retailers to develop and maintain a positive relationship with youngsters while simply recognizing that retailers, as adults, have a cognitive advantage over children. Just as some products are child-approved or age-graded, retailers also could be certified as child-centered stores by some interested and credible group. Such a group would be sensitive to the potential abuses of children that could occur in the retail store setting. A "Child Centered" sign on the retailer's door and in its advertisements could signal to children and parents alike that the store welcomes children, provides appropriate safeguards for their welfare, and actually wishes to make a positive contribution to their consumer development. Perhaps the certification program could contain incentives for many of the large number of retailers that are not children oriented to become so. In like manner, the absence of the sign would remind children and parents that the store seeks an adult market target or at least does not seek the patronage of children.

5
Advertising to Children

I n order to study the role of television viewing in the home life of children, some lengthy conversational interviews were undertaken. Children were interviewed at their schools by visiting with them in a small room set up for this project. Following is an excerpt from an interview with Lisa Ann, a third-grader, who attends a private school in a major southwestern city.

INTERVIEWER: How often do you watch television?

LISA ANN: About every day.

INTERVIEWER: What time of day do you usually watch it?

LISA ANN: After school. When I get home from school I always watch TV.

INTERVIEWER: Do you eat anything while you are watching TV?

LISA ANN: Sure. I'm starved when I get home, so I eat a lot.

INTERVIEWER: Eat a lot?

LISA ANN: Sure. I drink a Coke and eat chips and cookies and usually a big sandwich.

INTERVIEWER: A big sandwich?

LISA ANN: Yeah, a big sandwich with meat and stuff.

INTERVIEWER: Do you usually eat each time you watch television?

LISA ANN: Yeah, always, I eat breakfast when I watch TV.

INTERVIEWER: You eat breakfast while you watch TV?

LISA ANN: Yeah. When I get up I always watch *Tom and Jerry* and *The Three Stooges* and eat a big bowl of cereal.

INTERVIEWER: A big bowl of cereal?

LISA ANN: Yeah. Sometimes two, and sometimes I get bacon with it and toast.

INTERVIEWER: So you watch television in the mornings, too. How often?

LISA ANN: Every day I go to school.

INTERVIEWER: Oh. You don't watch it on those mornings when you don't go to school?

LISA ANN: Sure I do, but I watch it all morning then.

INTERVIEWER: All morning? When do you watch it all morning?

LISA ANN: Saturdays when I don't go to school.
INTERVIEWER: You watch it all morning?
LISA ANN: Yeah. It goes all morning on Saturdays with kids' programs.
INTERVIEWER: How about Sundays? Do you watch it then?
LISA ANN: Yeah, but there's not much on. Then I have to go to church.

Lisa Ann is not atypical of young television viewers today. During an ordinary week children watch television around twenty-five to thirty hours; it is somewhat more for those five and under. According to A.C. Nielsen television network studies, children may watch television much of the entire telecasting period, and in fact their peak viewing time is in the evening, the same as that for the general population (Banks, 1980). Other major viewing times are after school and on Saturday mornings.

The well-known Saturday morning television viewing of children actually constitutes only 8 percent of their total viewing, but it is the time when they are most concentrated in front of the TV. For example, children make up 53 percent of total viewers during Saturday morning, as compared with only 14 percent during prime time (Banks, 1980). Consequently, Saturday morning is also the viewing time when advertising to children is most prevalent, with after-school hours being the second most important period. By advertising to children on Saturday morning when they are most concentrated, advertisers keep their cost-per-thousand low compared to other time slots.

Best estimates suggest that during their television viewing children are subjected to around 20,000 advertisements per year and pay attention to around 10,000 of them at a rate of approximately 200 per week (Ward, 1978B). Why are there so many advertisements aimed at children? Simply, it is good business for many marketers. As observed in the last chapter, children constitute three markets for business's goods and services: a primary market of children who buy things with their own money—over $4 billion a year in total; a future market for *all* goods and services that can be cultivated now; and an influential market that business believes can have substantial impact on mom and dad's purchases.

Children love television and parents like it, too, for their children and for themselves, but the advertising that comes with it and makes most of it possible is not as well loved. Parents, consumer advocates, and policy-makers alike often have harsh words for television advertising that is aimed at children, both for its contents and its effects. In this chapter we want to examine these two broad aspects of television advertising to children, and decide if the criticism it receives is justified.

There is a problem with trying to draw judgements about the impact of television advertising on children, because numerous conflicting judgements already exist. Also, the amount of information about the topic is overwhelming. There appear to be ten studies of effects of the television advertising on children for every one study of other aspects of children's consumer behavior. It is possible, however, to look at all the studies and draw conclusions on the basis of the findings of the majority. That will be our approach in this discussion of the topic.

Model of Children Interacting with Television Advertising

In order to place in perspective the research findings about children as audiences for television advertisements, as well as criticisms and concerns, a model that depicts the important elements of the activity is shown in figure 5-1. The model, based on many reported studies, begins at the point that children decide to watch television. What program they will watch will determine to a great extent what advertisements they will see; if they choose a public television channel or a pay-TV channel, such as Walt Disney, they will see little or no advertising. In such cases, the question of the influence of television advertising on children consumer behavior is moot. (Recognition is given to the fact that advertising is seeping into public television; this is under investigation by the Federal Communications Commission.)

The model shows that the decision to view television is not just the child's. Parents may determine what their children watch on television and how often it is viewed. In fact, advertisers and broadcasters are eager to declare that they do not force children to watch television; their TV viewing is in the hands of their parents, who often abdicate the responsibility. Parents may not be the only persons who influence their children's TV viewing. Peers to some extent, and often to a great extent in homes where there is no parental supervision, determine what programs a youngster will watch. Children enjoy getting together to watch television and may take turns deciding what to watch, or a dominant child may determine the programs for others.

The result of the child's decision to watch television is a flow of advertising messages. In a three-hour sitting, which is common, a youngster will be subjected to around thirty minutes of advertising. This amounts to twenty to forty ads an hour, depending on their length. The model in figure 5-1 indicates that public policy can influence the advertising messages children receive. Policy makers, either through law or pressure, can determine the length of the advertising message, the nature of its content, and, of course, whether there is any message at all, as done in Quebec, for example. The extent to which advertising to children is regulated, however, often seems to depend on the atmosphere on Capitol Hill more than it depends on the welfare of children. During the 1970s, for instance, the Federal Trade Commission was so outraged with television advertising that it was ready to shut it down to children under eight and severely limit it to children under twelve. In

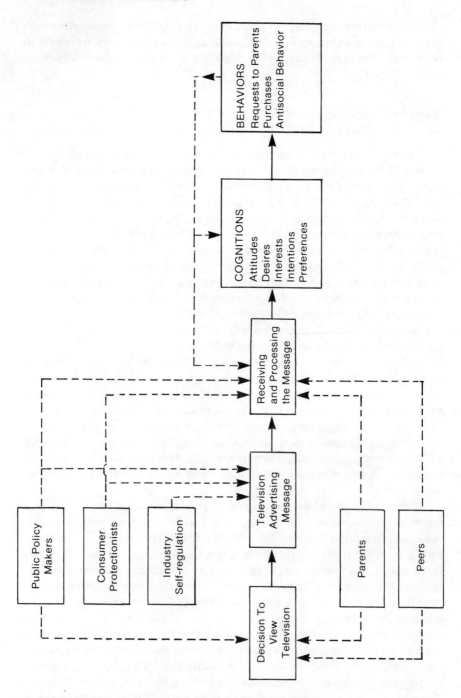

Figure 5-1. A Model of Children Interacting with Television Advertising

the 1980s, in contrast, the Federal Trade Commission (FTC) seems to be in a live-and-let-live mood, and children are seeing more advertisements than ever.

The model also shows that industry self-regulation can influence the actual television advertising message. In fact, self-regulation is in theory the ideal solution to protecting children from undesirable advertisements. When developing advertisements, advertisers need only to consider the standards that the public holds for advertising messages, which probably are the true standards of most advertisers, too, because many have children; the result should be advertisements that are acceptable to most everyone. Alas, such is often not the case. There are often other standards used by industry that relate only to sales, profit, and share of the market. Industry self-regulation may emanate from trade associations such as the National Association of Broadcasters or the Better Business Bureau or it may be on a company-by-company basis. Therefore, there is potentially a great deal of self-regulation. However, in a giant toy company, for example, it is possible for one self-serving person to circumvent the firm's ethical standards. Chapter 10 will discuss self-regulation and effectiveness.

Finally, consumer protectionists, as the model indicates, may influence the nature of advertised messages on television. Consumer protectionists attempt to represent the interests of the children and are active in petitioning law makers and regulators for help in imposing standards on advertisers. Action for Children's Television (ACT) is an organization that pushed the FTC for a ban on television advertising in the 1970s. Consumer protectionists also solicit self-regulation on the part of producers and retailers in all their relations with children.

After an advertising message is broadcast, figure 5-1 shows that the next event is the child's receiving and processing of that information. Much research centers on this step; the youngster's ability to understand the information and intent of the information in an ad is often questioned. In fact, there is concern about whether many young children can even distinguish advertising from programming. What information the child actually receives from advertisements may be a function of parents, peers, public policy makers, and consumer protectionists, in addition to the advertiser, as the model shows. Parents may interpret the advertising messages for the children, particularly if they view TV together. Even if they do not watch programs with their children, they may still voice agreement or disagreement with the messages and therefore influence their intended meaning. Peers also can confirm or deny ad messages either through joint viewing or simply through conversations. It is possible that public policy makers and consumer protectionists can influence the information that is processed by the youngster by being the source or cause of counter messages, perhaps as public service messages, that may effect the meaning of the advertisements to the child. Industry members, of course, do not want anyone or anything coming between the child and his reception and interpretation of the messages presented. To do so, according to them, is tantamount to abridging First Amendment rights.

The results of the information processing of advertised messages by children are, according to research, the formation of attitudes towards or against products and sometimes their makers or sellers, interests in certain products and brands, intentions to buy certain items, desire to buy certain products (usually by brand), and preferences for brands of some products and for some stores. These cognitions are all "behaviors of the mind" and generally are viewed as antecedents to the children's actual behavior, as the model illustrates. To explain the formation of these various cognitions, researchers look back to the content and intent of the message and to the social and physical setting in which the child received the message. There is concern among researchers about how rigid these cognitions are and what forms they are in. It is widely held that the extent and nature of children's information processing and the form and firmness of the resulting cognitions are a function of the maturity of the mind as expressed in age or in cognitive development stages.

The last event in the flow model in figure 5-1 is the behavior that occurs among children as a consequence of television advertising. The principle behaviors of concern to investigators are children's purchase requests to parents, children's purchases, and antisocial activities such as conflicts with parent or conflicts with peers. Two major intentions of advertisers are to get children to buy or to get children to ask their parents to buy, and in either case there is the question of whether or not the child should have the product. Thus parent-child conflicts may transpire. The three primary areas of parental concern have been with foods that contribute little to good health, toys that do not perform as the children anticipate, and unsafe products.

The behavior step in the model in figure 5-1 shows lines and arrows returning to both the cognition step and the information processing step. These indicators are intended to suggest that resulting behavior has an influence on cognitions, reinforcing or changing them, and on information processing in terms of causing children to want more information or less and causing them to be more receptive or less receptive to certain advertisements. For example, children may be disappointed with a toy once they obtain it and play with it, and consequently change their attitudes about its brand and tend to disbelieve future advertisements of it.

It is hoped this model places in perspective such concepts as regulation of television advertising, the impact of television advertising on children's thoughts and behavior, and children's information processing activities. These topics and several others will be considered as we assess the results of the interaction of children with television advertising. Regrettably, there are not comparable studies of children's interactions with other media, such as newspapers, comic books, or radio. There is no reason to believe, for example, that radio does not impact substantially on children's attitudes given the number of "jam boxes" we see on their shoulders and the number of earphones caressing their heads. Television advertising receives most of the concern of caring adults, however, and thus it is the medium in focus here. One notable study regarding other media will be described at the end of this chapter.

Children's Decision to Watch Television

Children watch television, and consequently television advertising messages, because parents permit it and usually encourage it (Kay, 1974). If by chance a child is not permitted very much television viewing, he or she usually can visit a friend's house where it is a normal practice. Whether or not children actually watch television is not usually a conscious decision by parents, and the amount of viewing and the programs viewed are not actually known by one-half or more of parents (Kay, 1974).

While parents may permit their children to view television, it is not their intent that their children be subjected to either harmful programming or advertising. For a majority of parents, the television set is a good friend to their children; it entertains, sometimes educates, and almost always cooperates by providing children-oriented programming at just about any time of the day. Parents, up to 64 percent of them according to a study by Cosmas and Yannopoulos (1981), would prefer television for their children without commercials. Consequently, pay TV for children, such as the Walt Disney channel, is growing in popularity. However, the "hot shows" are still on the networks where the advertisments are, and that is where you will find most children in spite of their reluctant but indulgent parents.

As noted in the discussion of the model, children watch television more than just after school and on Saturday mornings. They watch it during prime time and even as late as midnight. Banks (1980) reports that more children view network television during prime time (7 to 11 P.M.) than on Saturday morning, and there are over 1 million children watching television after midnight. It is apparent, then, that children's television viewing is generally blessed by parents, and it follows that children's viewing of commercials is expected by the parents, also. It follows, too, that parents do not expect these commercials to have a bad influence on their children. While parents agree that the airways are public and advertising is permitted, they do not agree that they can be littered like our highways. Nevertheless, advertisers are quick to point out that television viewing is or should be in the control of parents who determine whether or not and to what extent television advertisements actually reach children.

The Television Advertising Message

Once the television set goes on, unless it is tuned to a public broadcasting channel or a pay channel, children will be subjected to commercials. They may be commercials aimed at children or adults, they may be for products or services, but their ultimate intent is almost always to make a sale.

Who Determines the Message

The television advertised message to children is mainly the determination of the advertiser. The television networks such as ABC, CBS, and NBC are obviously in a position to decide if they will permit a particular children's advertisement to air, but rarely seem to exercise this responsibility. The National Association of Broadcasters (NAB), a trade association and lobby organization of the broadcasting industry, at one time played a major role in determining what messages could air to children. Its self-regulatory influence essentially ended, however, when NAB was found guilty of violating antitrust laws in 1982. Still a major self-regulator of the content of children's television advertising is the Children's Advertising Review Unit (CARU) of the National Advertising Division of the Council of Better Business Bureaus. A number of national advertisers submit their ads to CARU for review prior to their airing, thus giving its panel of experts a chance to determine the taste and ethical character of the ads. Given the fact that it is a member of the business community, however, and that it is not a legal entity, CARU appears reasonably effective in screening out commercials or parts of commercials deemed undesirable by parents and consumer advocates.

On the official regulatory side, the Federal Communications Commission (FCC), which is very much in a position to regulate television advertising to children, practically ignores it. In fact, the FCC during the past few years has taken the position that television advertising should be deregulated (*Advertising Age*, 1983).

Potentially the most powerful regulator of television advertising is the Federal Trade Commission (FTC). After being petitioned in 1977 by two consumer interest groups, Action for Children's Television (ACT) and the Center for Science in the Public Interest (CSPI), to limit television advertising to children, the FTC began proceedings aimed at that purpose. These consumer protection groups, and subsequently the FTC, were particularly concerned with television advertising's encouragement of youngsters to consume sweetened cereals and sweetened snacks. In its proceedings the FTC recommended banning all television advertising for any product to children too young to understand the selling purpose of advertising, banning advertising for sugared food products to older children, and requiring counteradvertising in the form of nutritional and/or health disclosures to counteract the ads for sugared food (*Advertising Age*, 1978A). The importance of the issue of television advertising to children was most dramatically illustrated in these unusually strong recommendations of the FTC. The banning, of course, never took place because of a variety of political reasons, but the mere possibility demonstrates the potential of the FTC's power to regulate "kid-vid."

As the model in Figure 5-1 shows, the actual advertised messages to children can be determined by public policy makers, industry self-regulation, and consumer protectionists, but policy makers are not dependable and self-regulators have an inherently self-serving bias. Consumer protectionists, because they have no authority and only limited clout, have to work slowly and on a case-by-case basis in order to have any impact on television advertising to children. For example, ACT complained to the FTC that Hudson Pharmaceutical Corporation was using a child's hero figure, Spider-Man, in vitamin advertising aimed at children after several other vitamin producers had agreed not to do this. The FTC pursued the matter and was able to get a consent order against the firm that prohibited it from advertising its product to children at all (Feldman, 1980). Thus, consumer protectionists have had limited impact on television advertising to children, but it appears that their clout has diminished during the 1980s.

Principally, as the model shows, televised advertising messages to children are a function of the advertisers. What the messages say and how they say it depends mainly on the motives and morals of advertisers. The amount of time for advertising on children's programs and the number and length of the advertisements are mainly a function of the broadcasters and their arrangements with advertisers. The nature of television ads during the greatest part of children's television viewing, during prime time, is not children-screened by anyone other than advertisers in spite of the need to monitor its many adult-oriented ads. For instance, advertisements for certain drugs and alcoholic beverages have potential for harming children, but advertisements during this time period are of concern to public policy makers only if the ads are harmful to adults. Even though consumer protectionists are strongly concerned about the ads that children see during this time, they have been able to do little about it.

Content of the Messages

In spite of the great concern for television advertising to children, analysis of its contents has not been common. Perhaps many researchers in this field feel that advertising to children is like advertising to adults, only simpler, or maybe they believe that if you have seen one content analysis, you have seen them all. Both views are too simplistic, although somewhat correct.

Two products, toys and foods, constitute most of the advertising to children. During the Christmas selling season the predominance of toys is apparent. One study of television advertising content during Christmas time found that toys made up 50 percent of ads one year and 66 percent the following year

(Atkin and Heald, 1977). A recent analysis of television advertising during the Christmas season by Bohuslav, Egan, and Morgan (1985) revealed that when public service announcements (PSAs) were included, 48 percent of ads were for toys. WIthout the PSAs, the amount for toys was 55 percent.

Within the food and beverage category, cereal is the largest advertiser to children. It was the heavy television advertising of sugared cereal that prompted consumer protectionists to petition the Federal Trade Commission for the removal of ads for all sugared foods. Robert Choate, a consumer advocate of the 1960s and 70s, demonstrated to a Senate hearing that advertising dollars spent on cereals was inversely related to the cereals' nutritional value—the less nutrition the more advertising (Feldman, 1980).

Table 5-1 lists all the products nationally advertised on children's television programming on the three major networks during one Saturday morning in November 1985. It is apparent that toys and foods make up the bulk of the products. In fact, if clothing for dolls can be counted as toys, and if we eliminate one toothpaste ad, 100 percent of the ads were for toys and foods. Of the food goods, only two out of forty-five were for non-sugared items. These were for hamburgers and spaghetti.

The study that produced the list in table 5-1 analyzed the needs appealed to in the Saturday morning ads. Using psychologist Henry Murray's taxonomy of needs in a two-step judgement process, the needs determined most important to satisfy among children according to advertisers are itemized in table 5-2. Sentience—to seek and enjoy sensuous impressions—was the most predominant need. It was the main appeal in foods and was manifested by such terms as pure, rich, delicious, smooth, creamy, and crunchy and by such sounds as mmm, and yum-m-m. Sentience was occasionally used also as an appeal with stuffed animals in which the children were encouraged to "Hug 'em. They're so soft!" Another need that was very frequently appealed to was the need for play. It was most obvious in the toy ads. Thus, according to this study, the two main need appeals in children's advertising are sentience and play and they are principally related to food and toys, respectively. Almost all ads appealed to more than one need; consequently, the percentages in table 5-2 total to more than 100. For example, it was common for advertisements of dolls to appeal to both the play and nurturance needs, to give the youngsters an object to play with and care for.

The 1985 study found that 95 percent of television commercials contained some kind of music, usually background music. This compares with 75 percent found in an earlier study by Doolittle and Pepper (1975). The heavy use of music reported in both studies is intended to create moods, for example, aggressiveness with certain robots or adventurousness with others and fun and play with games, dolls, and fast foods.

To describe briefly the content of advertising aimed at children as we have done here can be misleading because a major viewing time for children is

Table 5-1
Products Nationally Advertised during Children's Television
Programming, November 1985

Toys and Accessories

Kenner

Boulder Hill play set
M.A.S.K.
Hug-a-Bunch dolls
Care Bears
Cabbage Patch dolls
Cabbage Patch World
 Travelers
Care Bear Sit-n-Spin
Care Bear Cousins AM
 Radio
Care Bear Wear

Mattel

Peaches and Cream
 Barbie
Princess of Power
Baby Kickie
Barbie Workout Center
Barbie Office
He-Man
Swift Wind Horse and
 She-Ra
Heart Family
Puppy Brite
Hot Wheels Crackups
Rainbow Brite, Starlite, and
 Lurky

Hasbro

My Little Pony
G.I. Joe doll
G.I. Joe bridge layer
Transformer Microscope
 Autobot
Transformer
 Communicators

Tonka

Go-Bot
Mighty dump truck
Mighty loader
Pound Puppies
Pound Puppy Outfits

Schaper

Stomper Monster Water
 Demon
Stomper Bully
Speedsters Twistrack

Coleco

Sesame Street Parade Cycle
Sectaus Dragon and
 Dragonflyer
General Spidrax and
 Spiderflyer

LJN

Thunder Cats
Thunder Cats action
 figures

Fisher Price

Family Farm play set
Construx builder set
Zoo play set

Tomy

Sportboat
Leggos

Panosh Place

Voltron

Playskool

Muscle Machines

Milton Bradley

Hungry Hungry Hippos

Crayola

Crayon caddy

Parker Brothers

Nerf pool

Food

Cereal

Cheerios
Cap'n Crunch
Alpha Bits
Fruit Loops
Honey Combs
G.I. Joe
Sugar Smacks
Count Chocula
Frankenberry
Rainbow Brite
Sugar Pops
Cinnamon Toast
Golden Grahams
Honey Nut Cheerios
Frosted Flakes

Sweets

Fruit Roll-ups
Rice Krispie bars
Extra (gum)
Fun Fruits
Hostess donuts
Bubble Yum
Fruit Bars
Oreos
Hostess cupcakes
Twinkies
Granola Dipps
Fruit Pies
Almost Home cookies

Candy

Hershey chocolate bar
Reeses Pieces
Bonkers
Rolos
Reeses peanut butter cups
Butterfinger
M&M's
Kit Kat
Twix cookie bar

Other Food

Spaghettios
McDonald's
Kool Aid Koolers
Nestle Quik
Hershey's chocolate syrup
Ovaltine
Slurpee
Kool Aid drink mix

Other

Aqua Fresh

Table 5-2
Needs Appealed to in Television Advertising during Children's Programming, November 1985

Need	Advertisements Appealing to Need (%)
Sentience (to seek sensuous gratification)	64
Play (to relax or have fun)	52
Affiliation (to have cooperative relationships with others)	33
Nurturance (to protect and care for others)	21
Achievement (to accomplish something difficult)	14
Harm avoidance (to avoid physical pain or harm)	9
Aggression (to overcome opposition)	9
Understanding (to analyze or experience ideas or objects)	8
Exhibition (to make an impression)	8
Dominance (to influence behavior of others)	5
Autonomy (to resist influence or coercion)	4
Infavoidance (to avoid embarrassment)	4
Deference (to admire or support a superior)	4

prime time when the advertisements are targeted primarily to adults. Therefore, the content of advertising that actually reaches children is probably more extensive than that reaching adults. It contains messages about most adult-oriented products such as beer and cars plus all the children's products. There are some apparent pros and cons to this situation from a family perspective. Children may develop preferences for products intended primarily for adult consumption. There is, however, much to be said for the contribution of all this advertising to the consumer socialization of children if values are not considered.

Finally, it is interesting and useful to reflect on what products usually are not advertised to children. As examples, it is uncommon to see children-oriented ads for clothing, books, green beans, school supplies, or personal hygiene products. So one could argue that advertisements for these items should be aimed at parents who usually buy them, but we would have to say this about cereal and toys, also. Perhaps limited available advertising time combined with the advertising buying power of the giant food and toy companies preclude many other national advertisers from appealing to children during television programming oriented to them.

Deception in the Message

"Advertisers, regulators, and critics are agreed in principle that children are special and that those who approach them as potential consumers must seek to be honest and fair" (Griffin, 1975, p. 17). In fact, any advertiser who stoops to deceiving children stoops to the lowest level of deception because children are by psychological definition the easiest of human beings to deceive, yet we frequently hear of deception in children's television advertising. Five ways that advertisements targeted to children have the potential to deceive are the following.

1. They may use celebrity presenters, which can exploit children's trust in authority figures.
2. They may present products such as candy bars, toys, and hamburgers, without reference to a scale which may exploit children's limited perception skills.
3. They may focus on premiums rather than the product, which may cause children to use the wrong standards for assessing the product.
4. They may use adult terminology and contrived terms, which take advantage of children's limited knowledge.
5. They may make excessive use of emotional terms and/or intense sounds or colors, which may exploit children's gullibility.

The mere fact that a camera is used in television advertising means that there is much opportunity to deceive. How many fishermen, for example, have wanted to hold their catch closer to the camera to make it look larger? Who has not noticed that when the camera angle is varied, the speed of a vehicle can appear to increase? Thus, the potential dishonesty of the camera can come to life in the hands of a dishonest person. When combined with the natural limitations of children's cognitive abilities, the potential for deception becomes great. Therefore, even advertisements that have the potential to deceive must be avoided in the case of children.

This is not the view of everybody, however. A representative of Hershey Foods, in addressing the possibility of banning advertising to children, said that the FTC must first prove that advertising causes substantial harm to children (Mazis, 1979). Other critics may choose to ignore the potential deception by noting that advertising is a First Amendment right (Barry, 1980). In a very elaborate model that determines deceptive advertising to children, Barry (1980) said that deception must cause economic or psychological impact on children before some corrective action is taken. Hopefully, pretests of advertisements against an ethical set of standards could determine this impact before it actually occurs and thus prevent it. These standards are already in the hearts of most people and only need to be applied.

Separators and Disclaimers in Messages

Advertisers like to present their products in the best possible light, and therefore they show them in full use and completely functional. Then the advertisers will insert a disclaimer, such as "some assembly required," "batteries not included," or "accessories sold separately." Consumerists sometimes believe that these disclaimers do not have their intended result, that is, of actually removing a misleading impression that may be placed in the minds of children. Further, this incorrect impression may be passed on to parents and in the process may cause some parent-child arguments. Studies show that these disclaimers often are not understood by children, particularly those under six. However, these studies also show that the disclaimers can be reworded so children *can* understand them. For example, in a study by Liebert et al. (1977), it was found that the disclaimer "partial assembly required" for the Walt Disney Haunted Mansion Game was not understood by more than one-half of the five-year-old children. However, when this disclaimer was changed to, "It must be put together before you can play with it," 100 percent of the five year olds understood it.

Although studies reveal that disclaimers can be misunderstood and that adjustments in them can improve the communication of their meaning, the adult-sounding disclaimers still prevail. Probably, pretests of advertisements containing such disclaimers would reveal the same results. Advertisers, however, seem intent on doing it the way they always have with little regard for the results.

In the case of separators, which are those statements made by an announcer or printed in the lower portion of the picture to inform the audience that a commercial is forthcoming, there is concern similar to that for disclaimers, that is, children may not understand them. This concern is related to the notion that children ought to be able to separate programs from commercials, and some cannot because of cognitive age. Research is inconclusive about separators. It does appear that by the time children understand the difference between programs and commercials, they understand the purpose of separators. Further, it appears, also, that separators cast in children's language are easier to understand. For example, in a study by Stutts, Vance, and Hudleson (1981), seven year olds more quickly recognized commercial material when "The Bugs Bunny Show will be right back after these messages" was changed to "Hey kids. The next thing you'll see will be a commercial and not part of the program you've been watching."

For both the research on separators and disclaimers, a lesson for advertisers is apparent; we might assume it would be known by them. That is, when you speak to children and want them to understand, speak their language.

Processing the Advertising Message

When an advertising message is directed to children, regardless of who determines its contents, there are major questions about the nature of the children's interaction with the message. Primarily, there is a desire to know the extent to which the advertising message is received or attended to and the extent to which it is understood by children. The Federal Trade Commission's intent to bar television commercials was based on the belief that young children often could not understand them and could not discern their intent. Research has addressed both of these issues somewhat, although most of it has focused on children's understanding of commercials.

Children's Attention to TV Advertisements

Even if a television commercial is designed by the very best creative talent, it has no effect unless children pay attention to it. It is well known that the human being has the ability to selectively attend to stimuli. This is true of children; just ask the parent who is calling to his or her children at play to come home. Children, like adults, theoretically direct their perceptual processes to those stimuli that promise the most satisfaction. Television advertisements that promise satisfaction of such needs as sentience and play should logically attract children's attention, particularly when presented in a "bells and whistle" environment. Research shows, however, that children attend to only around 50 percent of TV commercials, and this number declines as more ads are presented in sequence (Ward, 1978B). A partial explanation for this relatively low level of attention is that the children, particularly as they get older, get irritated by commercial interruptions and therefore may devote less attention to the ads. Additionally, as children get older, they mistrust ads more, and this mistrust combined with irritation can easily cause the children to be distracted.

There are a number of factors that can influence the level of attention that children give to television commercials. They can be divided according to whether they are related to personal or to media characteristics. The important factors, according to research, are personal and stimulus.

Personal Factors

Level of motivation—The child may desire to watch commercials, or certain commercials, for information or entertainment value.

Attitudes toward commercials—Children may have developed negative feelings toward ads because the ads interrupt programming or because they are perceived as generally dishonest.

Influence of parents and peers—Parents and peers can distract children from commercials because of conversation that may begin at commercial time or because of warnings about commercial intent.

Lack of knowledge about commercials—Children's attention may remain constant as programming changes to commercials because the youngsters do not know the difference between the two.

Stimulus Factors

Programming nature—Attention to commercials may vary because programs are boring or interesting; for example, boring programs may invite attention to entertaining commercials.

Commercial content—Advertisers use a variety of practices to get and keep children's attention: music, singing, jingles, sound effects, animation, celebrities, and well-known characters. Some are more effective than others.

Product advertised—Certainly the involvement children have with the products in the commercials will influence their attention to the ads, for example, attention might be expected to vary depending on whether the products advertised are for children or adults.

Public service announcements—Because public service announcements are different from commercial announcements (they may even be contrary to them), children may give them special attention.

Studies of children's attention to television commercials are not plentiful, and most have some methodological shortcomings according to the investigators. For example, in the best-known study of attention, the investigators noted that the experimental situation itself probably biased the results (Wartella and Ettema, 1974). Another problem in assessing children's attention to TV commercials is their dual channels of attention in terms of hearing and seeing. Most measures have been on a visual basis only because the simultaneous assessment of both sensory systems is difficult.

In general, television commercials directed to children are well done by any standards. They almost always are elaborate productions, particularly when compared to adult-oriented ads. Overall they appear to elicit more attention from children than their counterparts do from adults. Children also have a more personal relationship with the television set than do adults, and consequently they freely, almost lovingly, give it their attention. It is apparently not until adolescence that they learn that commercial breaks are just that—time to load up on snacks or go to the bathroom.

Children's Understanding of TV Advertisements

There is no doubt that very young children ages two, three, and four pay attention to television commercials but understand very little about them. The Federal Trade Commission has said that children even up to age eight do not possess reasonable understanding of commercials. Research over the past decade or so has considered this issue and provided some useful findings.

For children to objectively respond to ads, they must understand three major dimensions of them, according to researchers. They must be able to distinguish them from programming, discern their basic purpose or intent, and make sense out of their basic messages in terms of what they are saying, asking, or explaining.

Distinguishing Television Commercials from Programs. It is generally conceded that if children cannot tell the difference between commercials and programming, they are at an unfair advantage. There have been investigations of children's ability to discriminate between commercials and programming at most age levels. Butter et al. (1981) studied preschoolers. These researchers divided boys and girls into two age groups whose average ages were 4.13 and 5.15 years. Among the younger groups, there was a 70 percent recognition rate for commercials; for the older group, it was 90 percent. These figures would, at first glance, surprise the FTC commissioners, for example, who believe that children of this age are not able to discriminate between ads and programs. A close examination of their methodology, and that of other researchers, shows that what these very young children identified were probably not commercials per se in the sense that they knew that they were commercials, but "something different from the program," to quote the authors (Butter et al., 1981, p. 56). It seems that preschool children recognize that the program stimuli change to another set of stimuli, perhaps helped by a separator, but knowing that the change is to a commercial, that is, to some audiovisual presentation with a different purpose from the program, is ordinarily not within these young children's cognitive abilities (Stephens and Stutts, 1982).

These findings are confirmed and extended by an earlier study by Ward (1972B). He found that children ages five to eight years generally could not differentiate between commercials and programs, but that children ages nine to twelve years could. Again, in the case of the younger children, they knew there was a change to something else, but not usually to a commercial per se. For example, they knew it was a change to something "shorter than programs" (Ward, 1972B, p. 40).

Discerning the Intent of Commercials. Although young children cannot usually distinguish between commercials and programming, it may be possible for them to discern differences in intent between them. Further, the age at which children do understand the intent of commercials is important to advertisers and to advertising regulators.

In general, research shows that understanding of the purpose of advertising moves hand-in-hand with understanding the difference between commercials and programming. Ward's 1972B study revealed that "kindergartners showed no understanding of the purpose of commercials" (p. 38). A study by Rubin (1974) found that 75 percent of first graders could not discern the purpose of TV ads. Many of the children thought that the commercials were "for fun," "for children," or "for cartoons" (p. 415). It is not until around age eight and above that the selling intent of ads becomes apparent to children. Ward (1972B) found that 53 percent of eight to ten year olds could discern the selling intent of ads, and for ten to twelve year olds this measure rose to 85 percent. The Rubin study (1974) concurs, with around 71 percent of third-graders and 88 percent of sixth-graders being able to discern commercial intent.

Understanding Content of Commercials. Children generally may understand the selling intent of commercials by the time they are eight or nine, but for the advertisements to be effective the youngsters must understand what the ads are selling in terms of their main points. For example, as a result of a typical cereal ad, children might be expected to see cereal as good tasting and fun to eat and to ask their parents to buy some. The Rubin (1974) study addressed this issue in the area of cereals. He found that children from the first grade on understood the concept of a cereal product; it is to be eaten, enjoyed, and purchased. Apparently, the wide use of this product and the frequent advertisements of it make it a normal part of the child's environment at a very early age. However, Rubin discovered that it is not until the third grade that children's understanding of cereal advertising contents go beyond the product concept to such other notions as "having a good breakfast" (p. 446). A 1979 study of public service announcements to children showed that 58 percent of preschoolers (ages four to six) comprehended at least part of the message and 92 percent of those seven to nine understood the main points (*Advertising Age,* 1979).

In all, the notion that children go through cognitive levels of development is upheld in the many studies of understanding television commercials. Also, the viewpoint of the Federal Trade Commission, that children under eight do not understand TV commercials, appears valid. It is a large step for children to take from understanding the entertainment function of television programming to understanding the selling function of commercials. Young minds simply are not able to make this transition until around age eight or nine. Implications of these findings will be discussed at the end of this chapter along with the implications of findings from the following section.

Cognitions among Children Caused by TV Advertising

The fundamental purpose of advertising to children is to make a sale or to persuade, according to Robertson (1972), or to encourage trial and repeat purchase in the words of the Children's Advertising Review Code of the Council of Better Business Bureaus (1977). Before advertising can persuade children to purchase, however, it must cause them to form favorable attitudes toward the advertised goods and services and to want them. Several studies have examined advertising's influence on children's cognitions and generally found it very effective in accomplishing its goals.

Just one Saturday morning of television viewing of children's programming will convince the curious of television advertising's intent—to plant favorable attitudes in children's minds so that they will want the products advertised. There is not just one brand of each product advertised, however; there is all-out competition among several brands seeking favorable positions in the minds of children. This takes place on all networks simultaneously, so in case the child does switch channels, he is still subjected to essentially the same ads. Consequently, not only will youngsters probably like several brands of a product, but they will hold favorable attitudes toward the product category in general. This is a fact that concerns consumer advocates. They state, in effect, that whatever is advertised to children obtains a favored position in the minds of children. For example, they believe that if unsweetened cereals were given the promotional backing that is given to sweetened cereals, the former would be preferred, and if fruits and vegetables were advertised as are sugared snacks, children would have more desire for fruits and vegetables. Is this true? Will mere exposure to a product cause a liking for it? It appears so. A well-developed study by Goldberg, Gorn, and Gibson (1978) exposed children to advertising for either sugared products (cereal and drinks) or nonsugared products (milk, juice, eggs, and toast). Results showed that the children's preferences were definitely in the direction of the product advertising they received. This was true although the ads for the nonsugared items were public service announcements and not done with the flair of the cereal and beverage ads. Further, these investigators felt that repeated exposure to advertisements for "a given set of products can result in increased demand for a nonadvertised but related set of products" (p. 77). Thus, advertisements for certain sugared cereals probably carry over favorably to sugared cereals, in general; likewise, ads for certain fruit juices probably produce favorable attitudes among children for other juices. This is an advertising principle.

These kinds of research findings lead to another question. Would children develop favorable attitudes toward products advertised even though the products were not for children or not currently consumed by children? Although the research is limited, the answer to this question is in the affirmative direction. Gorn and Florsheim (1985) conducted an experiment among nine- and ten-year-old girls in which they were shown ads for lipstick and diet drinks. The results were that the girls demonstrated a more favorable general attitude toward diet drinks and more favorable general and specific attitudes toward lipstick, the latter being more easily viewed as a potential product for the girls. Robertson, Rossiter, and Gleason (1979) studied the effects of the advertising of proprietary medicines in children and found a mild but positive relationship between exposure to the ads and belief in the efficacy of medicine and a positive attitude toward taking it.

Of course, the positive attitudes displayed by the children in these studies were influenced to some degree by others, particularly parents, but these studies took the additional influentials into consideration wherever possible before drawing their conclusion. Thus, it certainly appears that television advertising is a major contributor to children's attitudes toward brands of products and toward product categories. These are the *exact* results that marketers want and expect. Naturally, favorable attitudes do not necessarily translate into action. A positive attitude toward lipstick, for example, may not cause a child to express a demand for it if she has been taught by parents that lipstick is an adult product. Repeated exposure to lipstick, however, could possibly overcome parent-instilled attitudes toward the product. (Children currently consume cosmetics at the rate of $10 million a year, according to a 1981 report by Weil.) It would certainly seem easier for favorable attitudes toward such products as sugared cereals, candy bars, and soft drinks to become purchases simply because, in general, they are very acceptable products for children.

Children's Consumer Behavior Induced by Advertising

Tom Robertson, a noted researcher in the field of children's consumer behavior, stated in a report by Ward (1978B) that it was not necessary to show behavior effects in order to prove the impact of television advertising on children as consumers. He suggested that just its mere reinforcement of *existing* preferences is significant enough. Television advertising also creates *new* consumer-related attitudes and desires among children, as described in the preceding discussion. They are likely to produce consumer behavior when the opportunity arises. Further, as Moschis and Moore (1979, p. 109) point out, "Many of the orientations and norms about consumption that young people learn" from such sources as television advertising "have little practical value at the time they are learned" but are "saved until a later time."

Still, there are charges made by consumer advocates that television advertising does induce behavior among children that is undesirable in many instances, and there can be no doubt that marketers who advertise to children often expect certain consumer behavior as a result. Figure 5-1 shows that television advertising may indeed produce three types of behavior among children: purchases, purchase requests, and antisocial behavior. Let us briefly consider each of these.

Purchase Behavior

As described in chapter 3, children have money of their own to spend as a result of gifts, work, and allowances. Data in chapter 5 revealed that perhaps

one-third of major retailers are cognizant of children's income and seek business from them, sometimes through television advertising. However, most
television advertising to children emanates from manufacturers of toys and
foods. Their advertising has several goals, only one of which is to encourage
children to make purchases.

Studies of advertising-induced consumer behavior among children are
scant, just as they are among adults. It is very difficult to design a study that
will show that advertising is the main cause of purchase behavior because
there are so many variables, such as parental influence, that intervene between
the advertising and the purchase. Nonetheless, research results do indicate an
advertising/purchase relationship among children.

In 1954, the Kroger Foundation sponsored a study in which children
were permitted to shop in a Kroger supermarket "as grown-ups do" (p. 1).
The report noted that "children really looked for specific items and brands"
that they had seen advertised on TV and, further, that "most of the children
selected cereal" that they had seen advertised on TV (pp. 9, 10). A 1964 study
by McNeal noted that "over half of the children" interviewed reported buying
or asking their parents to buy goods they saw advertised on television (p. 22).

Resnik and Stern (1977) conducted an experiment in which children
viewed television programs along with a commercial for a new brand of
potato chips. Afterward, the children were rewarded with a choice of two
brands of potato chips, the new one that was advertised or another new one.
Fifty-seven percent chose the advertised brand, causing the authors to conclude that "a child is more likely to choose a brand that he has seen advertised
on television over another previously unknown brand that he has not seen
advertised" (p. 16).

In another more elaborate experiment, Goldberg, Gorn, and Gibson
(1977) subjected children to various combinations of a Fat Albert animated
program on junk food, public service announcements that encourage good
nutrition, a Yogi's Gang cartoon, and several 30-second commercials for
snack foods such as Hershey bars and Cracker Jacks. The children then were
permitted to select a set of three snacks from the following: a banana, peanuts,
raisins, Mounds candy bar, jelly beans, and Lollipop Lifesavers. The authors
reported that "those who viewed material stressing the attractiveness and
value of eating more nutritious foods selected significantly more of these
foods than those who viewed commercials stressing the attractiveness and
value of eating less nutritious foods" (p. 543).

Finally, a study of actual rather than experimental consumer behavior of
children by Gorn and Goldberg (1982) demonstrated the power of television
advertising to induce choice behavior. Children from low-income families
who attended a summer camp were subjected to four different treatments
during their voluntary television viewing: (1) candy commercials for such
sugared items as M&M's and Three Musketeers bars, including Kool Aid; (2)
fruit commercials for orange juice, apples, and grapes; (3) public service

announcements on the value of moderating sugar intake and eating a balanced variety of food; and (4) no commercials messages. Each afternoon after their quiet period (television viewing), the children went to another room where they could select beverages and snack foods. Overall, children who watched a morning set of candy/Kool Aid commercials picked the most candy/Kool Aid and the least fruit/orange juice, and those who watched no commercials or fruit/orange juice commercials tended to select fruit/orange juice more than candy/Kool Aid. The authors made what appears to be a significant observation about their results. They said that the young children in the study knew what they *should* eat, but "whether they *acted* upon this awareness and actually chose more fruit seemed to be a function of whether or not they had been exposed to commercials for candy" (p. 204).

Purchase Request Behavior

A particular concern among parents is that television advertisers may cause children to make purchase requests that the parents do not want to fulfill, either because the item requested is expensive or it is viewed by the parents as undesirable. Further, such purchase requests can produce substantial pressure when they are made in the store. For example, Galst and White (1976) conducted a study in which children averaged a purchase-influence attempt every two minutes while in the shopping environment with parents. Moreover, the rate of attempts showed an increase when children watched more television.

Purchase requests made by children typically do vary according to television viewing. Robertson and Rossiter (1977) divided children into low and high TV exposure groups and studied their purchase requests for toys and games during the Christmas season when ads for these items are most intense. The high-exposure group requested significantly more toys and games than the low-exposure group. The researchers found, also, that purchase requests vary by age, with decline occurring in both groups as the children get older. A later analysis by Rossiter (1979) disagreed somewhat with this finding and has more logic. He concluded that purchase requests do not decline with age per se, but just for certain items. For instance, they appear to decline for toys but increase for bicycles. One characteristic of the parents—education—was found to mediate the children's purchase requests. The more educated the parents, the less that TV seemed to persuade the children to make requests to parents. The study results caused the investigators to conclude that television advertising has its greatest effects on the youngest children in families with parents of low education and most likely low income.

It seems appropriate at this point to embellish this discussion of television's influence on children's purchase requests to parents. There is a great deal of literature showing that children influence household decisions through suggestions to parents. For example, Jenkins (1978) found in a study of 105 families that children have a lot of influence on family vacation decisions, and a study by Nelson (1978) revealed that children have extensive influence on the family decision to eat out. It is quite possible that television advertising to children actually is a determinant of some of the children's suggestions to parents and therefore a determinant of parental purchases for the family, not just for the children. Not only do fast food chains advertise during children's programming, but children are exposed to many of the advertisements targeted to adults, such as those for motels, airlines, and vacation places. It has already been shown that television advertising can create desires among children for products normally considered adult products.

Antisocial Behavior

Behavior induced by television advertising may not always be positive. The advertiser may expect a positive outcome and surely he has a positive outcome in mind when he reaches out to children, but it is not possible for him to predict all of the actual impact of his ads on children and their families.

Robertson (1972) noted in an analysis of television advertising's impact on children's behavior patterns that where the advertising pressures children to make purchase requests to parents, the results can be unpleasant conflicts between parent and child. Another result may be disappointment among the children when requests are denied, as Robertson and Rossiter (1976) discovered in around one-third of a group of children, with the disappointment being greatest among the younger ones. This finding was supported by a later study by Sheikh and Moleski (1977).

In a frequently cited study by Goldberg and Gorn (1978), children were shown to be so influenced by a toy ad that the children would prefer to play with the toy rather than a friend, and it even increased their preference for a peer described as "not so nice" rather than a "nice" peer, presumably in order to play with the former child's toy (p. 27). Additionally, this research confirmed the notion that children whose requests are denied experience unhappiness.

It does appear, then, that advertisers' good intentions may actually result in substantial antisocial behavior among family members and among peers. The advertising additionally can, instead of producing happiness, produce sadness and disappointment within the child whose requests are denied. Finally, advertising also may cause unhappiness for parents who do not want to deny their children's requests, but must because of limited economic resources.

Advertising to Children in Other Media

The foregoing discussion of advertising to children has centered only on the medium of television because that is where most of the ad dollars targeted for children are spent and that is the medium of most concern to parents, policy makers, and consumer advocates. This single-medium focus by business as well as the general public also has resulted in television being practically the only medium researched by those interested in children's consumer behavior. One study by Lindquist (1978) is the primary exception. Lindquist's research focus was on children's attitudes toward advertising in the four media of television, radio, comic books, and children's magazines and how these attitudes varied by age through school grades three to six. His essential findings were as follows:

1. Children overall view advertising in children's magazines as most truthful, followed in order by radio, television, and comic books.
2. Children do not feel that advertising in children's magazines encourages them to buy things they don't need to the degree that comic books, radio, and television do.
3. Within all these four media, children's attitudes toward advertising become progressively more negative with age.
4. The shift in attitudes toward advertising in the four media from favorable to unfavorable as children get older is most dramatic for comic books.

The investigator concludes that the overall favorable attitude that children hold toward advertising in children's magazines is due to the reputable organizations (e.g., Boy Scouts, Girl Scouts, National Geographic) associated with some of the magazines, the fact that these magazines are often given as gifts by parents and grandparents, and the fact that the sanctity of the printed word is being felt by the children. He might have added that advertising is not so common in children's magazines, and this relative scarcity may give it an air of quality. He might have mentioned, also, that schools and school teachers, which are very credible sources of information to children, often endorse children's magazines.

The rapid decline in credibility of comic book advertising as children reach preteen years is interesting. Probably, as Lindquist points out, the picture-dominance of comic books appeals to younger children who are just beginning to read, but by the time they reach the fifth and sixth grades the frequent negative remarks about comic books by parents are accepted and assigned to advertising in the comic books. In an interesting inventory of children's books and magazines, Duke (1979) notes that there are around 225 different comic books, and their sales are estimated at two hundred million copies a year. They are an entertainment medium like television and like television are a potentially great medium through which advertisers may reach children. Also like television, they carry a somewhat negative image among children, particularly older children, that probably limits their advertising effectiveness. James Shooter, editor-in-chief of Marvel Comics Group, states,

"Unfortunately, comics are not accepted in this country as a legitimate medium" (Alsop, 1985, p. 33). There is an effort on the part of the industry to get more acceptance and to make it a more viable advertising medium, however. The industry is seeking more distribution outlets, such as bookstores and supermarkets, and it is also attempting to get more acceptance in libraries and schools.

Discussions and Implications

Writing in the *Wall Street Journal* five years after the Quebec government banned all advertising aimed at children under thirteen, Freeman (1985) observed that the law was "winning the praise of consumer advocates" but "toy makers, packaged-food companies and fast-food concerns say the ban makes their selling job harder and more costly while stifling freedom of speech" (p. 23). Similar statements would no doubt be made if advertising to children were banned in the United States, as once attempted by the Federal Trade Commission. Such an action would be tough on advertisers, although pleasing to consumer protectionists. Therefore, serious consideration of this nationwide matter is needed before there is a lopsided victory by the protectionists. The victory would be lopsided because the protectionists appear to have the stronger case, and if a new wave of consumerism cycles in again as it does every 30 years or so, they are likely to win.

Let us look at the evidence presented in this chapter.

1. Children under the age of eight are far too vulnerable to the skills and expertness of Madison Avenue. Children at this age level tend to believe advertising unconditionally, tend to see advertising as a logical part of programming, and tend not to perceive the selling intent of advertising.
2. Separators that identify the approach of a commercial tend not to be effective for children under eight. However, these separators probably would serve their purpose if advertisers would put them in language that children understand.
3. Advertisers still all too often insist on procedures that are misleading to children, particularly to those under eight. For example, they use separators and disclaimers that are often not understood by young children, although research confirms that rewording them would make them effective.
4. Advertising to children is virtually all emotion and persuasion. Advertisers put to work all the creativity they can muster to create a fantasy environment in advertising to children with very little regard for useful information expressed in ways children can understand.
5. Advertisers have the ability to convince children to like and desire practically any product, yet this ability is applied mainly to toys and sugared foods, not to many other product lines.

6. Regulators and self-regulators of children's advertising are not as effective as they could be. Federal regulators are often limited by political bonds, while self-regulators, who are in a position to be almost perfect controllers of advertising, limit their effectiveness by their self-imposed boundaries.
7. Parents are often displeased with certain elements of advertising to children, such as deceptiveness, excessive persuasion, emphasis on undesirable products or product features, and emphasis on premiums. This general negativism is gradually parroted by the children as they get older, and by adulthood there is another generation of consumers who are skeptical and mistrusting of television advertising to children.
8. Finally, advertising is in a pivotal position to participate substantially in the consumer socialization of children, yet, while it is teaching children a great deal of consumer behavior, it continues to mar its own image among them.

What all this means is that advertising to children is doing a fantastic job of practicing good advertising principles. It is more proficient than the proverbial Pied Piper. However, it is doing only a fair job of practicing good business principles. The three-in-one children's market is so exciting and appealing to advertisers that their anxieties are causing them to err by forgetting to be consumer-oriented. Our economy is founded on the fundamental principle of consumer sovereignty: business exists for the benefit of consumers and can serve itself only so far as it serves consumers first. Therefore, a rethinking of children's advertising is needed.

Somewhere between Quebec and Madison Avenue is a vital midpoint that must be sought. Advertising to children has too much value to society to eliminate it as they did in Quebec. It plays a very important role in the consumer socialization of children and it provides much entertainment and baby-sitting in the form of Saturday morning and after-school programming, but it must become consumer-oriented. Its consumers are children who are not yet as skilled as the adults who do the advertising. Children are consumers in training. They should be treated this way. Just what form advertising should take to be acceptable to all parties—to children and, of course, their parents and to advertisers—can be worked out so that the advertisements remain and the children and their parents are satisfied. Probably the final form for children's advertising, particularly to children under age eight, should be one that consists mostly of information rather than persuasion. In Quebec, after five years without advertising to children, the toy industry reports sales "about the same as before the ban," fast food chains still describe sales as "great," and only the presweetened cereal industry is reporting possible lower sales than expected (Freeman, 1985, p. 23). It may be that sweetened cereal sales are not as large as would be, but perhaps cereal sales in general are fine. After all, the cereal companies are probably not so concerned with sales of sugared cereals as much as with cereals in general. For instance, discoveries in medical science have caused increased sales in bran cereals during the 1980s that no doubt were accompanied by decreases in sales of certain other cereals. It is most likely that overall the cereal companies are not disappointed by this switch among consumers because the end result is still profits.

Advertisers are skilled at producing informative ads, and who has better information about the products than advertisers. Emphasizing information and deemphasizing persuasion may cause a loss in sales of one product at the expense of another, but such sales are then on much more justifiable grounds. Advertisers can still compete with one another, television networks can still sell time at very high rates, and children can still have their Saturday morning cartoons. The First Amendment rights of advertising do not become an issue, and probably they should not. In the final analysis, the right to advertise to children is not necessarily the right thing to do, to paraphrase a more eloquent statement by Paine (1984).

6
Features and Functions
of Products for Children

Focus group interviews were held with groups of three or four boys and girls who were playmates in order to elicit their opinions about signature clothing, defined as clothing with a quality-endowed brand name. A portion of an interview among three sixth-graders follows. All three boys live in the same upper-middle-class neighborhood.

INTERVIEWER: I would like to know your favorite brand of shirt.

LEE: Izod.

T.J.: Ocean Pacific.

TIM: Izod.

INTERVIEWER: Now I need to know why those are your favorite brands of shirt. Why is Izod your favorite brand, Tim?

TIM: Izods last a long time and they are top quality.

INTERVIEWER: How about you, Lee. Why do you like Izod best?

LEE: I don't know. They are just better. My dad wears them.

T.J.: One thing's for sure, an Izod doesn't look as classy as an OP (Ocean Pacific).

TIM: What? What do you mean? An Izod has class. It has more class than any shirt. That's why it costs more.

LEE: Let me ask you this, T.J., would you wear an OP shirt to church? You wouldn't, would you?

T.J.: Sure I would. That black OP I have looks as nice as any shirt. I've worn it to church.

LEE: I wouldn't wear that thing to church. It looks like something break-dancers wear.

TIM: I agree with Lee that an Izod looks nicer than OP. I have some OPs, but I like the Izods better. I don't wear any of them to church, but I would wear the Izods if my parents would let me.

LEE: My parents let me. Even my dad sometimes wears Izods to church. You think God cares?

These brief remarks indicate some of the emotion that may be generated among children by certain products and their brands. Children often take their products and brands seriously, even to the point of bringing God into a discussion of them.

In chapter 4, we described children's interactions with retail outlets and the resulting purchases. Here in this chapter we will spotlight those purchases by examining some of the products that marketers offer and children buy. Separate treatment will be given to the product attributes of brand and price.

Why Children Want Products from the Marketplace

Children aren't born wanting commercial products (although some parents might almost think it, because one of the first sentences children learn is, "I wantta"). Products are imposed on children by their culture as the principal means of satisfying their needs. Children are apparently born with need imprints and, as the needs mature and require satisfaction, children are taught to depend on commercial products. More precisely, the child, as an infant, first looks to his parents for the satisfaction of needs, but the child eventually realizes that his parents rely on the marketplace for his need satisfiers. At just what age this transference takes place is not clear. Probably, it is determined by the periodicity of marketplace visits with parents.

As an infant, the soon-to-be consumer discovers that his crib is filled rail to rail with stuffed toys, noise-makers, and teethers. Moreover, he discovers that many of these items also accompany him when he is taken from the crib. By the time he is old enough to sit erect on the floor, he is surrounded by a field of toys that squeak, squawk, roll, and bounce and almost always smile back. When he is able to try out his legs, he can practice with strollers, rollers, go-cars, and push cars that have been obtained from the marketplace. During all this time, he is being turned into a giggling gourmet as his mouth is introduced to every flavor and fragrance imaginable. In only a few years, however, his mother in a moment of frustration may respond to one of his requests with, "I can't understand you. All you do is want, want, want!"

Almost unknowingly, the parents begin transferring to the child the concept of being his own consumer. He is unintentionally introduced to all the kinds of stores in which his parents have been obtaining the many toys and sweets they give him. He is introduced, also, to the product selection and exchange activities, often from his vantage point high atop a shopping cart. Intertwined among many store visits with his parent is a continuing education in money, its use and value. By age five or six, he is able to put it all together by making his first visit to a store on his own. Now it is only a matter of time before he will be making requests to parents for money to buy for himself many of those products, such as candy bars and soft drinks, that they once bought for him. As he continues his purchasing practice, the world of marketing unfolds to him and reveals an endless array of things to want and buy.

Although a child seems to view everything generally from his own per-spective—for example, the moon is seen as following him (Piaget, 1932)—the products he values and wants to buy are determined principally by his social setting. Thus, what a youngster wants to eat, for example, is taught to him by significant social agents. If he wants the wrong things he is punished, although usually subtly; if his wants are socially correct, he is rewarded with the products and with signs of approval. Early in their life children do not know, for example, that paper and dirt are inedible, so they often place these things in their mouths. If not corrected, they may even learn to like them; this is a practice called pica (Lourie, Layman, and Millican, 1963). Three-year-old children will invariably put coins in their mouths, and parents must scold them in order to teach them this is dangerous. Only a few years later, however, parents will begin teaching the children that coins are not really bad but good and in fact have purchasing power. In a classic study many years ago, Bruner and Goodman (1947) found that ten-year-old children consistently overesti-mated the size of coins, and the larger the coin's denomination, the greater the overestimating. For instance, children overestimated the size of a nickel, but overestimated the size of a quarter even more. Further, the poorer the child, the more the size of coins was exaggerated. What we see here is not only the value that children have been taught to place on certain pieces of metal called coins, but the gradations in value they have been taught within their social setting. Similarly, a child learns to like bubble gum, for example, as it is purchased and given to him by parents, and within a short time he learns that two pieces in his mouth are better than one because they produce a bigger bubble and elicit a bigger sign of approval from observers. Because there are so many products to learn about and because many of these prod-ucts are age-related, part of each year of childhood is involved with under-standing products and their value to different groups of people. Belk, Bahn, and Mayer, for example, studied the individual's "ability to recognize the social implications of consumption choices" among a wide range of subjects (preschoolers to adults) and found that the ability hardly exists at all among preschoolers, is significant by the time children reach the second grade, and is almost fully developed by the sixth grade (1982, p. 13). If children did not learn what products are for what people, obtaining need satisfaction from the marketplace would be very difficult.

The fact that children desire commercial products at all cannot be ade-quately explained then on the basis of needs theory alone but is better under-stood by combining need theory with a cultural or social perspective. Chil-dren quickly learn in our society that it is not only correct to satisfy most needs by going to the marketplace, it is a cultural requirement. Sometimes in their disgust with children-oriented advertising, parents tend to think that marketers started this system of need satisfaction rather than it being a part of the cultural fabric.

Both motivation theory and social theory are necessary to explain why children want a lot ("a whole bunch") of different products. Motivation theory suggests, for example, a need for variety (Faison, 1977) as an explanation for children wanting many different products. The need for variety—also termed need for new experience, novelty, sensation, and curiosity—has adequate empirical support and is intuitively appealing as an explanation for a good deal of children's behavior. It seems, according to this theory, that products have quick "wear-out" for children; they become bored with their present toys, candy bars, cereals, and so on, and want different ones. Because most children in our society usually do not have to worry about essentials— mom and dad provide these without even asking—their minds have plenty of time for mental playfulness to produce new ideas, new wants, and new directions for satisfying their desire for stimulation. They tear their toys apart, they play curiously with their cereal, they dip their chocolate bars in the peanut butter, all for the experience of it. They make requests for new items, which often differ only slightly from articles they already have, in order to have more novelty in their lives. In one experiment by Harris (1965) three-, four-, and five-year-old children had new toys introduced into their play setting. Afterward, the children insisted on having the new toys, and the experimenter had trouble drawing the children's attention back to the familiar toys. This is not unlike the problem that parents experience after their children have seen a new toy in a store. The youngsters often insist on having the new item, and when reminded that they have similar items at home, respond, "I don't care. I want that one." Perhaps what the child is really saying is that what is similarity to the parent is variation to him.

There are many other needs in addition to the need for variety that children satisfy by owning "a whole bunch" of things, including, for example, the needs for affiliation and achievement. However, once we have worked our way through a list of needs and demonstrated how they are met by children with an endless array of products, we are still left without an adequate explanation for why children want specific products and not others and want certain brands of particular products. Social theory can provide this explanation. Social theory tells us that children want certain products for two reasons: identification with and/or separation from others. Children identify with other children, but also with adults, mainly parents and certain celebrities. Consequently, children often want what other children have. By having the exact products that peers have, the children can be equal to or just like them. Thus we may hear the child justify to his parents the need for a certain product by saying, "Everyone has one." Children also want to be grown up and having things like those that mom and dad have is a way to act out grownupness. In the process of attempting to satisfy this need to be adult, some marketers offer children socially undesirable products. One example is look-alikes. These items are confectionary copies of strictly adult products, such as candy cigarettes, gum that looks like chewing tobacco, and candy in cans that are designed like well-known brands of beer (Brackin, 1982). Children also may demonstrate maturity by buying products related to celebrities and therefore identifying with them. These products may be something unusual, such as a Star Wars ray-gun used by one of the characters in the movie, or they simply may be products routinely used by a celebrity, for example a brand of cereal or candy bar eaten by Mary Lou Retton.

Children also can practice separation or differentiation by buying and owning certain items. Children have negative reference groups, just as adults do. Certain age groups, such as preschoolers, may be negative to youngsters in another age group, such as sixth graders, and those in the latter group can separate themselves from the younger ones by owning certain products. For instance, a bicycle separates a child from those younger ones that own tricycles. Being first to own something can be another way to differentiate oneself. Hence, the advertisements that shout to children, "Be the first on your block to own one," probably appeal to children's needs to be different from some certain other children.

In order for children to use various products for satisyfying such needs as identification and separation, the children must be informed of available products that serve these purposes. Learning of these products is usually easy. Children can discover what products are significant for satisfying certain needs by observing what products other children are using. These products are displayed by the children at school and at play. If by chance some youngsters live in isolation, they can still be informed of their peers' products use through television. Practically all advertisements aimed at children contain children in them displaying and demonstrating products. Also, actors in programs targeted to children often provide young viewers with guidelines for product ownership and use. Children also can find out about product use through catalogs sent to their home from, for example, Sears, Penneys, or a large number of giftware houses. Magazines, such as *Highlights for Children, Jack and Jill,* and *Penny Power,* will indicate what products are "in." Finally, the retail store is a great place for children to discover what is new and to be able to actually touch what they see advertised on television.

In a study by Frideres (1973), children were asked where they first heard about new toys. Over three-quarters answered television, while the remaining named playmates. In another study, Caron and Ward (1975) found four major sources of Christmas gift ideas used by children; they were television (27 percent); catalogs (19 percent); stores (22 percent); and friends (26 percent). Studies do not seem to cite parents as a typical source of information about products for children. This may be because parents are so natural a source that children fail to mention them, or, to the contrary, that children prefer other sources such as peers, at least after a certain age (Hawkins and Coney, 1974). Advertising media other than television are seldom mentioned by children as sources of product information, no doubt reflecting the over-whelming influence of television.

Products in the Consumer Socialization Process

Chapter 2 observed that products are a major factor in the consumer sociali-zation of children. By owning, using, and just being around products, children learn the nature and functions of the products. As a result of experiences with products, children also learn more about other children, about the consumer role, and about other roles such as marriage and working. Products often are major sources of conflict between parents and children and between children and their playmates, but products are also a means of communication and affiliation between children and others. Hence, products are very fundamen-tal in children's consumer socialization. According to Belk, May, and Driscoll (1984), products form a symbol "language" for children by suggesting char-acteristics of their users.

Products, of course, do not teach in the sense that a person teaches. They teach in the sense that a maze teaches a rat. They are culture-bound instru-ments of learning that give direction to behavior. Their influence on chil-dren's socialization—on the transference of culture from one person to another and from one generation to another—can be assessed, to some extent, if we just try to imagine life without them. Therefore, we will portray them as things from which children learn, just as we may describe people from which children learn. We should note that while learning from products is often incidental for children, both marketers and parents may use them for pur-poseful teaching.

From an investigative perspective, the importance of products in the development of children, like most elements in the consumer socialization process, is overshadowed by the attention given to advertising and its sociali-zation effects. This in fact seems somewhat naive of researchers because they are overlooking such a fundamental contributor to the development of chil-dren. Often researchers unintentionally study products while studying other elements of the consumer socialization process. Ward, for example, reported that he studied children's "perceptions, judgements, and explanations of TV advertising" (1972B; p. 37), yet many of his findings were in terms of prod-ucts. He asked children, "What is a TV commercial?" Children's responses however, were often in product-related terms, such as, "tries to get people to buy products" and "informs people about products; shows things to buy" (p. 39). When he asked children, "Why are commercials shown on TV," his largest groups of responses were of this nature: "to make people buy things" and "to sell products" (p. 39). When Ward asked his young respondents what commercials they liked least and best, he classified the answers in terms of products (p. 40). Consequently, Ward's conclusions often were related to

Table 6-1
Some Skills, Knowledge, and Attitudes that
Children May Learn from Owning a Bicycle

Physical aspects
   It carries people and things
   Its wheels turn; you can steer them
   You can sit on it
   You can stand on its pedals
   It has variable speeds

Comparative aspects
   It moves like a motorcycle, tricycle, and automobile
   It is slower than an automobile, faster than a tricycle
   It is faster than walking
   It can be raced with other bicycles

Social aspects
   Some are for girls; some are for boys
   Two people can share one
   It permits group behavior such as riding together to school
   It serves both children and adults
   It facilitates occupations, such as newspaper carrier
   It is for older children

Psychological aspects
   It attracts attention to the rider
   It suggests physical prowess
   It confirms the self concept of being youthful, fast, daring,
      self-sufficient, social

products. For example, he observed, "Among young children . . . a substantial number of answers indicated that a commercial was liked because the product was liked" (p. 41) and "They may evaluate truthfulness (of commercials) in terms of their experience with products" (p. 42). Thus, Ward and other researchers have indirectly demonstrated the fundamental role of products in the consumer socialization of children.

   To emphasize the importance of products in the consumer socialization of children, table 6-1 prosaically enumerates some possible skills, knowledge, and attitudes that children may learn from owning a bicycle. With this list in table 6-1 as a reminder, consider the hundreds of products owned during childhood and the hundreds of products owned by the children's parents but used by the children; then the extent to which products may impact upon children's learning can begin to be appreciated. Let us classify some of the important things learned from products that contribute to the consumer socialization of the child.

Product Nature and Functions

In describing what cognitions a child might learn from owning a bicycle, table 6-1 notes first the physical aspect of a bicycle. Although a child may learn about a bicycle before owning or riding one, actual experience with one is the most logical way to know its physical characteristics. This is generally true for all products. To know the pleasure of a video game, the cold refreshing taste of a frozen dessert, and the tasty crunchiness of a cereal, a youngster must experience them. It is this experience that ultimately determines whether the child will be a consumer for specific products. He may want a particular product before he has ever had one, but he is a consumer for that product to the extent he wants more after he has experienced one. A study by Robertson, Rossiter, and Gleason (1979B) showed that most children wanted medicines when ill, and after experiencing illness and presumably taking medicines their intent to take medicine increased. In a landmark study over one-half century ago (1931), Dr. Clara Davis for a period of five years allowed fourteen children ages one to five to eat whatever they wished among a wide assortment of foods and to eat as much as they wished. As the children discovered and experienced the actual tastes and textures of many kinds of foods, they settled down to eating what they particularly liked. She stated:

> Definite likes and dislikes have not been much in evidence during the first week or two but have become apparent by the end of this time and thereafter when the trays have been placed before them the babies have quickly looked them over as one does the food counter in a cafeteria and promptly reached for what they wanted, regardless of its position on the tray, generally making their meals of three or four articles and ignoring the rest (pp. 631-632).

Thus, in order for children to continue to want a product—to have a product preference—they must understand its utilitarian functions and these functions must benefit the children. Experiencing products and learning their nature is probably the most fundamental aspect of children's consumer behavior. Most retailers have learned this fact well and display products of interest to children within hand's reach and at eye level. Kroger's supermarkets have considered discontinuing this practice at the checkout counter because of frequent complaints from parents.

Social Functions of Products

"At some point . . . material goods acquire social meaning . . . and children begin to see goods as being instrumental in achieving social goals rather than as simply filling a functional need . . ." (Ward, 1974, p. 10). A rose is indeed more than just a rose when it is given by a child to mother on Mother's Day. In this case, the product, perhaps purchased at a nearby supermarket, is beautiful and fragrant, but additionally it is a social bond between child and parent.

The social aspects can be great for any product regardless of its cost. A Coke or a pack of M&M's, for example, can be just as instrumental in forming friendships as a bicycle or video game. Although children can learn the social implications of products from such agents as parents and advertising, only through owning the product and experiencing it can the social outcomes be confirmed. "This is because more experience with a product affords more opportunity to see how others treat the product's owners, regardless of whether the owners are self or observed others" (Belk, Mayer, and Driscoll, 1984, p. 386).

Products are instrumental in children's learning of sex roles. Barbie dolls and G.I. Joe dolls almost always elicit different responses between boys and girls, whereas a game such as Monopoly probably elicits similar responses. Boys and girls also discover that they can buy makeup to accompany the Barbie doll, but not G.I. Joe. Experience with products such as these contribute substantially to the understanding of sex roles among children and will eventually contribute to their sex typing of other products. The net result is that they learn that they can purchase some products to reinforce their own sex roles, purchase some products to reinforce the sex roles of others such as parents, and buy some products to switch sex roles or even neutralize them.

Another very major social aspect of products is their ability to permit children to identify with reference groups and role models. A youngster has many different reference groups at various times, such as older children, rock stars, children at school, and athletes. Products facilitate easy identification with these groups. Ocean Pacific T-shirts and Nike running shoes, for example, can place a young man in good standing with his fellow fifth-graders. A young lady in the same grade can wear Tinkerbell eye shadow in order to show her association with teens, and a signature tennis racquet can help both sexes identify with certain pro players. Marketers are certainly aware of these social implications of products. The children's cosmetic industry is a $10 million a year business and is expected to grow to several times that figure (Weil, 1981). A ten-year-old miss can go to a department store and be shown how to apply Tinkerbell cosmetics at a "grooming session," and if she is well-to-do she can purchase, for example, a skin care regimen kit by Organica Jeunesse that includes "a cleanser, moisturizer, and head-to-toe shampoo . . . each containing nine herbs, vitamins A, D, and E" (Weil, 1981, p. 28). If children wish, they also can copy some bad habits of role models at low prices. Boys can chew Big League Chew ("shredded Bubble Gum in Stay-fresh Pouches and Man Size Wads") and imitate some of their favorite baseball heroes (Brackin, 1982). If these baseball stars also drink, then the boys can pretend to be like them by buying jelly beans in a whisky bottle labeled nonalcoholic Strawberry Daiquiri or candy in a beer can labeled But Wiser (Brackin, 1982).

Children also learn through the vehicle of products the concept of social status. That is, the owning of certain products will cause a child to be assigned more or less social status relative to other children. In one study, "There were

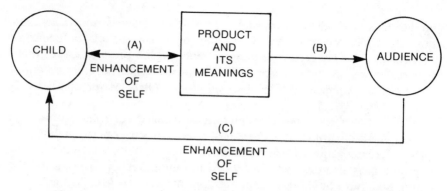

Relationships:
A. The child transfers the meaning of the product to himself, thus enhancing his self-concept.
B. The child communicates to an audience with a product and its meanings.
C. The audience attributes to the child the meanings communicated by the product. Thus, his self-concept is enhanced again.

Figure 6-1. Products Can Enhance a Child's Self-Concept in Two Ways

indicators that there was prestige value associated with such toys as air rifles, football uniforms, and miniature rockets powered by realistic fuels," and that "generally the prestige of the item was related to its cost and its approximation to the real thing" (McNeal, 1964, p. 19). In this same study, about 40 percent of nine year olds were concerned about automobiles and stated preferences for "prestige cars, considering them beautiful, fast, fun to ride in, and worth having because their friends' parents owned one" (p. 20).

Psychological Functions of Products

Holbrook and Hirschman observed that "all products, no matter how mundane, may carry a symbolic meaning . . ." and "project important nonverbal cues . . ." (1982, p. 134). It has long been known that people utilize the symbolic aspects of products to say things about themselves and to enhance their self-image (Grubb and Grathwohl, 1967). Self-enhancement can take place in two ways, by buying goods that one knows are recognized publicly and classified in a manner that supports and matches one's self-concept and by using the products in the interaction process to cause desired reactions from other individuals (Grubb and Grathwohl, 1967, p. 206). Figure 6-1 presents a flow diagram depicting how a product can serve to enhance a child's self-concept in two ways. First, by owning and displaying a product (*A*), such as a G.I. Joe toy, a child enhances his self-concept by communicating to himself (*A*) the meanings of the product that have been assigned to it by advertising and by other children. Second, the product conveys symbolic meaning to an audience (*B*), such as the child's friends, and the audience assigns the product's meanings to the child who displays the product (*C*), thus enhancing this self-concept again. For example, if the product is a G.I. Joe toy machine gun that has been imbued with the attributes of masculinity and maturity by advertising and by other children, simply owning and displaying the gun makes the child feel older and more manly. When these meanings are fed back to the child by peers who see him with the gun, his self-concept receives an additional enhancement.

Probably most branded products targeted primarily to children possess symbolic meaning that has been added through repeated advertising messages. Their meanings can be communicated easily providing the products are conspicuous, as are most toys, clothing, shoes, and soft drinks. There is concern among consumer advocates over what they term "self-concept appeals" in advertising in which children are promised certain personal benefits from using or owning certain products. According to Rossiter (1980), "self-concept appeals" occur in 27 percent of television advertising to children.

Products that Teach Specific Consumer Behavior

Ordinarily, when we think of teaching children consumer behavior, we think of the activities of parents and those of elementary and secondary school. As noted in chapter 2, schools and parents are the most important agents in the consumer socialization of children. Chapter 4 noted that retailers, also, are potentially very important socialization agents. In addition to these, advertising as described in Chapter 5 is a very important socializer of children as consumers. There are some products, also, that apart from being for sale in stores or being the focus of advertising play a specifically important role in the consumer socialization of children.

To say that products have specific influence on the consumer socialization of children may sound like a contradiction because the term *socialization* implies people influencing people. The products that we are referring to here, however, are no more or less inanimate than some advertisements. As with advertisements, there are people behind the products that are responsible for the influence.

Table 6-2 lists a large number of products that were found as a result of a search in two toy stores. The list is hardly exhaustive, but it does present a number of examples of products that appear to teach particular consumer behavior to children. The products are placed in four classifications: (1) products that teach children how to buy or shop; (2) products that teach brand names; (3) products that teach their use in tandem with other products that require purchase; and (4) products that teach something about business operations. These classes are not mutually exclusive.

There is no research available that tells us to what degree these products actually are intended to teach particular consumer behavior to children and whose intention it is. For example, is the children's plastic trailer for super cabs that has the brand name Exxon emblazoned on its sides intended to teach children brand name awareness, and specifically the Exxon brandname? If so, is it the intent of Kidco, the company that makes the toy trailer, or the intent of Exxon? If it is the intent of either of these business firms for children to learn brand names, is the motive social service, profit, or both? That is, do the firms feel an obligation to help children learn such consumer behavior as brand name awareness, or do they see this as simply an opportunity to develop customers for Exxon by creating awareness of its brand name among children. One toy store manager stated that he assumed that the various toy companies had produced these toys that teach consumer behavior simply because they believe that children are interested in business matters. He went on to say that he was impressed with these kinds of toys because they were so realistic.

Let us briefly consider some of these toys and their potential for teaching specific consumer behavior. Keep in mind that the actual intent of these toys is not known. However, their potential to teach certain dimensions of consumer behavior seems apparent.

Products that Teach How to Shop or Buy. There are many aids that teachers use in the elementary school classroom to teach children consumer behavior, but it is unusual to see similar items in the store for sale to children. The Milton Bradley game Bargain Hunter, which is intended for children beyond age nine, certainly could teach children about shopping, credit, types of stores, and debt. The object is to buy a variety of items for the home and to get them paid for first—to get out of debt. There is a credit card machine with the game that simulates those used in stores, but this one also accepts or rejects one's credit. Among other toys that teach something about shopping or buying are two brands of shopping carts, Lil' Powder Puff and Tuff Stuff, that permit a child to act out the product selection efforts in a supermarket or discount store. Banks, such as the Handy Candy Bank and the Toy Gumball Machine bank, can help children learn money management. There appear to be several books for reading and coloring that teach a variety of aspects of consumer behavior. The one listed in table 6-2 appears to have the purpose of acquainting children with the various retail stores they may find near their homes.

Products that Teach Brand Awareness. It is understandable that toy companies would want children to learn the brand names of their toys, but the items in table 6-2 potentially teach children brand names of many items such as cars, trucks, and motorcycles. The lines of miniature cars and trucks are

Table 6-2
Toys that Teach Consumer Behavior to Children

Description	Manufacturer
Toys That Teach How To Buy or Shop	

My First Purse: Just Like Mommy's
    with keys, credit card, compact, comb, lipstick, pen, change
    purse
	Arco Preschool

Lil' Powder Puff Shopping Cart pink and white, handle and wheels, rustproof	Empire
Tuff Stuff Shoppin' Basket 3-year warranty, 22 × 16 × 19 inches, plastic with seat	Mattel
Toy Gumball Machines Bank-O-Matic, takes 1¢, 5¢, 10¢, plastic shatter-proof dome	Arrow
Handy Candy Bank w/Reese's Pieces	Arrow

Play Phone
    hangs on doorknob, like a pay phone, plastic 5¢, 10¢, 25¢
    coins, slots for coins, change dish
	Playschool

Bargain Hunter Game "the smart shopping game with lots of fun in store for you"	MB

Sesame Street—People in Your Neighborhood
    golden melody book talks about the baker, cleaner, barber,
    grocer
	Golden

Toys That Teach Awareness of Brands and Company Names	

Hot Wheels
    Corvette
    380 Sel
    Pontiac J2000
    Aries Wagon
    Ford Escort
	Mattel

Pocket Cars
    Jaguar XJS
    Datsun 280ZX
    BMW 320i
    Continental Mark IV
    Toyota 4WD Pickup
    Custom Chevy Van
	Tomy

Power Devils
    Bronco
    Toyota
	Mattel

3 Wheel Riding Pedal Motorcycle
    Kawasaki KLT 250
    Harley-Davidson
	Empire

Battery Powered Motorcycle
    Honda "Follow the Leader"
    Tomy Poweride (electronic idle and high rev sounds)
	Tomy

Tough Wheels
    plastic trailers for super rig trucks, side-labels: Exxon,
    Kool-Aid, Barnum's Animal Crackers (Nabisco), Chips Ahoy
    (Nabisco), Mounds (Peter Paul)
	Kidco

Table 6–2 *continued*

Description	Manufacturer

Plastic Toy Cars
  decals: Mountain Dew, Bronco II-XL9, Skoal Bandit,
  Porche 928
	Gay Toys Inc.

Rail Master 72 train set rail cars: Santa Fe, Union Pacific, Texaco	Tyco

Kaleidoscopes
  cardboard cans with real-looking labels: Campbell's
  Vegetable soup can and Pepsi
	Steven Manufacturing Co.

Toys That Teach Consumption of Complementary Products

Easy-Baker Dual-Temp Oven Betty Crocker oven, two round pans, pan handler, cookbook	Kenner
Make Believe Silverstone Set 17-piece pots with lids with Silverstone Sticker	Chilton-Globe
Toy Replicas Corningware Cookware pots and plates	TMA
Revere Ware Aluminum Replicas	Chilton-Globe

Betty Crocker Easy-Bake
  Strawberry Shortcake Party Cake Set with Betty Crocker
  Cake and Icing Mixes
	Kenner

Easy Bake Mixes—Betty Crocker 4 pack	Kenner

Ohio Art Play Pfaltzgraff
  four place settings, 26 pieces, 2 patterns, Village (brown)
  and Yorktowne (blue)
	Ohio Art

Kellogg's Snap! Crackle! Pop! Breakfast Set
  27 pieces, 4 place settings, 4 bowls, milk pitcher, 4 cups, 4
  plates with "Snap! Crackle! Pop!" characters on them and
  one small box of Kellogg's Rice Krispies cereal
	Ohio Art

Fashion Doll Barbeque Party Set
  with two small Pepsi plastic bottles, dishes, BBQ grill, chair,
  picnic table
	Arco

Toys That Teach Business Operations

Snoopy Sno-Cone Machine
  machine with metal ice shaver, one syrup bottle, one
  package unsweetened soft drink mix, paper cups, shovel
  scoop, instructions
	Hasbro

Tom Thumb Cash Register steel construction, cash drawer with bell, paper money	

Fisher Price Cash Register
  "It's fun to make a sale," "Place coins in slot matched to its
  size, push register key that's color and number coded to
  coin, register displays amount, coin disappears. Push Sale
  key, coin drops into drawer, register displays sale. To return
  coin, turn crank on side, drawer pop open, bell rings." Two
  coins each 5¢, 10¢, 25¢, sturdy plastic
	Fisher Price

Play Family Action Garage
  elevator, ramp, 4 cars, 4 play people, gas pump, grease
  rack, stop signs
	Fisher Price

Table 6–2 continued

Description	Manufacturer

Gas & Go Service Center
  small 1½ ft. plastic pump with nozzle, turn crank and
  numbers move, "motorized" gas pump
	Fisher Price

Hot Wheels Service Center
  car wash with turning rollers, dynamo meter, spins car
  wheels, pump-bell rings when cars pull up, movable
  elevator, ramps, "Larry's Towing, Mike's Transmissions"
  stickers on center: Shell, Pennzoil, Goodyear, Champion
	Mattel

Happy Pumper
  pump with nozzle, gallons & price on register, flexible air
  hose with handle for checking tires, plastic hammer and
  wrench for tune ups, rear shelf for storage of oil and water
  cans, oil and water plastic with spouts
	Little Tikes

Take Along Town Sweet Shop ice cream store with truck, chairs, table	Arrow

Barbie Dream Store
  70-piece fashion department with jewelry, hats, belts, shoes,
  mirrors for trying on items, dress rack, purse, glasses, furs
	Mattel

Barbie Loves McDonald's
  "the fun place where Barbie doll and her friends go to eat"
  plastic McDonalds' counter and benches, trash bin with
  thank you on it, drink machine, plastic trays, menu lists
  quarter-pounder, fries, breakfast items, etc., plastic
  McDonalds cup, hamburger and french fries packages,
  breakfast packages
	Mattel

Barbie Beauty Salon
  hair color, scissors (plastic), tissues, phone, mirror, counter
  and swivel chair
	Mattel

apparently popular with children; several were found in toy stores. On these toy vehicles are such well-known brand names as Chevrolet, Ford, and Toyota. In addition to brands of vehicles, there are brands of just about everything associated with the toys, such as candy, tobacco, soft drinks, and snack foods. If a manufacturer of any product wanted to develop customers, these toys suggest that it could start by arranging for a toy company to place the manufacturer's brand name on toys with the goal of teaching awareness of the brand name to children. The freedom to do this, however, particularly for items deemed possibly dangerous, such as tobacco, should be questioned. Apparently, however, only the social conscience of the toy company or the toy industry can prevent misuse of this freedom.

Whether it is the intent of these toy firms to teach brand awareness or to provide children with realistic toys, the potential for raising the brand consciousness among children seems substantial.

Products that Teach Use and Purchase of Other Products. There are several toys that have the ability to teach somewhat complex product relationships that children will have to know about as adults. These toys often are kitchen-related and permit children to learn something about related products required for food preparation. For example, the Fashion Doll Barbeque Party Set by Arco suggests that soft drinks, in this case Pepsi Cola, go with cooking out. The Betty Crocker Easy-Bake set by Kenner offers an understanding of baking a cake, using a cake mix and icing (Betty Crocker, of course). Kellogg's Snap! Crackle! Pop! Breakfast Set by Ohio Art teaches an awareness of breakfast preparation with emphasis upon serving cereal with milk. In all these cases, the youngster may learn mini-systems in which products that can be purchased in stores fit together. Of course, there is also much potential for learning brand names from these items.

Products that Teach Business Operations. To become successful consumers, children need to learn about business operations as well as learn purchase behavior. There are a large number of toys that have the potential for teaching children about business behavior, particularly that of retailers. There is, for example, a Hot Wheels Service Center by Mattel that washes cars, aligns their wheels, does transmission work, and, of course, sells several name brand items, such as Pennzoil and Goodyear. Fisher Price toy company also offers similar items, so car care appears to be important to children, no doubt reflecting the importance of cars to their parents. There is a Snoopy Sno-Cone Machine by Hasbro that shaves ice and comes with the mix and dishes for producing a sno-cone. There are two brands of cash registers, one by Fisher Price complete with bell, coins, and price display, that should give children an idea of what it is like to be on the other side of the store counter.

Toys such as these actually could facilitate children's entry into the consumer role. The toys reinforce some of the business activities learned by children while accompanying parents on shopping trips. Conversely, visits to stores may confirm what the children learn from the toys.

The Role of Brands in Children's Consumer Behavior

It is difficult to speak of products without mentioning or inferring brands. This was the case in the preceding discussion. Brands make modern marketing possible, and marketing, in turn, makes brands a normal part of our language, including that of children. For example, in an interview with an eleven-year-old boy, some merchandise in a chain sporting good store was referred to by the youngster as "K-Mart-y." When the youngster was asked what this term meant, he answered, "Stuff that's not very good." In a study by Belk, Mayer, and Driscoll (1984), it was found that children assigned more favorable evaluations of people who owned name brand items than those owning store brands.

Table 6-2 lists a number of toy store items that possess well-known brand names (in addition to the toy's brand name). For example, there is a Corvette miniature car, a Barbie doll set that has a McDonald's motif, and a Hot Wheels service center that "sells" such brands as Goodyear and Shell. Presumably, these brands are made an integral part of these toys by the toy manufacturers because the brands have significance to children. Lester Guest (1942), a psychologist, demonstrated many years ago that brands do have importance to children. He discovered that three-quarters of children ages seven and eight had awareness of brand of such diverse products as cereal and automobiles and that this awareness increased in depth and range with age. Rossiter (1976) also discovered children's brand awareness in an indirect but vivid way. He was interested in the stored images that children possess in their minds. In one part of his investigation, he asked children to draw a cereal box. To his surprise, 67 percent of first graders and 100 percent of third and fifth graders spontaneously provided brands within their cereal box drawings (p. 524). The mere fact that children hold a large number of brands in their mind, termed the *brand repertoire* by McNeal, McDaniel, and Smart (1983), suggests the significance of brands to children.

The fact that "as early as the third grade youngsters are as conscious of the importance of an Izod alligator or a Calvin Klein label as are adults" (Sloan, 1982, p. 24) may be explained by the children taking cues from parents, peers, and promotion. Parents consistently subject their children to brands, often unknowingly, by discussing brands of products and by using brand names conversationally, almost as generics, such as "Hand me a Kleenex" and "We'll make some Jello." In addition, a major portion of the goods that parents buy and display and that their children may experience are brand items. Parents also may intentionally teach children brand information. According to Ward, Wackman, and Wartella (1977A, p. 128), "Parents may teach which attributes are important in brand choice, the relative costs of different products and brands, the availability of products in different stores, and ideas about the quality of products and stores."

Children also are subject to brand display by each other. In McNeal's 1964 study referred to earlier, it was found that "Almost all the children in the study voiced the desire to own material goods possessed by other children . . ." (p. 19). Often these goods were referred to by brand name.

Marketers surely must be credited with causing much of the brand awareness that exists among children. In the study of children's consumer behavior by Ward, Wackman, and Wartella (1977A, p. 57), children were asked where they could find out about three kinds of new products, toys, snack foods, and clothing; and marketers were the principal source. Kindergartners relied primarily on in-store experiences as their main information source, whereas third and sixth graders relied on mass media, mainly television. James Frideres (1973) asked children what toys they would like to have if they could have them and where they found out about these toys. Over three-quarters credited television advertising as their source; the remaining quarter said they heard about the toys from peers (p. 24).

The influence of marketers on children's brand knowledge is obvious and can be expected. Rarely do marketers approach children with messages that say "buy candy" or "buy toys." Instead, their messages are very specific: "Buy Mattel toys," or even more specific, "Buy Hot Wheels by Mattel." The brand name is about the only thing that marketers possess that another marketer cannot copy. Consequently, marketers of very similar products are constantly approaching children with sales messages that are distinguishable only by their brands. Children seem to follow suit by emphasizing brand names among products that parents often see as very similar and substitutable. However, reports such as the one by Coulson (1966) suggest that parents are indeed aware of their children's brand preferences and commonly take them into account when purchasing for children.

In our marketing society, the brand concept is firmly in place when children are born, and they inherit it along with the language. Names such as Coke and Pepsi are as commonplace as Matthew and Jennifer. Children use them to identify products and distinguish among similar products much as they do people. This is what they are routinely taught during socialization. The fact that children are aware of many brands, prefer some brands over others, and are even loyal to some (Jacoby and Kyner, 1973) is not just a function of "scientifically designed persuaders" (Choate, 1973), as consumer protectionists call advertisements, but is a result of our entire social system.

Children's Responses to Product Prices

We have observed here that wanting and purchasing products are very natural things for children and are learned in earliest childhood from parents. Further, they learn that within product lines there are brands that can be used to identify products with varying attributes. Children, like adults, tend to find certain brands more desirable than others and demonstrate preferences for these.

We also learned in chapter 3 that children's product desires are as great as their income; consequently, they spend almost all the money they receive. Price of products, therefore, theoretically appears to be an important matter, because it is the main limiting factor in how many products children can buy with their money. Research, meager though it is, does not seem to support this assumption, however.

Although children know that prices may vary among different stores (McNeal and McDaniel, 1981), they do not appear to be very price knowledgeable in regard to individual products (Stephens and Moore, 1975). Their lack of price knowledge may result from a lack of price concern. In one study, for example, children were asked, "Suppose you wanted to buy a new television set. What would you want to know about it?" On the average, only 30 percent of the children wanted to know about price. Their main concern was with the physical attributes (Ward, Wackman, and Wartella, 1977, p. 69).

Although parents generally want their children to be economically conscious (Ward, Wackman, and Wartella, 1977A) and consumer educators want to teach children proper economic reasoning (Kourilsky and Murray, 1981), economic responsibility may be an unrealistic expectation because of the generous responses of both parents and business to children's consumer behavior. To overstate it only slightly, business is saying to children, "Buy our products, and never mind the price," and parents are forking over the money in agreement and often with encouragement. In a thorough analysis of the content of all Saturday morning television commercials, there was no mention of price for toys (Atkin and Heald, 1977). Advertisers clearly do not try to raise the price consciousness of children, and price-oriented advertising does not appear to be a major concern of parents. Under these conditions, it seems difficult for children to behave with much regard for price of products.

Children usually do not have to worry themselves about necessities. As was observed in chapter 3, all their money is discretionary; it can be spent on anything at any price. When their money runs out, it usually does not matter, for they have few monetary obligations. Such a circumstance does not encourage children to be concerned about the cost of goods.

Finally, it is significant to note that research generally does not show most parents to be economic in their behavior. In a classic study by Gregory Stone, replicated with similar findings by others over the years, not more than one-third of adults were considered to be economic shoppers (Stone, 1958). It is not likely, then, that their children will differ substantially.

Conclusions

There is no better evidence of the fact that children are considered a viable market by the business community than to watch Saturday morning television. The enormous number of toys and food goods aimed at this market, as displayed in commercials, unmistakably constitutes a marketing blitz. Moreover, these ads do not talk quality or price; they simply shout pleasure. The response on the children's end is elation and motivation. Children at that moment are keenly aware that the product world is theirs for the taking, and they do take it, fulfilling the destiny that was initiated by their parents during their crib days.

As if to perpetuate this marketing dream, many toys are designed in such a way that they will teach children such consumer behavior as brand awareness and retail store procedures. If toy marketers are in business for the long haul, they can stimulate children to buy a toy and that toy in turn can be designed to be instrumental in stimulating the children to want other products, even into adulthood. This is materialism in motion.

7
Packaging and Premiums for Children

A series of lengthy, in-depth interviews were conducted with children in their homes to determine their viewpoints and preferences about packages and such accompanying items as premiums and contests. Following is a small portion of one of these interviews with a ten-year-old boy named Sam whose parents own a large successful motel. This part of the interview is related to packaging graphics.

INTERVIEWER: I believe you said that your favorite cereal was Kellogg's Frosted Flakes. Is that correct, Sam?

SAM: Well, yes, Frosted Flakes and maybe Cheerios.

INTERVIEWER: I want you to think about Kellogg's Frosted Flakes and tell me what all is shown on the box.

SAM: You mean what all it says?

INTERVIEWER: Well, yes, and anything that comes to your mind that is on the box.

SAM: Well, there is the list of things that's in it such as vitamins and corn flakes.

INTERVIEWER: Good. What else?

SAM: Well, it tells about a contest where . . . , no, it tells about a free Dairy Queen sundae, a free Dairy Queen chocolate sundae.

INTERVIEWER: Great. What else?

SAM: I think that's all.

INTERVIEWER: Do you recall any pictures on it?

SAM: Oh sure, Tony the Tiger! He's gr-r-reat.

INTERVIEWER: You do have a good memory. Do you recall any other things shown on the Frosted Flakes cereal box?

SAM: No, that's about all. Oh yes, the name!

INTERVIEWER: What name?

SAM: Frosted Flakes. Kellogg's Frosted Flakes.

INTERVIEWER: That's great. Do you remember what color the package is?

SAM: Blue and white, isn't it?

While this ten-year-old boy's memory is not perfect, he demonstrates good knowledge of the package of his favorite cereal. It is remarkable that he could remember the colors (mainly blue and white), the Tony the Tiger character, something about the contents, and of course, the premium of a Dairy Queen sundae. It is unlikely that an adult could remember more. This high degree of recall reflects the child's intense interaction with the package, whose image is no doubt reinforced by advertisements of the product.

Packaging is a major marketing element in children's lives. Even more than advertising, packaging pervades the kid's world. It is on his breakfast table (cereal), beside him while he watches TV (soft drink), in the lunch kit he takes to school (cookies, cakes, and chips), at the school cafeteria (milk), perhaps along his walk home from school via the convenience store (candy and ice cream), and on Saturday when he goes to the movie (popcorn). All the time the package is giving him a visual sales talk.

Because of this intense involvement with packaging by children and their limited judgmental abilities, package designers must be extremely careful about not misleading children. Experiments by Soldow (1983), for example, indicate that children judge the size or extent of a product in a package by the shape of the package.

At one time the package was an unimportant marketing element, mainly designed to contain and protect the product. With the advent of self-service retailing and a multiplicity of brands, the package assumed the promotion functions of differentiating the product and stimulating purchase. It became the "silent salesman" in the store and in the home. It also became much more consumer oriented. In addition to the functions of containing and protecting, the package may also provide the following functions for consumers:

1. Facilitate use of the product—for example, the squeeze bottle makes it easier for the youngster to apply catsup or mustard to his sandwich or the pump container of toothpaste makes tooth brushing easy and almost fun.
2. Facilitate handling—for example, the indented shape of some soft drink bottles makes them easy to grip or the foil inner wrapper in several brands of cereal permit easy resealing.
3. Facilitate carrying—such as the handle on the six-pack of many soft drinks and juices or the multi-pack of candy bars and gum.
4. Provide reuse—for instance, the jelly jar that becomes a drinking glass or the toy carton that can become part of the play setting.
5. Provide information—such as the nutrition contents on cereal packages or directions for play on the packages of many games.
6. Give additional value—such as the coupons on cereal boxes for free ice cream, candy, and soft drinks or the surprises inside many cereal boxes.

This list of functions of packaging is not intended to imply that all packages are functional or do what they are supposed to do. There are many

Table 7-1
Recent Examples of the Wide Range of Premiums Found with Children's Cereals

Premium	Cereal
Care Bear Cousin's Cards	Trix (in pack)
Personalized T-shirt ($3.50 and 2 UPCs)	Cheerios (on pack)
Pitcher of Pepsi at Pizza Hut	Cinnamon Toast Crunch (on pack)
Baskin-Robbins ice cream cone (coupon for one "free" cone with one cone purchased)	Honey Nut Cheerios (on pack)
Four 2-ounce cans of Play-Doh ("free" with 3 Kix UPC symbols)	Kix (on pack)
Official 11 × 7 *Sports Illustrated* poster	Honeycombs (in pack)
Surprise Inside (not described on package)	Cracker Jack Cereal (in pack)
Twix Candy bar	Frosted Krispies (on pack)
Dairy Queen Sundae	Frosted Flakes (on pack)
Wacky Wallwalker	Apple Jacks (in pack)
Star Wars Rebel Rocket	C3POs (in pack)
Tidal Wave bubble gum	Cap'n Crunch's Peanut Butter Crunchy Sweet (on pack)
Mr. T sticker	Mr. T (in pack)
Rainbow-Brite night shirt ($4.95 with 2 proofs of purchase)	Rainbow-Brite (in pack)
Cabbage Patch Kids sticker	Cabbage Patch Kids (in pack)

exceptions, and some of these will be noted in a study of children's interactions with packaging. In view of the fact that probably around 7 percent or $294 million of children's annual expenditures go to costs of packaging, the problems with it should be few.

Premiums often are an integral part of the package. They usually are described in glowing detail on the package and then are often included in the package. They add value to the product as noted in the above list of packaging functions. They are a bonus for buying a product. The classic premium is the prize that is placed inside the Cracker Jack box. Cracker Jack (now owned by Borden) has given away over 16 billion prizes since it began in 1912 and currently packs more than 500 different novelties in with its popcorn blend (Norris, 1984). Today, premiums come in several forms. Table 7-1 lists some recent examples of premiums found in and on cereal packages. The Dairy

Queen sundae giveaway that Sam describes in the opening dialog to this chapter is just one example of a new kind of premium that provides children with other treats that are obtainable almost immediately after the purchase of the cereal. Other available snack foods offered as premiums that are noted in Table 7-1 include ice cream, soft drink, candy bar, and bubble gum.

The premium concept is in a dilemma. It is an effective marketing tool, and children love it. Many parents and policy makers, however, detest it. We will discuss some research related to these positions after we examine children's response to packaging.

Packaging in a Child's World

In a study by Rossiter (1976), 60 children ages six to eleven were asked to take felt pens and draw a cereal box. Although seemingly a difficult task, particularly for the six- and seven-year-old children, over two-thirds of the youngest children and all of the others placed a brand on their cereal boxes. Even the color schemes were correct 40 percent of the time for the youngest children and 63 percent of the time for the oldest children. Such well imprinted visual images in the minds of children indicate that the cereal packages are very significant to children. Although similar information is not available for other products, similar results might be expected for other desirable food items, such as candy, soft drinks, and gum. The plain fact of the matter is that packaging plays a memorable role in the consumer life of children, just as it does with adults.

Because of the importance of packaging in the consuming process of children and because of the increasing attention to children as consumers by marketers, a study was undertaken to determine if children were having any problems with packaging (McNeal, 1976). It was hypothesized that packages containing products primarily for children would be easy to handle and use, whereas packages containing products primarily for adults might be difficult for youngsters to handle and use. These expectations were based on the apparent differences between children and adults in skills, knowledge, and dexterity and on the belief that packages usually will take these differences into consideration.

The children in the study consisted of two four year olds and two ten year olds. They were selected on the basis of their convenience to the investigator. It was anticipated that some comparisons of responses could be obtained between the younger and older children. It first was decided to simply observe the youngsters dealing with packaging of any sort as frequently as was possible for the investigator. Later, it was decided to inject some small experiments as well. Observations were obtained over a three-month period. Anticipated findings were expected in three areas: opening and closure of packages, interpretations of package graphics, and handling qualities of packages. It was hoped that judgements could result in terms of good and bad packaging from the child's standpoint.

During the three-month period, 105 meaningful observations were obtained. The observations ranged from a simple single act of unwrapping a piece of chewing gum or candy to a series of acts such as "putting up" a sack of groceries. When an observation was made by the investigator, a written note was made afterward as soon as practical that described the act and accompanying comments, if any, by the youngster.

Opening and Closure of Packages

Observations about the opening and/or closing of packages seemed to be very significant because of consistent problems and negative comments noted in this category of child consumer-package relationships. Included in this category of responses also were wrapper or package removal from the product and replacement of the wrapper or package.

There was no particular type of product package that was intended to be the focus of the study, but a large number of observations of reactions of the children to packages of dry cereal causes cereals to be of significance to the investigator. Dry cereals were a favorite product of the children. They were eaten consistently at breakfast and frequently as snacks throughout the day and night. The children clearly perceived dry cereals as products for them. This fact was made evident by such statements as "my," "mine," "You can't have any of my Cheerios," "Leave mine alone," and "Get some more of my Freakies."

One problem was obvious about cereal packages; they usually were poorly designed for opening and closing by youngsters. The typical cereal package with the top that opened totally was generally torn upon the initial opening unless done by parents, who also tore them occasionally. This of course, made closure more difficult. The inside package, often a lightweight waxed paper bag, was equally a problem. There was no obvious way for the child to open the inner package except to rip it. Again, this added to closure problems. The net result was improperly closed cereal packages that further resulted in cereal often being made inedible from humidity. This was not considered a desirable situation by parents. Consequently, there were frequent harsh words between parents and children about opening and closing packages.

One bright spot among cereal packages was Skinner's Raisin Bran. It has a pouring spout on the side of the package. The initial opening of the spout was somewhat difficult, but the continued opening and closure were easy for the children. This was pleasing to the parents, who wondered why other cereal packages did not employ such a device. Ironically, it has been discontinued.

There were other product packages that were troublesome for children in terms of opening or closing. Wrapped candy was one of these. The Brach's

Pick-A-Mix variety of wrapped candies is a good example. These candies seemed to have had appeal to the children because of the variety, flavor, and because all pieces were individually wrapped, but removing the wrapper was not always easy. Often the candy stuck to the wrapper and the child had to do battle with the wrapper using both hands and teeth, sometimes consuming part of the wrapper along with the candy. From the parental point of view, the result often was a mess. There were sticky hands, faces, clothes, and households. Here again was a good product desired more by the children than the parents because of the negative results of packaging.

Candy bars, such as Hershey Bars, Milky Ways, and Baby Ruths, were little trouble for the youngsters to open. They just ripped them open. However, if the entire bar was not eaten, saving the remainder was a minor problem. This was not true, as a rule, for those candies that were packaged in hand-size boxes such as Milk Duds or Sun-Maid raisins, which were purchased as a candy substitute. In these cases, the remainder was easily stored in the original container. The investigator wondered why many other candies might not be packaged in hand-size boxes for the convenience of storing left-overs. Although the wrapper is traditional for candy bars, this does not mean it is the best package.

Frozen desserts on a stick, generalized as Popsicles by youngsters, presented opening and closing problems. Most of these products are wrapped in paper that is difficult to remove because the product is stuck to the paper or vice versa. Like some of the candies, this meant a messy product to parents. Further, there was the obvious problem of left-overs because the wrapper was destroyed in the opening. A pleasant exception was the aluminum foil package of the Eskimo Pie ice cream bar. This wrapper was easily removed and replaced.

Beverage containers presented opening and closing problems for the children, too. The capped bottles of Coca-Cola, Pepsi-Cola, and Royal Crown Cola, as examples, generally could not be opened by a child with a hand opener without much effort and often spillage. Closures for the bottles is not a problem because several manufacturers provide a variety of bottle closures for left-over beverages. Another solution could be the twist caps usually found on larger bottles of soft drinks. These would provide fairly easy and effective opening and closing.

Beverages in cans with lift tabs were more of a problem than capped bottles. The four year olds could not do more than pull the tab half-way. Among all of the children there was frequent spillage and spewing during opening. Closure was almost impossible, although there are a few manufactured items for this purpose. In addition to spillage, there were also two incidents of cut fingers.

Other packages that were observed to have opening-closing problems for children included chips, luncheon meats, and sliced cheese. In one "test" by the investigator, the two four year olds and two ten year olds were seated for a snack. Each was given an individual-size package of Doritos along with a glass of soft drink. Difficulty in opening the bag of Doritos resulted in pulling, tugging, and finally tearing with the teeth.

Another "test" was conducted by asking the two ten year olds to stop off for a sandwich. The investigator nonchalantly tossed an unopened 8-ounce package of Oscar Mayer bologna on the table with the statement to the boys, "You open the meat while I get the bread." One of the youngsters, after wrestling unsuccessfully with the package of meat, gave it to the other, who had to give up and resort to a sharp knife. Skin packages such as are commonly found on luncheon meats were typically difficult for the youngster to open. Closure often meant wrapping the remainder in some type of wrap or container. (In effect, two packages are required for some products, one furnished by the consumer.)

In one other "sandwich test," the sandwiches were prepared for the two ten year olds. Once the sandwiches were placed before them, the investigator invitingly asked, "Does anyone want a slice of cheese on theirs?" The response by both was yes. Each was handed an individually wrapped slice of cheese. The investigator was curious to see if they would have much trouble finding the open slit in the wrapper. They did. About a minute was needed by each child to unwrap the cheese. Each had performed the act many times before.

Graphics

The term *graphics* as used here means any pictures, words, or other symbols attached to the product package or label. It was observed throughout the study that the children interacted with packaging graphics with varying and interesting responses. It was decided to note some of these responses that seemed to be significant in terms of the probable intent of the printing on the package. Two facts become apparent: (1) some children, because of age or training, generally cannot read, yet are able to correctly interpret many symbols on packages; and (2) children tend to lend literal meanings (denotative more than connotative) to packaging graphics, particularly the four year olds.

Reading printed words on packages was naturally difficult for the four year olds. These youngsters usually were able to recognize well-known brand names, however. It was interesting to note, also, that these children easily recognized the word *free*. Probably most of this recognition was due to advertising and frequent product use. The four year olds could not always point out the actual printing of the brand name on some packages, but recognized the package as containing a certain branded product because of other symbols on the packages. For example, Freakies, a cereal by Ralston Purina, was recognized easily by the young children because of the monsters on the package. When asked, "What is the name of the cereal?" the children immediately answered, "Freakies!" When asked, "Where does it say Freakies?" both of the four year olds pointed to a monster. The same questions received the same responses about Quisp, a Quaker Oats cereal. Again, a symbol, in this case a very large picture of a little man from outer space, was the key symbol. It is interesting that neither of these cereal packages actually showed a prominent picture of the cereal. It was almost as if the symbols were the products. Perhaps this confirms the statement often noted in marketing books that "The package is the product."

Related to the earlier comments about opening and closing packages, the directions for these functions were not read or were not easily read. This may explain partially why packages were not opened or closed properly. If these directions were in picture form, they might be more effective.

Two particular observations represented the literal interpretations of package symbols. The investigator was having a bowl of Skinner's Raisin Bran for breakfast when the four year old asked for some. The youngster enjoyed the taste of the raisins, and he immediately recognized them in a graphic on the package. The graphic was a bowl of the cereal with the raisins prominently displayed. A few mornings later, the investigator was having a bowl of Nabisco Spoon Size Shredded Wheat when again the four year old asked for the same. While pouring the cereal into his bowl, he asked "Where's the raisins?" He was told that this cereal did not contain raisins. He quickly pointed to the package, which illustrated the cereal in a bowl with blueberries, and said, "Yes, it does. Here's some." To him, the blueberries appeared similar to raisins and generalized the picture on the package to the raisin bran package. He even insisted upon looking into the package for the raisins. It was explained to the youngster that the cereal was suggesting that it would be enjoyed with blueberries. The youngster did not want the cereal then. As a check on this generalization, this child was shown a box of Cheerios, a General Mills product, and asked what the cereal was like. He answered, "It is little doughnuts." He was then asked if it contained raisins. He answered, "No." The package showed a bowl of Cheerios with strawberries. The investigator pointed to this picture and asked what the red things were. The child answered, "Strawberries." "Are they in there?" the investigator asked. He responded "No, they leave 'em out." The response seemed to indicate that he felt they should be there but for some reason were not. As another check by the investigator, a ten year old was asked if there were strawberries in the Cheerios. He soberly responded, "No, they don't put 'em in." "What about the picture?" he was asked. "They just try to fool you," he answered. "Do you like it anyhow?" was the question, to which he answered, "Sure."

Several observations regarding, again, mainly cereal packages indicated that the packages that contained some type of premium were very important to all children. In fact, the premium, usually some toy of little monetary value, often decided the cereal selected. Knowledge of these premiums was derived from the advertising and illustrations on the package. For example, Freakies contained a "Free Freakie Magnet Inside." The word *free* was understood correctly by the four year olds as well as ten year olds. On the other hand, the Quisp package showed an illustration of a fire truck on the package front, and around the picture were the words, "free truck offer, see back." The four year old assumed that the fire truck was in the package and looked for it several times. Actually, it was necessary to mail "three proof of purchase seals" in order to obtain it. Again, there was a literal interpretation of the picture showing the fire truck because the four year old could not read the print and had been conditioned by other cereal packages. None of the children even commented about an offer on the Froot Loop package (a Kellogg's cereal) that said, "Win five dollars a week allowance for a whole year." The four year old could not read it, and the ten year old showed no interest. When the ten year old was asked about the offer, he shrugged it off with, "So what, they ain't gonna give you a bunch of five dollars." In sum, premiums in a package were far more important than those that must be requested by mail. If there was a hint, such as an illustration, that there was a premium in the package and there was not, disappointment resulted among those children anticipating a premium.

Regarding other printing on cereal packages, all the children seemed to ignore it. This included mail premiums (placed elsewhere than the package front), contents, nutrition value, and an occasional cut-out premium. Whether there was any nonverbal interaction with these printed elements was difficult to judge, but there were no comments generated by them. Apparently, the children viewed most information on the package as mainly for the edification of adults. One might wonder about the results of this perception.

It was noted by the investigator that neither of two brands of milk purchased had any illustrations on their packages. That is, there was not a picture of a glass of milk, for instance. Because all the children were frequent milk drinkers, it was decided to try to ascertain any perception of the milk cartons' graphics. Two four year olds were shown three half-gallon cartons of milk, one being chocolate milk. Two private brands, Kroger and FM (Fedmart) were used. None of the three packages contained any pictures, just printed words. The youngsters were asked which milk they liked best. They both responded that they liked the chocolate milk best, even though the investigator had not identified the chocolate milk separately. They were asked how they knew one carton was chocolate milk and both responded that they had drunk it (that brand) before. It was apparent that the base color of the carton was the determinant of chocolate milk that was derived from use. They then were asked which of the two brands of "plain" milk they liked; one replied, "The red one," and the other responded, "I don't know." Finally, they were asked what were the names of the milks. Apparently, this question was not meaningful because they replied, "Milk." They were then asked who made the milk; one said, "I don't know," and the other child answered, "Farmers." It appeared to the investigator that neither advertising of milk, to the extent it was done, nor usage had much influence on the learning of brand names by these children.

Handling Qualities

Handling qualities, as used here, refer to those characteristics of a package that involve holding, lifting, emptying, and transferring the product from the package. Several problems were observed in the handling of some packages by children, although some packages had good handling features.

Some of the major problems in package handling by children were as follows:

Holding wet containers. Glass and metal packages that were refrigerated became wet when removed from the refrigerator. The wet package was observed to be a serious problem. Soft drinks were items handled daily by the youngsters. Most of those containers are round for easy gripping, but it was the roundness combined with wetness that was a problem. When wet, the beverage can was sometimes dropped by all youngsters. Spills from cans of soft drinks were observed. Some soft drink bottles were slippery, but the shape of the Coca-Cola bottle seemed to prevent dropping and spilling. Glass quart containers of soft drinks presented a serious problem. They were heavy as well as slippery, and one was dropped and broken. Perhaps this was a reason that they were replaced with plastic.

Other wet packages that presented some problems were sandwich spreads, pickles, mustard, and milk. Milk was in a cardboard container, but a half-gallon was still too heavy and slippery.

Holding heavy or large containers. The wet heavy containers were mentioned above as a problem, but heavy packages generally were a problem. A 24-ounce glass bottle of mouthwash was dropped and broken. As with the large beverage containers, the purpose behind the large size of mouthwash was economy. Other economic but inconvenient packages for children to handle included a 9-ounce tube of toothpaste, a 24-ounce bottle of syrup, a 19-ounce package of cereal, and a 32-ounce bottle of catsup. It should be noted that the syrup was in a plastic container, which was a reason for the purchase of that brand. It was thought to be unbreakable.

Measuring and pouring. The younger children encountered problems in measuring and pouring liquids. This was also true occasionally with the older children. The problem arose because of the shape and/or size of the package and viscosity of the liquid contents. In terms of measuring or pouring the needed amount of liquid, the thicker liquids seemed to be most troublesome.

A real culprit was the 16-ounce can of Hershey's Chocolate syrup (now available in a plastic squeeze container). The children could not judge correctly the amount of syrup to pour. The can always dripped, leaving a sticky mess to be cleaned. Catsup, also a thick liquid, presented a similar problem. The classic problem that adults have always had of pouring catsup was exhibited among the children. Holding the catsup bottle, patiently waiting for catsup to pour, and finally shaking the bottle usually produced too much catsup on such targets as french fries and hamburgers. This problem was compounded when the 32-ounce bottle was used because of the additional weight and difficulty in grasping the container. The viscosity of salad dressing such as Seven Seas Thousand Island also caused a pouring problem. The container shape and size seemed adequate, but the results were similar to the catsup situation.

Pouring thin liquids was not necessarily easier. Large bottles of soft drinks were difficult to control. Splashing and overfilling of glasses often resulted. This was also true of pancake syrup and particularly milk. Little hands and not fully developed motor skills were not matched with many packages.

For those products that had to be removed from the package with a utensil, the package often made removal of the product difficult. The problem was most prevalent with glass containers because of container shape or size. Jellies and jams, frequently consumed by the children, seemed most troublesome. The nature of these products was part of the problem. From a package standpoint, small openings, deep containers, and containers with shoulders caused problems. Results were sticky hands and jelly on items such as the table, floor, and clothing. Because jelly was such a frequently consumed product, the problem was very noticeable. If glass containers are to be used, the mouth of the jar should be at least the same diameter as that of the jar. Large size containers should be wider rather than taller.

Products such as jelly, pickles, mustard, sandwich spread, and peanut butter are examples of products widely used by children, and containers for some brands of these products are very inappropriate. The wide-mouth jar of Peter Pan peanut butter made removal simple. This was true, also, of the shallow, wide-mouth container of Koogle (Kraft). A contrast that may indicate an obvious lack of consumer orientation was Bama jelly. The 18-ounce container possessed a mouth that was conveniently wider than the rest of the jar, but the larger 32-ounce size was deeper and had a mouth smaller than the lower part of the jar. The latter container was a nuisance in spite of its economy. It was presumed that the smaller mouthed jar was designed to be more stable for shelving. However, such a design was a deterrent to product removal for children. It would be simple, it seems, for Bama to note the large jar of Peter Pan peanut butter that was used with the jelly in order to see what a difference in convenience exists.

Potentially Dangerous Packages

It was not anticipated that the study would indicate any human dangers from packaging. However, over time it did sensitize the investigator to some potential packaging dangers. Most have been suggested above, so they will be noted only briefly.

1. Glass containers are potentially dangerous because they are breakable and may produce sharp edges and flying glass. They can be dangerous to both the user and elements of the environment. This situation is particularly true when the glass containers are used by children. The danger is even greater when the child handles a wet and/or heavy glass container.

2. Pull-tab beverage cans may cut an inexperienced finger. The sharp edge produced by this type of opening has the potential for cutting lips. If the child drinks from the can, which is common, a straw is recommended.

3. Aerosol cans are potential hazards to the child. One observation made this fact clear. The household contained several aerosols of room air freshener. One four year old attempted to use one that was located in the bathroom. When he pushed the button, the mist ended up on the side of his face because the container was pointed in the wrong direction. Whether this product could have injured the skin or eyes is not known, but other aerosol products such as insecticides might.

4. Potentially dangerous products must be packaged with the user in mind. Households have dangerous products because they are needed. Manufacturers encourage the sale of such products. Therefore, both parents and manufacturers must be responsible for these items. Prescribed drugs are now available in containers that are difficult for the child to open. This effort must be applauded. However, the same is not true of many nonprescribed medicines, such as pain and cold remedies. Neither is it true of most detergents, bleaches, and seasonings, as other examples. In sum, potentially dangerous products could be better controlled with improved packaging.

Implications

This study described some significant problems that children may have with packages. The problems were more significant among the younger children, but existed among all of the children. This is a regrettable situation because parents encourage their children to be consumers as early as possible and the youngsters like this idea; it is adult. This fact was noted three decades ago by Riesman et al. (1953) and two decades ago by McNeal (1964). Yet it would appear that packaging for children has not adequately recognized this social change.

Some criticisms can be made about packages with which children interact frequently. These criticisms result in blame to the producer of the packaged products.

1. Cereal packages need improved opening-closing devices or procedures that would make them more convenient to use and reduce spoilage. The Skinner's Raisin Bran package with its pouring spout was a good model for other producers to copy.

2. Snack packages such as chips and cookies also need improved opening-closing devices or procedures for the same reasons.

3. Packages for many candy bars and frozen desserts need to be designed for storage of the unused portion of the product. A box, rather than a wrapper, might be the answer.

4. Soft drink containers need to be improved to prevent slipping from the hands. Perhaps a rough finish on the exterior of the bottles and cans might help.

5. Those products such as sandwich spread, peanut butter, and jelly need wide-mouth containers with no shoulders. There are several good examples available.

6. Large containers purchased on the basis of economy by families with several children are generally inconvenient for children's use. This is a conflict that needs consideration in many product categories. At least, attention should be given to reducing the package weight. Multi-packaging (several regular packages in one large package) may be a better solution than the very large package if economy can be maintained.

7. Packages for naturally sticky products such as some candies and frozen desserts need to be made "sticky-free." The aluminum foil wrapper on the Eskimo Pie is an example of a better package for this group of products.

8. Skin-wrapped products such as luncheon meat and sliced cheese need improvement in their opening and closing. A zipper-type opener is suggested, and a closure that prevents spoilage is badly needed.

9. Directions for opening and closing should be produced in picture form when possible on all packages aimed at the very young.

10. Premiums included in the package should be illustrated on the package front. If premiums are not actually in the package, they should be described on the back side of the package.

All the above packaging problems result mainly because they are not matched with children's dexterity, strength, or knowledge. Those packages intended for use by children should give more consideration to the more limited abilities of children as compared to adults. Those products consumed by both children and adults, such as milk, present very special problems for the packager.

Parents must share the blame for many packaging problems. They can train their children in the use of problem packages, or perhaps consumer education in elementary school can treat problem packages. Both of these ideas, however, suggest that the problem packages will not be changed. This assumption need not prove correct; the packaging industry has often demonstrated its ability to produce problem-free packages.

A few things are certain, and this small study demonstrates them. The youngster is a consumer. As such, he interacts frequently with packaging. In the process, he encounters problems. These problems are also usually problems for parents. The astute producer of products used by children can create much more satisfaction among children and parents by devoting more attention to the package.

Although packaging plays a major role in the consumption process of children, there are few studies of children's responses to packaging. The preceding study is one of the few; although meager, it does hint at some difficulties that children have with packaging. The greatest source of packaging problems for children is the package designed for adults that contains a product targeted to children. This is analogous to the problem children have in most retail stores that sell products targeted for children in an environment geared to adults.

The most notable example of an adult package/child product is cereal. Most of the boxes are difficult to open and close properly, and the inner package is often fragile and only slightly functional in the hands of children. Indirect evidence of this problem can be obtained by observing the packages for the various adult cereals, such as Fruit and Fiber and Special K. These packages are the same design as those containing children's cereals. This adult package/child product situation exists with many other products to various degrees, such as peanut butter, jelly, chips, cookies, and soft drinks. In defense of the producers of these products and their packages, it may be difficult and uneconomical to provide packages for children. If the products are targeted to children, however, it is not illogical to expect the packages to be compatible. This expectation can be extended to package-related premiums and contests; this will be discussed shortly. There are at least two problems with those offers that are directed to children. First, children normally approach things literally. When the package says free in regard to a premium, it should be free in the box in the minds of children, not indirectly free with three proofs of purchase that may entail a long period of time before the premium can be obtained. Second, contests should be simplified. A recent contest, for example, on Post cereal packages offered children a free shopping spree in a toy store. The actual directions, however, filled an entire side-panel in printing the size of fly-specks and in words and sentences that were very complicated to children.

Package-Related Premiums

In children's terms, a premium is a "bonus," "something extra," "something-for-nothing," a "prize," or a "surprise." In marketing terms, a premium is "an item of additional merchandise that a customer receives for purchasing a particular brand of product or purchasing it at a particular retail outlet" (Dommermuth, 1985, p. 583). The most familiar premium is probably the one that comes in the cereal box; marketers call this an *insert* or *in-pack* (Norris, 1984, p. 36). Children seem to be emotionally involved with these inserts, often wanting then as much as the product itself. There is no simple explanation for the special attractiveness of premium inserts among children. Children seem to see them as something especially for them, probably as a result of advertising emphasizing this, and they do not cost anything. Therefore, they may reason that parents should not complain about the price or ever refuse to let children have them. Finally, they are oriented to fun. It may be, also, that children feel that the premiums please their parents because many of the items do not cost anything additional. Thus, the children's need for play can be satisfied without any extra costs.

There are many other children-oriented products that may offer premiums in addition to cereal; these include bubble gum, candy bars, ice cream bars, powdered drinks, and juices, to name a few. These products do not receive the attention given to cereals, perhaps because they do not offer premiums as consistently as cereals do and because the premiums they offer often do not accompany the product but must be obtained through the mail or in some other manner. Actually, premiums often do not come with the product. The Dairy Queen sundae described by Sam in the interview at the beginning of this chapter, for example, can be obtained by going to a participating Dairy Queen restaurant. Normally, the premiums are acquired through the mail by sending several proofs of purchase or UPCs (universal product codes). Consequently, these premiums are never free, even though they are traditionally described this way. In fact, they may cost a good deal and require a lot of time if a number of proofs of purchase are required. Some premiums are offered at near what they would cost if purchased separately. These are referred to as self-liquidating premiums because the money the youngster must pay covers the cost of the item.

There are sharply different viewpoints about the use of premiums with children's products, particularly cereals. In general, the case against them is that they attract too much of the child's attention away from the product that provides them. Consequently, the child may not evaluate the sponsoring product correctly or carefully and may in fact want the premium as much as or more than the product. Thus, when children-related products with premiums are advertised, it is believed by the antipremium group that the children "will exert pressure on their parents to purchase the product advertised not for its own sake but for the premium, thus resulting in a social or economic cost to society" (Hallaq, 1977, p. 65). Many parents probably can support this view. This also has been the position of the Federal Trade Commission (FTC). In 1974, the FTC issued a request to television advertisers asking them to voluntarily discontinue describing premium offers in their advertisements because such ads were, in the minds of the Commission, unfair and produced harmful effect on children (Shimp, Dyer, and Divita, 1976). It should be noted that the request of the FTC was not a proposed ban on premiums, per se, but on the advertising of them. The rationale for wanting to prohibit advertising of premiums, rather than the premiums themselves, is not clear, because the FTC specifically declared that "the premium's main purpose is to distract the buyer's attention from (the product's) attributes and to motivate purchase not on the merits of the products but in order to obtain the premium" (as quoted by Shimp, Dyer, and Divita, 1976, p. 2). Presumably, the FTC was concerned with the potential benefits of advertising and believed that advertising without a focus on premiums would permit children to make a more correct assessment of the product. This is probably true if the advertising focuses on salient attributes of the product presented.

Even if premiums were eliminated from consideration in television advertising, they could be advertised in other media, as the tobacco industry did when TV advertising of cigarettes was banned. Perhaps just as important as advertising is the presentation of the premium offer on packaging, and this would still remain. It is the package that holds the premium if it is an insert or permits the premium to be ordered via a coupon on the package. The package can and often does make a very persuasive presentation of the premium offer, and it is on display on supermarket shelves and, more important, on the breakfast table at home. If the premium is offered in any medium, children will find out about it and inform others. Probably every mother has heard these or similar words: "Mom, pleeeeze buy me some Honey Smacks." "There's a secret decoder inside." "Eric and Joey have one . . . everyone but me" (Norris, 1984, p. 36). Word-of-mouth advertising is always more powerful than media advertising.

The propremium view, in contrast to the antipremium view, is much less emotional and is mainly that of the premium industry. Its view simply is that premiums are just one form of promotion and should not be singled out for criticism or special regulation. There are studies that show that premiums do not significantly enhance children's evaluations of a product, and there are very few public complaints about premiums (Hallaq, 1977).

There are three studies that shed some light on the premium controversy. None are funded by either side, rather, they are unbiased academic studies with the simple goal of inquiry. All of the studies have serious limitations, as noted by their respective investigators. They are not field studies; they are based on small rather than national samples, and each has certain methodological shortcomings. All three studies are in response to the FTC's desire to regulate television advertising describing premium offers to children.

The first study of the effects of premium-oriented commercials on children by Shimp, Dyer, and Divita was published in 1976 and had as its purpose "to test empirically the legitimacy of the FTC's proposed premium guide" (p. 1). The study was conducted among 197 children in grades one through six. The children were shown a 30-second advertisement for a hypothetical cereal, Snappy Fruit Smacks, either with no premium information (the control group) or with 10, 15, or 20 seconds of premium information. The premium, which is typical of premium inserts in cereals, was a National Football League (NFL) team patch.

The findings were somewhat contrary to what antipremium advocates would have expected. The control group of children exposed to a commercial containing only product information did not exhibit any more product information recall than any of the three experimental groups subjected to varying lengths of premium promotion. The experimental group exposed to a ten-second presentation of the premium demonstrated the highest level of product information recall, suggesting that "a relatively short presentation of a premium object in a commercial will not interfere with children's processing of product information and, perhaps, might even encourage children to rehearse and retain product information" (p. 7). This tentative conclusion should be tempered by the fact that the children exposed to the fifteen- and twenty-second premium presentations recalled less product information than either the ten-second or control groups. Also, those exposed to longer presentations of premium information tended to prefer the cereal more, which tends to support antipremium views. As might be expected, older children remembered the product information better than the younger ones, suggesting that premium information interferes with learning processes less as age increases. This finding also gives encouragement to the FTC regulation of premium-oriented advertisements to younger children. Finally, the study did indicate that the longer children are exposed to premium-oriented advertisements, the more they desire the sponsoring product. The premium advertising, of course, does not make the product desirable per se; it makes the premium more desirable, and the only way for the child to get the premium is to buy the cereal. Therefore, a time limit on premium information within a product advertisement is suggested by this study. It should be noted here that as a result of this study by Shimp, Dyer, and Divita, the FTC rejected its suggested ban on premium advertising (Heslop and Ryans, 1980).

A year after the Shimp, Dyer, and Divita paper was published, another study of children's reactions to premiums was published by Hallaq (1977). Hallaq's investigation was mainly concerned with the influence that premiums have on cereal selection. He subjected one sample of 119 elementary school children to four brands of sugar-coated cereals and four small premiums and another group of 99 similar children to four brands of "adult" cereals displayed with four large premiums. Hallaq did not explain his rationale for using "adult" cereals (Wheaties, Total, Special K, and Spoon Size Shredded Wheat) with one group as compared to more desirable sugar-coated cereals (Sugar Pops, Cocoa Puffs, Trix, and Honey Comb). Perhaps they were to show that children would select not so desirable products in order to obtain a premium.

What Hallaq seemed to find was that small premiums (game, iron-on patch, bike reflector, and panda bear poster) did not influence cereal selection differently when compared with choices in the market place (share of the market in that region). However, large premiums (play-do, puzzle, doll, and racing car) were found to influence selection when compared with market statistics. What appears to be shown here is that relatively expensive premiums can sway children to redirect their choices to products they do not really like. If the study were methodologically sound, this conclusion might be stretched to say that "good" premiums can sell "bad" products, which was one of the concerns of the FTC.

In a third study, Heslop and Ryans (1980) challenged the Shimp, Dyer, and Divita study as being "not very realistic" (p. 416)—even though it was the basis for the FTC changing its mind about banning premium-oriented advertising—and set out to provide a more realistic study environment by including parents. They studied 280 children ages four through eight. Children were exposed to a thirty-second commercial for an actual cereal that did not mention a premium (the control group), another that promoted only the premium, and another that devoted eight of the thirty seconds to a premium. All of these were arranged in a twenty two-minute cartoon. After viewing the cartoon and commercial film, the children along with their mothers (the element of realism) were taken to a product selection area where the test cereal was displayed along with two other children's cereals; they were told they could have one as payment for their participation. Three measures were obtained: the child's stated cereal preference, the mother's report on what cereal the child requested to take with them as payment, and the actual cereal taken. On "none of the three independent measures did the degree of premium emphasis in the advertisement have any significant effect" (p. 418). Although the premium-oriented ads appeared to influence preferences somewhat, they did not influence the cereals requested. Thus, these findings are supportive of the Shimp, Dyer, and Divita findings, although perhaps richer because of the behavioral dimension of requesting. The authors concluded that "the implications of the research on premium advertising are that cereal advertising and the use of premiums may affect the child's preference, but are less likely to influence the child's requesting behavior and even less likely to affect the cereal purchased by the mother" (p. 420).

Conclusions

In this chapter we have considered packaging and premiums because in the case of children the two are very closely related. In a study of children's visual memory, Rossiter (1976) had children draw cereal boxes from memory. In one part of the exercise in which children were instructed to draw the backs of the box of cereal, 39 percent of first-graders, 55 percent of third-graders and 75 percent of fifth-graders included a premium, thus indicating that at least in the case of cereal the package and the premium are almost inseparable.

Packaging is a very integral part of the product in our market economy and a very expensive part. In many processed foods, such as soft drinks and cereals, the cost of the package exceeds the cost of the product, according to food and nutrition specialists at Texas A&M University (*Bryan-College Station Eagle*, 1985). An investigation into package management practices revealed that the median expenditure on a new package was $50,000; $35,000 was spent on package modification (Hise and McNeal, 1985). In spite of these enormous costs and the importance of packaging in the consumer world of children, we have produced very little empirical knowledge of the effectiveness of packaging among children. The case study of four children's interactions with packaging does suggest that the possible functions that packaging may perform for children are many but often are not accomplished. It appears that packaging for children's products is planned, designed, and produced by adults with adult views and uses in mind rather than those of children. An investigation by Schneider (1977) into the abilities of packaging to prevent accidental poisoning among children showed a wide range of new possibilities, yet it does not appear that any of his ideas, although simple and inexpensive, have been put to use. This may be due to the difficulty of package designers to think in children's terms.

The design of packaging for children may take place at any one of three sources, the producers of packages, the producers of products, or the specialists in package design. Therefore, there should be no shortage of talent or ideas for producing functional packaging for children. A major problem for packagers is designing packages for products consumed by both children and adults, such as soft drinks. The economic solution to this problem generally has been to produce packages for adults and force their use on children. Perhaps as children increase in number and in buying power, more packaging will be oriented to them.

It does appear that premiums that come with the package are much more children-centered than are the packages. To make sure of this, the producers of children's products and the producers of premiums screen the premiums for acceptance among children. A child psychologist at National Creative Merchandising, a producer of premiums, said this: "We discovered that creative people designing and trying to anticipate what kids liked just didn't work. Children are better able to tell us what they like and why" (Norris, 1984, p. 37). For example, National Creative Merchandising discovered that gender becomes a factor in preferences for premiums as early as age four and takes this into consideration for almost all of the premiums it designs (Norris, 1984, p. 37).

It would appear that the premium industry has done too good a job of satisfying its markets. Children often want the premium more than the product. This seems to suit many producers of products just fine because it ends up selling their products. Public sentiment, however, does not strongly favor premium-sold products, and the FTC has even attempted to regulate their advertising on television. Research presented in this chapter suggests that the amount of time within a commercial that is devoted to premiums certainly should be limited, probaby to less than ten seconds.

The combination of the premium and other packaging elements, including games, contests, cartoon characters, nutrition information, brand names, and color schemes, has much opportunity for influencing the consumer socialization process of children. Although the package is intended to extend the promotional strategies of advertising, it seems to have a life of its own that transcends just the basic selling effort. As a frequent visitor to the breakfast table and snack setting of children, the cereal package may teach children much about product use, reinforce brand names of the cereal and related products of the producer, inform the youngsters about nutrition, give them practice in use and reuse of packages, and do all these things and more in a fun environment that also is created by the package. Cereal producers have been experimenting with the use of what is termed a *fifth panel* in order to have even more space on the cereal box with which to inform, entertain, and persuade children. The fifth panel on General Foods' Cocoa Pebbles and Alpha-Bits, "opens like a book on the back of the box to produce two more usable surfaces" (Giges, 1985, p. 82). In the case of Cocoa Pebbles,

> When the flap is opened, if the box plays "Happy Birthday," you know you're a winner, and Fred Flintstone and his friend Barney will bring video arcades, Jell-O Pudding Pops and Kool-Aid to your home for you and up to 25 friends. If you're not a winner, there are mazes and word games printed on the box and directions on how to get another chance to win a party (Giges, 1985, p. 87).

There are no studies that tell us of the impact that packaging and its premiums have on the child's learning of consumer behavior, but it might be estimated that it is significant over the span of childhood. The learning of a variety of knowledge and skills can result from intentional instructions from the producer to the child consumer through the package as a medium, by incidental learning on the part of the youngster through observation of information on and in the package, and by hands-on participation through handling the package and its contents. All these means of socialization may take place in an atmosphere of excitement created by, for example, a laughing Tony the Tiger, an absolutely free Dairy Queen chocolate sundae, and a yummy-tasting cereal that is fortified with nine essential vitamins and minerals! Such is the life of the child because of the wonders of modern packaging.

The combined forces of the premium seller and the product seller can be enormously persuasive relative to children, who are logically at some cognitive disadvantage. It is certainly easy for the influence of this alliance to be amplified even more by a good package and some creative television advertising. The child's chances of defending himself against this combined persuasive force are meager. If the premium industry chooses to sell its products through the medium of other products such as cereal and if producers of children's products believe they can better merchandise their wares through the use of premiums, then both are probably good ideas and should be combined. There must be full consideration of the market for which these items are intended, however. Children are new consumers, and although eligible for most marketing practices, cannot cope with all of them adequately. They often do not know, for example, that premiums are not really free and that they or their parents pay for them. They probably do not see anything wrong with wanting the premium more than the product. Perhaps equalizing the odds should be considered when the child is on one side of the cash register and the premium specialist, the packager, the advertiser, and the producer are arm-in-arm on the other.

Part III
Issues about the Consumer
Behavior of Children

8
Researching Children as Consumers

C hildren were interviewed in depth at their schools in order to determine the extent to which they participate in the consumer role. The
children were brought to a small room where they were given a
warm-up interview that revealed the purposes of the interview to them and
determined the children's willingness to talk freely. Following are excerpts
from a warm-up interview with Mary Ellen, a fourth-grader, assessed by her
teacher as very bright. Mary Ellen's father is a career officer in the Air Force;
her mother is a college-educated homemaker.

INTERVIEWER: I will be asking you some questions, Mary Ellen, about. . . ."
MARY ELLEN: What about?
INTERVIEWER: What I was going to say is that I will be asking you some ques-
tions about being a consumer, and I hope you will talk freely
about them.
MARY ELLEN: What do you want to know about me?
INTERVIEWER: We think what you have to say, Mary Ellen, is very important to
our research.
MARY ELLEN: What do you do with this information? Do you make money with
it?
INTERVIEWER: No, we don't make money with it. We use it to help us to better
understand the consumer behavior of children. Now tell me
about some shopping trip you took recently with your mother.
MARY ELLEN: I don't think my mother wants me doing this. Are you going to
talk to all the kids in our room?
INTERVIEWER: Yes, we hope to talk to them all, and we don't want any children
to talk to us if they feel they shouldn't. How do you feel about it?
MARY ELLEN: Are you going to give me something for doing this?
INTERVIEWER: Yes, we do have a small gift for each of you as a way of showing
our appreciation. Would you like to tell me about a shopping
trip you took with your mother?
MARY ELLEN: Another man came to our school and asked us about that.

INTERVIEWER: About shopping with your mother? What did you tell him?
MARY ELLEN: That I like it and I like to talk about it.

The above dialogue might be entitled "Who's Interviewing Whom?" It reflects some of the difficulties of conducting research among children. As children have become bona fide consumers, however, research into their behavior has become a marketing necessity. That is the topic of this chapter. Specifically, the kinds of research conducted among children as consumers will be described, along with its purposes and frameworks. Then some ethical questions about researching children in the consumer role will be discussed. Finally, some observations will be made about the research that is still needed in this area.

Background and History

It was observed in an earlier chapter that viewing children as consumers is a relatively new phenomenon. It received only an occasional mention in the literature in the 1950s, was noted somewhat more frequently but with caution in the 1960s, was presented as a legitimate new research topic of the 1970s, and is now a standard subject of discussion in the 1980s. It took root in the 1940s during World War II when children were asked to assume more responsible roles because all the able-bodied men had been drafted and even some women were serving in the armed forces. It was easy for children to earn money during this period, and many did. Consequently, some merchants began seeing them as a market for more than just penny candy. It took the baby boom of the late 1940s and early 1950s to make their numbers significant; then it took another phenomenon—Saturday morning television—to make it possible for marketers to effectively aim promotional messages at this market segment.

There is little question that business began to research children as consumers during the 1950s television bonanza; otherwise, manufacturers would not have committed millions of dollars of advertising to them. However, it was very unacceptable for business to pursue a typical business/consumer relationship with children; therefore, consumer research among children was not a topic of discussion in the 1950s trade journals, much less the academic journals. There was no way to know what research was being done by business then or what research concern it had. Business almost never publishes its research results (more will be said about this later), and it was not until the 1960s that academicians began publishing some of their studies related to children as consumers. An exception was a study conducted by the Kroger Food Foundation in 1954 that was briefly described in a previous chapter. This exploratory project was the responsibility of a business, Kroger, but observers from academia, government, and noncompeting businesses were invited. Its essential purpose was to obtain children's reactions to "food products" in the "environment of a self-service food store" (p. 1).

A year later, a study of brand preference and loyalty among children was published in the *Journal of Applied Psychology* by Lester Guest (1955). This study, which was later to become a classic, went almost unnoticed by business practitioners and academicians. It went unnoticed perhaps because it was in a journal not ordinarily associated with the business community or perhaps because the objects of brand loyalty were mainly adult items such as autos and gasoline; probably the reason it hardly made a ripple, however, was because it was done by someone who supposedly had a *legitimate* interest in children— a psychologist.

In 1964 the University of Texas published the first study to consider children as a current market for a variety of goods and services (McNeal, 1964). Later this study was published in summary form in a consumer behavior book (McNeal, 1965) and then in a marketing journal in 1969. Although the McNeal (1964) study had many shortcomings, it did take a position, with evidence, that children constituted a bona fide market of consumers.

In 1966, two years after the McNeal study declared children to be a market, a study by two psychologists, Wells and Lo Sciuto, was published in a marketing journal. It demonstrated that children may greatly influence parental purchase decisions for candy and cereal in the supermarket. Stimulated by this study and the earlier McNeal study, a business professor and his students conducted a study of children's influence on mothers' purchases of cereal. This study by Berey and Pollay (1968) showed that children did influence the mothers' selection of cereals and that this influence varied according to the children's assertiveness and the mothers' child-centeredness. In this study, it was assumed that the children's cereal preferences were a result of commercial persuasion.

In the meantime, the strongest wave of consumerism to ever take place in our nation was going full blast. A book entitled *The Hidden Persuaders* by journalist Vance Packard came out in 1957; it incensed the public. Packard, with great detail but little research, described how advertisers and marketing researchers were manipulating the public, including children, without the public realizing it. In 1962, President Kennedy gave the public a Consumer Bill of Rights in which everyone was assured of the right to safety, the right to be heard, the right to choose, and the right to be informed. These rights became badges for consumer advocates, such as the Action for Children's Television (ACT) organization that formed in the 1960s; in turn, the activities of the advocates stimulated some research.

The stage was practically set for legitimate research into the consumer behavior of children. Research had shown that children, the embodiment of innocence in our society, were acting as consumers and were influencing the consumer behavior of their parents, and the children, in turn, were being influenced by marketers, mainly advertisers. The final element of legitimacy for researching the consumer behavior of children was provided in 1974 by Scott Ward in a new journal, the *Journal of Consumer Research* (the title itself provides some sanction). In this article, a theoretical foundation was suggested for guiding such research. The article, entitled simply "Consumer Socialization," was a very thorough treatment of how various social agents, including advertising, contributed to the development of children. If the research movement needed any more legitimacy, it was supplied by Ward's credentials. He was a professor at the Harvard Graduate School of Business Administration. Research into children's consumer behavior blossomed.

Who Conducts Children's Consumer Behavior Research and Why

The above commentary about the development of research in the area of children's consumer behavior may imply that academicians are responsible for most of the research. This is not the case. Unquestionably, the greatest quantity of research into children's consumer behavior is being done by the business community to support its product development and marketing efforts. Because its results are not published, this research is not visible and it is difficult to appreciate its extensiveness.

The mere fact that children are three markets in one, a current market for certain goods and services, a future market for all goods and services, and a market of influentials, is a very attractive inducement for business to conduct research among children. Thus, researching them has become a competitive effort, just like pricing or advertising. In the toy industry, for example, there is much more sophistication in research as a result of the growing importance of the children's market. "Instead of rolling out new toys and hoping they sell, companies are doing upfront research, positioning their products, investing big money in sales tracking to see how they perform in the marketplace, and fine-tuning the marketing plan as needed" (Higgins, 1985, p. 1). One toy company, Mattel, uses "focus groups, diary panels, concept and theme testing, name and package testing, and simulated test models" among children as part of its research-reliant marketing efforts to capture its share of the children's toy market (Higgins, 1985, p. 1). Some producers of products for children turn over much of their research on new products and new advertising to research consulting firms that specialize in researching children's consumer behavior. One of these firms, the Gene Reilly Group, has been doing this kind of work for thirty years. Megan Nerz, a vice president and director of children's research for Reilly, states, "What we do with the younger kids is hold creative play sessions. We'll bring small groups together . . . set up a simulated in-store display and let them pick out toys to play with" as one technique for researching children's responses to a new toy idea (Schleier, 1985, p. 26). Although it is easy to see that this kind of research is not published because of its competitive importance, it is regrettable that it is not available to play a very major role in contributing to the body of knowledge about the consumer behavior of children. The published research findings about children's consumer behavior mainly originate in universities and could never match up to these "firing-line" findings. It is unfortunate that there is not some mechanism to permit the publication of such research efforts when their results are no longer deemed beneficial to the business.

Essentially, research into children's consumer behavior can be divided into applied and pure research, with the former being the domain of business and the latter that of academics. The main purposes of each can be summarized as follows.

Applied Research into Children's Consumer Behavior

To Support New Product Development. This type of research mainly consists of concept testing, in which a new idea for a child's toy or snack, for example, is subjected to examination. Procedurally, the product idea, in the form of words or pictures, is posed to children to obtain their opinions and level of enthusiasm. Usually, the format employs focus group interviews, which may be done by the company or a consulting firm. Concept testing, in addition to the product, may embrace the package, the product's price, and its brand name.

To Provide Guidelines for Effective Advertising. A typical advertisement on television is thirty seconds long. It may cost $50,000 to produce, and the company may pay a million dollars or more to networks for its showing. Therefore, it must effectively present the product, its name, and its general story—what it is, what it does, and why it should be purchased—in less time than it takes a child to open a new box of cereal. Research into impact of words, sounds, and colors and impact of the product in different presentations, such as camera angles and use, must be done, and the resulting commercial must be tested to see if it accomplishes what was intended. This research work is normally the domain of an advertising agency, but it usually also includes advertising and marketing research personnel from the sponsoring company.

To Determine Specific Regulative Action and Its Impact. A special kind of applied research into children's consumer behavior is that done when regulation by a federal agency via a new rule or law is proposed. Such research may be conducted by the regulatory agency or by the businesses affected; more likely, it will be done by academicians, either because of interest in the issue or because university professors are paid as consultants. For example, in 1974 the Federal Trade Commission (FTC) issued a proposed guide requesting that the advertising industry discontinue the television advertising of premium offers to children. Three university professors, Shimp, Dyer, and Divita (1976), decided to "test empirically the legitimacy of the FTC's proposed premium guide" (p. 1). Eventually the FTC used these research results, published in the *Journal of Consumer Research,* to assess the premium guide. Usually, regulatory agencies prefer to have their research done by the university community because it is inclined toward objectivity. Business rarely publishes its research results related to regulatory matters, but may describe it in public hearings as "our research."

Pure Research into Children's Consumer Behavior

To Lend Understanding to Children's Actions as Consumers. Probably most of the children's consumer behavior research conducted at universities has this purpose. Most university professors recognize the charge that is given to them—to contribute to knowledge—and a few choose to research the area of children's consumer behavior as a partial fulfillment of this obligation. Most of the research is done in research-oriented universities where publication is rewarded. A glance at the bibliography at the end of this book shows that only around a half-dozen academicians view the subject of children's consumer behavior as important enough to merit repeated research. Most of the research consists of one-shot studies reflecting simply a curiosity about the topic or perhaps an opportunity to publish because the topic is a hot one.

To Lend Understanding to a Body of Facts about Consumer Behavior. A few members of the University community see the study of children in the consumer role as making a contribution to the understanding of consumer behavior in general. In such a case, children usually are seen as simplified consumers or consumers in embryonic form whose understanding helps to explain the more complex adult consumer. For example, the classic study of brand loyalty among children by Guest (1955) may help consumer behaviorists to better explain brand loyalty among adults.

To Improve the General Welfare of Business and Consumers. A few university teachers and an occasional business person may study the consumer behavior of children because they feel it will ultimately help both business and consumers. This reason for doing consumer research among children is often combined with one or both of the other two reasons given.

This may sound unrealistically altruistic, but it does motivate the university professor particularly to conduct research studies about the consumer/business interaction. Some business persons agree with this reason for doing research, but feel that it would also benefit their competitors. Therefore, they are reluctant to do research or to do it for publication. This motive for studying children's consumer behavior is sometimes strong enough to encourage business persons and academicians to work together.

Theoretical Frameworks for Guiding Research

Among all the research studies of the consumer behavior of children there exists a wide variety of theoretical frameworks that directs them. These general viewpoints, if applied logically, cause the research to provide more meaningful results because they give the researcher guidance in the preparation, execution, and reporting of the study. For example, if a researcher states that he intends to study the impact of television advertising on children without stating his frame of reference, it will be difficult to predict the value of the measured impact because it is uncertain what he will do. For example, will he measure the impact of color, sound, appeals, spokespersons, animation, music, language, premiums, product brands, repetition, length of commercial, time of day of commercials, quantity of commercials, quantity of adult commercials, or some combination of these variables? Will he measure the impact on children's attitudes, behavior, motivation, perception, interactions with parents or peers, desires, interests, intentions, attention, learning, information processing abilities, awareness, understanding, or some combination of these variables? Will he measure the impact in accordance with age, school grade, cognitive development stage, sex, race, culture, geographic location, income of household, parental mediation, peer mediation, time of day or week, or some combination of these variables?

One can easily begin to see the problems that arise if there is no theoretical framework to guide a particular research effort regarding children. This seems even more important in a relatively new area like children's consumer behavior. Also, it seems exceptionally important to have a framework for this research in order that the results can be placed in inventory in an orderly way and thus be easily retrieved. As the large number of research projects referred to in this book are examined, it appears that most of them were guided by a theoretical framework, although occasionally the framework is implicit or only briefly described.

There is no such thing as one correct theoretical framework for guiding children's consumer behavior research, although there are some statements made in the literature that ring of this belief. It depends on the purpose and philosophy for doing the research. We have already shown some differences in

Table 8-1
Theoretical Frameworks that Guide
Consumer Behavior Research on Children

Attitude Behavior Theory
Attitude Consistency Theory
Attitude Formation Theory
Cognitive Components Theory
Cognitive Processes Theory
Cognitive Quality Theory
Decision Theory
Demographics
Developmental Theory
Economic Theory
Ethics Theory
Information Processing Theory
Learning Theory
Motivation Theory
Perception Theory
Situational Variables
Social Class Theory
Social Interaction Theory
Socialization Theory
Values

the research thinking of business practitioners and academicians, for example, simply because their goals differ. It is true, however, that an examination of the research on children's consumer behavior shows that two or three viewpoints, with slight variations, guide many of the efforts. Table 8-1 lists the theoretical frameworks that were gleaned from examining all the research for the preparation of this book. It is probably apparent to some of the readers acquainted with the literature in this area that several studies utilize combinations of frameworks.

One of the first concerns that arises about theoretical frames of reference used in researching children as consumers is the choice of an adult or child model to guide the research (Calder, Robertson, and Rossiter, 1976). This question is logical but troublesome. It is spawned by the recognition that a child, although possessing many similarities to an adult, is developing; an adult has developed. Therefore, the framework for research among children ordinarily should allow for this developmental aspect. There is also the question of whether the child is simply an adult in miniature or do children's minds work differently. Calder, Robertson, and Rossiter (1976), for example, posit that children differ in the type of memory codes used to store new information. It is obvious that children possess more similarities to adults than differences, but there is nevertheless wisdom in using the many child-centered models of thinking and behavior that exist as frames of reference for researching children as consumers.

One of the most popular research frameworks for children's consumer behavior is socialization. As noted earlier, it was eloquently suggested by Ward in 1974 as an appropriate model for studying children's consumer behavior; because it was the first, it stuck. It is a sociological concept that primarily focuses on the social agents who influence children's learning of consumer behavior, their learning setting, and what they learn. Developmental theory, another framework for research among children, is similar to socialization theory but dwells more on the changes in the child's motor and perceptual skills. Social interaction theory is a subset of socialization theory, but it gives consideration mainly to the relations between social agents and children. Studies of parents' influence on their children's television viewing or studies of children's influence on parental purchases often use a social interaction research framework.

Another very popular research framework is information processing theory. This theory, of which there are many components, posits that there are steps that a child's cognitive processes take from the time he is stimulated (by a television advertisement, for example) to the time at which he takes some action based on the stimulation (asks mom to buy an advertised item, for example). These steps are popularly described as attention, interest, desire, and action, or what is termed the AIDA concept. Information processing theorists usually select attitudes as their research focus. Thus, subsets of information processing theory are attitude formation theory, attitude consistency theory, and attitude behavior theory. Two other subsets of information processing theory are theories of cognitive processes (for example, how the memory works) and theories of cognitive components and cognitive qualities (for example, intelligence and its nature).

Demographics are also a frequently used base for guiding research among children as consumers. Research may be concerned with the demographics of the household in which the children live, such as income or number of people in a household, or demographics of the children, such as age and sex. A study by Bearden, Teel, and Wright (1979), for example, examined children's attitudes toward advertising and how they varied by income of their households.

Situational variables, another framework for guiding research into the consumer behavior of children, refer to those factors that occur in a behavioral setting that in the normal course of events could not have been predicted. Situational variables have been of particular concern to researchers of children's television viewing; for example, they are interested in whether or not there were snacks available or parents present during the viewing.

The set of research frameworks alluded to earlier that guide applied research are not shown in table 8-1. Many are not theoretical frameworks per se. They are mainly the marketing strategies of the companies doing product and promotion research among children, the research strategies and methodological theories that guide studies in the application of certain research techniques, and laws and ethics that direct study into such topics as advertising deception, deceptive package design, and persuasion.

The use of two or three of the research frameworks listed in table 8-1 is not uncommon and is needed for complex research work. In a study by Roedder, Sternthal, and Calder (1983), for instance, the investigators called on theories of decision making, attitude consistency, attitude-behavior relationships, and cognitive development. In contrast, some business researchers invoke no theoretical foundations, but simply let marketing strategy direct the research effort.

Although there are many theoretical frameworks used in studying the consumer behavior of children, there are some noticeably and surprisingly missing. Motivation theory and satisfaction/dissatisfaction theory are two frameworks that have had little or no utilization in children's consumer behavior research. Why these fundamental theories have not been used is unclear. Perhaps the bandwagon effect of other theories may have caused these simply to be overlooked.

The large variety of research frameworks used in researching children as consumers has been responsible for diverse and disorganized research results about their consumer behavior. Consequently, general behavior models, such as that used in chapter 5 to describe children's responses to television advertising, often are suggested as a way of systematizing the research results. Resnik, Stern, and Alberty (1979) developed such a model and through its application showed not only how to order the various research findings on children's advertising, but also were able to pinpoint important areas for future research efforts.

Methodological Concerns in Researching Children's Consumer Behavior

One can not go to a research techniques book and turn to the children's section. Essentially, all the techniques used in researching adults are also used for researching children. A variety of experimental laboratory studies have been utilized in studying children's consumer behavior; the direct observational method has been a technique employed in several studies, and a wide range of in-person survey research methods have been used. Only mail surveys and telephone surveys are not reported in the literature related to children's consumer behavior, and probably this is due as much to ethical considerations as to methodological ones.

Children are different from adults, however, particularly those children under age eight, and consequently there are methodological concerns that must be addressed when researching them. The chief ones are as follows.

Children Lack the Articulative Skills of Adults

"The judgements of children, like those of adults, are influenced by and often based upon their own experiences with people and social institutions," observe three researchers who are interested in methodological matters related to children (Neelankavil, O'Brien, and Tashjian, 1985, p. 41). They go on to note, however, that "whereas adults can reasonably be expected to articulate these background factors, one cannot reasonably expect this from children, especially the younger ones" (p. 41). Articulative skills are related to learning, motivation, and personality. Most youngsters simply have not lived long enough to have learned a great deal of vocabulary and syntax. Further, they often are not motivated to articulate well, and often they are shy and suspicious of adult researchers.

Children Possess Limited Knowledge

Researchers usually approach children from a children's perspective, but somewhere along the way to their research objectives the researchers too often reassume an adult perspective. This usually puts a lot of distance between the child's knowledge and the investigator's knowledge. In one of the best-known studies of children's consumer behavior (Ward, Wackman, and Wartella, 1977A, p. 69), researchers asked children, "Suppose you wanted to buy a new television set. What would you want to know about it?" The purpose was to "obtain a measure of children's product-information selection in a specific decision-making situation" (p. 69). The plain fact of the matter is, however, that children know very little about the purchase of a television set or any durable goods. Consequently, in this particular study, most of the children focused on physical attributes such as color versus black and white because that is where most of their knowledge is in regard to this particular item, that is, in the realm of the obvious. The children, for example, apparently did not ask about warranties and would not be expected to, as a rule, because of their limited knowledge, even though warranties are a major attribute of durable goods.

Children Have Very Limited Reasoning Powers

Children, particularly those below the age of eight, not only have less developed reasoning powers than adults, but may reason differently (Strauss, 1952). Therefore, research procedures that ask "why" of the children will obtain answers that often are not useful because of the youngsters' limited reasoning ability and because their reasoning networks may differ from those of adults. For example, a number of studies have asked children why companies advertise in order to determine if children are aware of commercial purposes. It may be possible that many of the answers given to this question by very young children may not be understood by adults who are "smarter." Moreover, the reasoned answers are compounded by the children's limited articulative skills. In fact, it may be, as Chestnut (1979) hints, that any task required of children that entails verbal responses may not produce much valid information.

Children Have Limited Reading/Writing Abilities

There is concern today with the reading ability of high school students, but it is a much more serious matter, particularly from a research perspective, among children. Researchers in the past have demonstrated a fondness for going into children's classrooms and administering questionnaires. Reading these questionnaires can be a real problem for children unless the instruments have been tested thoroughly for readability—an uncommon effort among marketing researchers. Equally a problem are the questionnaires in which children have to write responses. To deal with the writing problem among children, research instruments requiring that the youngster check or circle an answer, often on a scale, have been introduced. Understanding scaled responses such as "agree" and "somewhat agree" can be difficult, however, for children, who may be more literal and not see a difference between these two responses. Some consumer researchers have utilized questionnaires that permit children to make responses to pictures or faces, such as those in figure 8-1, rather than scaled statements, which should help with both reading and expression inabilities. The smiling faces in figure 8-1 that were introduced by Wells in the early 1960s have become popular among consumer researchers, and logically so. However, they can introduce unintended consequences into the research program, such as distracting the youngster, causing the youngster to be reminded of another who looks like the drawing, or misleading the respondent by suggesting laughter or sadness rather than agreeableness or disagreeableness.

Children Are More Self-Centered than Adults

Children's lives revolve around a particular and narrow social setting. Therefore, research topics selected by adults may or may not be of interest to them. For example, we can expect television commercials about cereals and snacks to be interesting to children, commercials about medicines to be less interesting, and the people and purposes behind the commercials to be uninteresting. When the research topic is not interesting, there are research problems, such as completion of the questionnaire, maintaining a conversation in a group interview or depth interview, and obtaining more than superficial thinking, for example. A related problem that often accompanies self-centeredness is short attention span. This additional problem may compound the research effort. Warm-up interviews, financial inducements, and an interesting research environment all may be necessary to cope with children's self-centeredness.

FOR BOYS

FOR GIRLS

Source: William D. Wells (1965), "Communicating with Children," *Journal of Advertising Research*, 5 (June), p. 4. Reprinted from the *Journal of Advertising Research*. Copyright 1965, by the Advertising Research Foundation.

Figure 8-1. A Smiling Faces Scale Used among Children to Accommodate Limited Reading and Writing Abilities

In view of these five methodological concerns about researching children as consumers, there are two research techniques that are particularly recommended. The first is the *observation* technique. "The principal advantage of direct observation," according to Wells and Lo Sciuto (1966, p. 227), is that "when it is done well it produces a highly detailed, nearly complete record of what people actually do." When compared generally with other techniques, the observation technique definitely has advantages. In conducting research into parent-children interactions in the supermarket, Atkin (1978, p. 41), a noted researcher in the field of children's consumer behavior, had this to say.

> The direct observation method provides a more accurate assessment of varying modes of interaction than would be obtained by self-reports elicited in interviews or direct measurement under laboratory conditions. Interview data would be subject to distortion and memory error, while laboratory behavior would be artificial compared to the real-life supermarket situation.

The observation technique, of course, avoids requiring the child to speak, thus nullifying the problems associated with children's limited skills in reasoning and articulation. Moreover, there is not the problem of children providing descriptions without much detail because it has been forgotten or because it does not seem important to the youngsters. Some studies have utilized parents as observers of children, but then there is the problem of an additional level of communications that may produce error and bias.

Observations do not have to be limited to the store setting. The findings in chapter 7 about children's interactions with packaging were produced through observation. It is one thing to ask children about difficulties they experience with opening or closing packages; it is another, and much more enlightening, to actually observe them using the packages in the normal course of events and witness the details of the difficulties. Unobtrusive observations of children's television viewing and radio listening may also be more productive than self-reporting when the focus is on attention and actual number of advertisements seen or heard. The observation technique is also useful in understanding children's problems and satisfaction with the actual use/consumption of products. No doubt this is how the Nabisco Company discovered the children's rituals when eating Oreos that are so affectionately demonstrated in Oreo's advertising.

The observation method, like any research technique, has its faults. It provides information on behavior but no explanations for it, it can be biased by its location or environment, and in real life it generally is difficult to control for the subjects contained in the research sample (Wells and Lo Sciuto, 1966). Nonetheless, overall it does overcome some of the serious methodological problems in researching children as consumers.

The other technique that is recommended for researching children's consumer behavior is the *conversational interview*. The conversational interview is more of a procedure than a technique and therefore has various titles, such as in-depth interview, informal interview, or focus group interview, depending on the format. Most of the vignettes reported at the beginning of each of the chapters in this book were obtained through conversational interviews. Conversational interviews may be on an individual or a group basis (three to six children) and are recognizable by their minimum number of direct questions. Once a topical discussion is under way, questions are used much as a counselor would, to keep the conversation going and to keep it going in the desired direction. The interviewer, who is better termed a moderator when interviews are on a group basis, rather than asking questions, repeats the last few words of a statement made by the respondent or makes utterances such as mmm-hmm or huh-uh in order to elicit continued conversation. Such a procedure focuses on the respondent and, in the case of children, capitalizes on their self-centeredness. It also capitalizes on the children's lack of articulation and shyness in the sense that its informal atmosphere encourages them to speak spontaneously and to speak in their own jargon. Finally, it takes advantage of children's natural honesty. If there is good rapport between interviewer and respondent (admittedly, children's shyness often prevents this, as

Wells (1965) so strongly notes), children will express exactly what is on their minds.

Conversational interviews may not be popular among those who call for more rigor in children's consumer behavior research, such as Rossiter (1978), simply because the technique does not produce easily quantifiable data. However, it does produce a great quantity of information, often very rich in meaning, that can be tested in structured procedures that are subject to strict quantification.

Ethics in Researching Children as Consumers

Doing right in researching children as consumers seems even more important than in adult researching because of children's limited understanding of the commercial world. The assumption here is that it is ethical to conduct consumer research among children, although there are some consumer protectionists who would disagree. They view such consumer research as part of an overall exploitation effort aimed at defenseless children by well-armed adults. However, as long as business is permitted to develop products for children, marketing research will be done to make sure these efforts are as effective as possible in meeting sales and consumer satisfaction goals. An ethical framework therefore should guide this research.

Most researchers who get involved in studying the consumer behavior of children are subject to codes of ethics of various professions, such as those of the American Marketing Association, American Sociological Association, and the American Psychological Association. These codes of ethics, however, are not laws and have very few punitive aspects. Therefore, they may be violated, just as codes of ethics of advertisers are violated. Further, they may not always embrace all aspects of research. For example, The Code of Ethics of the American Marketing Association appears to give more consideration to the client-researcher relationships in survey research than to that in experimental research, which is very common in children's consumer behavior.

An ethical framework for consumer behavior research among children is provided by President Kennedy's Consumer Bill of Rights. Part of being a consumer is the expectation that one will participate as a subject in marketing research, but another expectation of the consumer is that one's rights will be respected. These rights as provided by the Consumer Bill of Rights are the right to be informed, the right to be heard, the right to choose, and the right to safety. Protecting these rights is the ethical responsibility of all researchers who investigate the consumer behavior of children whether associated with a business firm or a university. Let us briefly look at these rights from a research perspective.

Right To Be Informed

Children and also their parents, or those responsible for them, must know the purposes of the research in which they are asked to participate, how it is to be conducted, and the expected performance of the children. This information permits the child or his or her guardian to make a rational decision about participating. If the parents or those responsible for the children feel that the research project has improper motives, then they can refuse to permit the children to participate.

After a research project is completed, the children who participated and their guardians should be debriefed, an often neglected responsibility of consumer researchers. If a researcher is testing to see if subjects can discern differences in brands of soft drinks, for example, and part of the study has children sample three containers of beverage, two of which are the same, they should be told these facts after the experiment is completed. Debriefing can provide an important learning experience for a child by just learning about some of the complexities of the commercial world, but most important it can keep the respondent from feeling foolish later on. If a reward at the end of the project is an integral part of the study, this information also should be part of the debriefing. Properly informing children and their parents of the nature and purpose of research projects among children and debriefing them afterward is not only ethical, but may also improve the image of marketing research. This is badly needed in the case of researching children.

Right To Choose

Just as children should have a choice of products, they also should have the right to choose to participate in a research study of their consumer behavior. Special caution must be used when the child makes the choice because of the impact that the adult researchers have on most children. The children may be frightened by an authority figure or simply believe that as children they must obey the request to participate. Therefore, saying yes to a request to participate may not be an actual choice of the child. Researchers should keep this in mind and always obtain a decision from a parent or guardian, although there may be an ethical question about whether children have expressed their choice when their parents have chosen for them, particularly if the parents or a classroom teacher received a payment or gift for the children's participation. Professional researchers should always confirm the child's choice as well as that of the parent or guardian.

Right To Safety

During the research project, the child's safety should be paramount. There should be concern for their physical safety and their psychological safety.

Safety from physical harm is more apparent. For example, children should be properly protected in a play environment in which a new toy is being tested. This may sound like a minor precaution, but just think of the toys that went through research only to be found unsafe for children when sold in the marketplace. Safety from psychological harm is another ethical issue. It can mean many things, but it particularly refers to freedom from humiliation and freedom from stress. For instance, both embarrassment and stress can result from children being unable to answer several of a series of questions. Debriefing often can be used to insure that the respondent will be protected against long-term stress as a result of the research procedures.

Right To Be Heard

Just as young consumers have a right to voice opinions and complaints about products and services, they have parallel rights as participants in a research project. If children are deceived, misled, treated in a harmful or rude way, not given the reward promised, not debriefed, or not told the purpose of the research, the children's parents or guardians should complain to an appropriate authority. This is not always easy. In the case of interviews in a shopping center, often termed *mall intercepts,* children or parents may be interviewed by persons who work part-time, who are paid on an interview basis, who may not have had permission to use the mall or center as a research location, and who did not give their names or the name of the firms who hired them. If they did provide the name of the sponsor of the research, that sponsor should be contacted. If that sponsor is a professional marketing research firm, the respondent can usually expect action, such as an apology and an attempt at correcting the error. Sometimes university professors use students who are not professionally trained for various research tasks. In such cases, errors may be made, but the professor is usually professionally conscious about such matters and will attempt to make things right.

Needed Research Among Children as Consumers

The large number of references listed at the end of this book suggest that the topic of children's consumer behavior is a popular one that is frequently researched. This is really not the case. A closer examination of the references will reveal that most of the entries are about the single consumer topic of television advertising, reflecting researchers' responses to the FTC's desire to severely limit such advertising.

Actually, there is a shortage of research on children's consumer behavior, particularly in view of its potential contribution to a body of knowledge about consumer behavior in general and children's consumer behavior, specifically.

Two reasons explain much of the shortage. The first is the widely held belief that it is somehow wrong to conduct research that will have commercial value on children. One does not help business make money off of innocent children who are inherently at an unfair advantage, seems to be the thinking. The second reason, related to the first, is the unavailability of children for research purposes. Parents are reluctant to permit researchers into the home to conduct consumer research among their children, schools tend not to permit it, and researchers themselves are inclined not to intercept children and interview them at shopping centers and stores. Therefore, there is still much research needed in this area.

Let us itemize the needed research in the consumer behavior of children. We will do this according to whether the focus is on behavior or cognitions. This division is strictly for the sake of description, because in reality the two are inseparable; cognitions always precede and follow behavior.

Needed Behavioral Research on Children as Consumers

The following is a summary of the behavioral research areas on children as consumers needing more investigation. Their order is random.

Children as a Current Market. Some of the television advertising research has viewed children as a market for goods and services, but most of it is concerned with children as influentials on parents. As chapter 3 indicated, children have quite of bit of money to spend and they are spending it. Chapter 4 documented retailers' efforts to get children's business. Nevertheless, research that recognizes children as a current market and examines their spending, saving, and purchasing behavior is in very short supply.

Children as a Peer Influential Market. Although children have been studied as a market of influentials, the focus has been almost solely on parents. We know that children influence each other and that peer influence starts at a very early age and grows, but we know little about peer influence on consumer behavior. Some items of information that would be useful to investigate are peer influence on meanings of advertising messages, store selection and preference, and product and brand preference.

Children as a Future Market. Although it is obvious that children will become markets for all products in adulthood, research does not reflect this. Research shows, for example, that children gradually develop mistrust of television advertising. It would be interesting to know what impact this has when they become adults. Equally important is the impact that current child /retailer relationships have on the children's future consumer behavior. This kind of research is difficult to execute, but as business management becomes more oriented to the long term, such research makes good sense. Consumer educators also should be interested in these data.

Children and the Retail Store. Although the store is essentially the only place from which children buy goods and services, we know almost nothing about this aspect of children's consumer behavior. Research is needed that tells us about frequency of store visits, factors in store choice, and in-store behavior. Also needed are studies among retailers that describe their side of the store/child interaction, in terms of their viewpoints about children as consumers, their activities aimed at this market, and the value of this market to various types of retailers. Particularly important in all these investigations is the retailer's contribution to the consumer socialization of children.

Sales Promotion and Children. We know a few facts about children's response to premiums, particularly to the advertising of premiums, but very little about many other types of sales promotion. Sales promotion is a term used to describe most promotion efforts except personal selling, advertising, and packaging and includes contests and cent-off coupons as well as premiums. For example, Post cereals ran a contest in which children could win a shopping spree in a Toys R Us store. It would be useful to study children's attitudes and responses to this type of sales promotion. Post also ran a coupon/contest campaign, no doubt aimed at parents, in which a person could spell POST and receive up to $6.00 in coupons toward different cereals. When children saw this coupon offer on their box of Fruity Pebbles, for instance, what impact did it have on them? In the case of premiums, we need to know much more. Children love premiums, often more than the cereals that offer them, but are some premiums more desirable than others, are in-box or by-mail premiums more important to children, and will premiums influence the sale of other items, such as toys, as they do cereals? These are important questions to marketers and to parents.

Children and Prices. One of the most important items of information, price, is a topic we know almost nothing about when it comes to children as consumers. We know that schools teach the concept of price in some of their courses, mainly math, and we know that parents help their youngsters to learn prices, although sometimes in negative ways, and we know children use price indicators during their store visits, but what do they know and understand about prices? Prices are never mentioned in advertising to children. Why not? Should they be? Wouldn't children learn prices faster if they were included in ads? Because price is such a fundamental topic of concern to consumer educators, marketers, and consumer protectionists, it should not be absent from consumer behavior research among children.

Children's Consumer Behavior in Environments of Ads Versus No Ads. Although we have many studies regarding children and advertising, we need more, but of a specific nature. There is need to know how children's consumer behavior differs when they are reared in an environment rich in television advertising as compared with one void of television advertising. Such a study or series of studies should help to settle the controversy surrounding television advertising to children. This is a great opportunity for a joint research project between some universities in Quebec and the United States. For example, several producers of children-oriented goods are complaining loudly about not being permitted to advertise to children in Quebec, while some observers are saying it does not make a difference in product sales. This disagreement and many others could be settled with the study proposed here.

Products' Contribution to Children's Consumer Socialization. As was observed in chapter 6, some toys, including games and books, appear to teach such consumer behavior as brand and store name awareness, shopping, and business operations. Whether their contribution to children's consumer behavior is intentional is not known. Their actual impact is also not known, and studies should be developed to assess this impact. In theory, it may be a fun way to teach children some consumer behavior and in fact could be utilized by consumer educators.

Needed Cognitive Research

The following suggested research topics have their focus mainly on the minds of children. As with the previously suggested research, there is no particular order intended.

Children's Motives for Their Consumer Behavior. Explaining the motives for specific consumer behavior is one of the most important efforts of marketing research. In turn, advertisements are then designed to show how a particular brand of product satisfies certain motives (needs). Chapter 5 presented some brief findings classifying the need appeals in children's television advertising. This is probably the first time that findings about children's needs have been published. Much, much more is needed. We need to know what needs children attempt to satisfy in the marketplace. Are they just parroting their parents' need expression in the marketplace or do they have their own unique set of needs to be satisfied? Are advertisers truly mirroring children's needs that can be satisfied with certain toys and snacks, or do they really know children's needs and which ones are best satisfied with certain products?

Children's Consumer Satisfaction. Satisfaction of consumer needs is the fundamental reason for the existence of marketers and of business. Just as there is no research on children's needs, there is no research on their satisfaction. We often hear retailers speak of "satisfaction guaranteed" and "your satisfaction is our primary concern." Does this include children too? Are children being properly satisfied with various products sold to them? To what extent are they experiencing dissatisfaction? Are there certain children's products that are consistently dissatisfying? We need to know these things. It is quite possible that the degree of consumer satisfaction/dissatisfaction experienced in childhood will favor general attitudes toward the marketplace in adulthood.

Children's Knowledge and Understanding of the Marketplace. Children are behaving as consumers. They are wanting things, buying things, consuming things. Marketers are encouraging all three activities, often to the displeasure of parents and consumer advocates. The latter say that children do not have a good enough understanding of marketplace behavior, particularly advertising, and therefore are at a disadvantage. Where, however, are the studies of children's knowledge and understanding of the marketplace? Granted, there are studies of children's understanding of the intent of advertising, but beyond that they are few. What about children's knowledge of the nature of our economy, the profit concept, channels of distribution, sources of products and services, and concepts such as production, marketing, and finance? Such information is not known to any extent. There have been small attempts to measure children's knowledge of some of these subjects and teaching children some of this knowledge has been the focus of consumer education, but where are the results? We need to know what children know before we can draw conclusions about their abilities as consumers.

Children's Intelligence as a Factor in Consumer Behavior. In the many studies of children's relationships to advertising, there are often extreme results. For example, if the study is to determine how much children learn from an ad, small percentage of the children learn very little, a major percentage learn about the same amount, and a small percentage learn a great deal. Because these kinds of studies usually control for age, perhaps intelligence level is a possible explanation for the extreme differences; that is, children's mental age rather than chronological age accounts for differences in learning. Much consumer research among children in fact recognizes the concept of mental age through the concept of cognitive age, but the latter is a more general notion, from a measurement standpoint, than intelligence. Studies involving a wide range of intelligence levels and a wide range of consumer behaviors, including responding to advertisements, are needed. What we may find is that some children in fact can operate quite well in the marketplace—much like adults—and some cannot operate there at all, while many can cope adequately. If such findings occur, then the concept of consumer protection perhaps should be revised to focus mainly on the groups that cannot function in the marketplace. Actual implementation of intelligence level in marketing or in consumer protection may be difficult, just as it has been in education, but research supporting such thinking is needed. It should also help to clear up conflicting findings about children's consumer abilities.

Discussion

The 1980s appear to be a nodal time for consumer research among children, a time when the hectic pace of the 1970s caused by the strong wave of consumerism in the 1960s gives way to a period of reflection and preparation for the 1990s. The prosperity of the 1980s has contributed to a calm among consumer advocates, while the spirit of deregulation on Capitol Hill has made quiescent those public policy makers ordinarily concerned with marketing to children. Consequently, there has been only slight encouragement for research of children's consumer behavior among academicians. In effect, consumer behavior research among children is in place; it simply needs to mature.

The very idea of researching children as consumers is no doubt offensive to some parents and consumer protectionists, but the facts are in. Children not only constitute a bona fide market for goods and services, but are pursued by business because they also constitute a large market as influentials and an ever larger market as future consumers. These facts logically stimulate a great deal of consumer research among children. This chapter has assumed these viewpoints and has examined some of the issues related to researching children's consumer behavior.

As one backs off and looks at the consumer research that has been conducted among children during the past two decades, it becomes apparent that there has been both too little and too much. There has been too little research into most aspects of the child consumer/marketer interactions and perhaps too much into children's interaction with television advertising. Too much is perhaps too strong a statement, in the sense that many of the research studies have shortcomings. The findings, however, tend to confirm each other and those of developmental psychologists for many years: children under eight are not capable of processing advertising messages appropriately. More studies are likely to produce the same results. In the meantime, researchers have practically ignored the influence of other advertising media, packaging, and sales promotion and the impact of products and branding on children's consumer behavior. There can never be an adequate body of knowledge about children's consumer behavior without substantial study in these areas.

There is another serious deficiency in the reported research about children's consumer behavior. Almost none of it comes from the business community. From a quantity standpoint, business has conducted most of the research done among children as consumers; except for that funded by business but conducted by universities, none of it has been published. Business has a standard defense: "For competitive reasons we can not disclose the information." Sometimes a businessperson will also respond by saying, "How can our research be important when it only shows children's preferences for toy concept A over toy concept B?" Of course, by itself such research is probably unimportant, but when combined with research about toy concepts C and D, it may take on theoretical significance. Also, when one reads statements such as, "Over the years my firm has developed special methods and techniques that enable children to express themselves freely and naturally" (Guber, 1976), one senses that the business community is doing research that has much significance. Perhaps one of these days a clearinghouse on children's consumer behavior research can be established that can be trusted by the business community to appropriately analyze, distill, and disseminate its research while protecting the anonymity of the research source.

This chapter's treatment of methodological matters carefully avoided the issue of shortcomings of specific children's research studies. It is easy to criticize some aspect of most of the research conducted on any topic. There is always someone to state, "This research does not provide conclusive evidence that. . . ." The literature itself contains a number of criticisms about the consumer research among children; they can be summarized as lack of detail and lack of generalizability. Both criticisms are related to a common deficiency in width and depth among investigations. A typical reported study can be characterized as one conducted among around one hundred children ages nine and ten in one geographic location, such as Chicago, during a short period of time, such as the month of August, focusing on one behavior or cognitive dimension, such as attitudes toward television advertisements of one product, such as cereal. Along comes the critic who tells the researcher that the results are not generalizable to younger or older children, to children in smaller or larger communities, to children in higher or lower income classes, to advertising in other media, and so on. Further, the critic will probably wrinkle his brow and ponder if the results would differ over time, would differ if conducted with another research instrument or in a different research setting, or would differ at another time of the year such as winter. All of these criticisms are probably valid.

There are two things that could be done to offset some of these criticisms, but never all of them. One is to conduct some case studies, just as Sigmund Freud did. Although case studies are not popular today as they once were, they do produce detail. The kind of case study referred to here is one in which the consumer behavior of one or a couple of children is studied for a period of time such as one year. Extensive records are kept, usually in diary form. Although observations are recorded without the knowledge of the child, the investigator does interact with the youngster, particularly in terms of seeking explanations. Case studies produce enormously detailed data on practically every aspect of children's consumer behavior—television viewing, interacting with packaging and products, in-store shopping, and responding to the influence of others—over a long enough period of time to allow for both changes and repetitions in behavior. Naturally, the case study has basic flaws. It is a sample of only one or a few and it is totally dependent upon the recording ability of the investigator. However, the case study is only intended to produce information that is almost impossible to obtain in any other way; then this information should be subjected to rigorous testing in formal studies.

The other research effort that can lay to rest many criticisms of children's consumer behavior research is the use of national samples. It is fairly uncommon to conduct research among any group on a national basis because it is so expensive. It seems unheard of among children. However, it is a sure way of quieting those critics who are concerned with generalizability. The kinds of studies that can be conducted on a national basis among children are limited by cost and by purpose. National surveys are usually done by telephone or mail rather than in person in order to save money. Yet studies among children usually are done in person by necessity. Care and time are required in order to get good quality data from children. A national survey of households with children is quite possible, however, if costs are not a major concern. It would require talking to parents first for clearance and also for help in setting up the interview. Therefore, telephone would seem more logical than mail. Also, much information about the consumer behavior of children could be provided by a national sample of parents, although critics sometimes call this second-hand information. It might be possible to establish a consumer panel of children on a national scale and use mail reports. Such a procedure, once cleared with parents, could provide on-going information about television viewing, daily purchases, and store visits, for example. In any case, the complexities and costs of national samples of child consumers need to be resolved in order to produce data that are representative of children in general.

Finally, we will never settle the debate over the consumer differences between children and adults until we start comparing data between the two. Rarely do children's consumer behavior studies do this. Several of them report information on children's consumer behavior and state that it is different from adults, but they do not produce the adult data to prove it. Clearly, children are very much like adults, and the actual differences need to be carefully documented with comparative studies.

9

Consumer Education for Children
as Consumers

During the spring of 1976, parents of elementary school children were interviewed to determine their attitudes toward the teaching of consumer education as part of the Social Studies course at each grade level. The interviews were prearranged and open-ended; they took place in the homes of the parents. Following is part of an interview with Mrs. Miller, who was one of a few who opposed a consumer education program. She sells real estate, completed two years of college, and is divorced.

INTERVIEWER: Would you favor this consumer education program in your daughter's school?

MRS. MILLER: Definitely not. It sounds like a waste to me and not something important that a third-grader should be learning. Put me down as being against it.

INTERVIEWER: Mrs. Miller, are you opposed to consumer education being taught in any grade or perhaps just in Bethany's grade?

MRS. MILLER: I don't see why they have to teach it at all. Why can't they just stick to teaching what they are supposed to teach—reading, math, things like that. There is so much for children to learn today if they are going to make something of themselves.

INTERVIEWER: As I understand it, then, you do not feel that it is the obligation of the school system to teach consumer education?

MRS. MILLER: No, I don't. As I see it, that's the obligation of parents. Bethany will learn those things from me as she grows older. Right now, I want to see her learning more important things.

INTERVIEWER: Then you do not feel that the program would have any benefit for most of the children, either now or in the future?

MRS. MILLER: No, I don't. The only people that will benefit are these stores around here.

INTERVIEWER: I'm not for sure what you mean. Would you explain?

MRS. MILLER: Sure. It's simple. If they learn more about it, they will want to do it more. I don't want Bethany thinking she can run to the Quick-Stop anytime she wants to or hanging around the shopping mall like I see some kids doing. She's not old enough for that sort of thing.

Perhaps Mrs. Miller's third-grade daughter is "not old enough for that sort of thing," but most children are doing it, old enough or not. According to the research in previous chapters, most children are consumers, particularly after they begin elementary school. They plan for purchases and go shopping for them. They petition parents for additional products or for the money to buy them. Most parents go along with this or even encourage it. They give their children money, as well as buy them the goods they request. Parents send their children to stores for household purchases, and they also take their children co-shopping with them for some household items. Business supports and encourages children as consumers. It advertises to them intensely, designs an array of products for them, packages the products with children appeal, and displays them in an inviting manner at eye level in a variety of stores.

There is a great deal of concern among some parents, policy makers, and consumer protectionists, however, about the child's ability as a player in the consumer game. Can little kids cope with all the magic of the modern marketing strategist backed up by sophisticated marketing research and represented by pied piper-like advertising? *They can if they have been put through a systematic consumer education program.* Consumer education, if appropriately and systematically introduced into the lives of children, holds the key to children becoming effective consumers in our type of political, social, and economic environment. We will discuss this possibility in this chapter.

Historical Perspective on Consumer Education for Children

The idea of consumer education has been around ever since we became an industrialized economy, but it did not gain much public attention until the 1930s. In general, the growth of consumer education has been tied to the three consumerism movements of the early 1900s, the 1930s, and the 1960s. The first of these movements seemed to center on health and wholesome foods and was highlighted by Upton Sinclair's book, *The Jungle,* in which he revealed the filthy conditions that existed in the meat-packing industry, and by the passage of the Food and Drug Act and the Meat Inspection Act in 1906. Just three years later, a paper presented to a meeting of what was to become the American Home Economics Association addressed "the need for educating people in proper health practices and sanitation" (Langrehr and Mason,

1977, p. 66). In fact, it is interesting to note that the founding leader of the American Home Economics Association, Mrs. Ellen H. Richards, was an instructor in the field of sanitary chemistry at Massachusetts Institute of Technology. The focus of consumer education in these early years was not on children—the child as consumer was unheard of—but on the household, and not on formal education to any extent but on self-education. So, consumer education was given life in this first era of consumerism, but very little structure.

The roaring 20s gave consumption a paramount position in American society that is still with us today. The emphasis on working and making money switched to spending the money earned. "Sales of autos, refrigerators, vacuum cleaners, radios and phonographs were brisk [and] consumers were flooded with advertising from billboards, electric signs, newspapers, magazines and the new medium of radio" (Herrmann, 1982). This national emphasis on consuming encouraged economists to give consumption a more prominent position in their writings and stimulated home economists to give more consideration to economics. The Great Depression hit in 1929; the consumption theories and concepts of the economists and home economists suddenly took on great importance and began appearing in the field of education. By the late 1930s, consumer education textbooks for high school students were fairly common. These books particularly emphasized how to get the most for your money, money that had decreased substantially due to deflated wages and extensive unemployment. According to Langrehr and Mason (1977, p. 67), "by 1939, 25,000 secondary schools were providing consumer education" although "two-thirds of the students enrolled in the consumer education courses were female." It should be noted that an appreciable amount of the consumer education literature was antibusiness, and particularly antiadvertising, probably as a response to a surge of almost unregulated and highly unethical promotion practices of business that began during the 1920s. This antibusiness attitude, although often understandable, has caused much misdirected effort among consumer educators.

While consumer education blossomed in high schools during the 1930s, there was no evidence of it as subject matter in the elementary grades. The idea that consumption was a life activity that commenced in the teen years and became important at marriage time still prevailed.

By the World War II years, consumer education was offered as a separate course in one-fourth of high schools. The war years caused the courses to give particular emphasis to "conservation, adjustment to scarcity, and rationing" (Royer and Nolf, 1980, p. 20). On the other hand, Royer and Nolf (1980, p. 21) report that the focus of consumer education shifted from a "cynical, anti-business philosophy" to a "rational approach to life." Still the high school rather than elementary school was the chosen target. This was equally true of the 1950s, during which time consumer education was in a lull, probably due to the post-war prosperity.

The last consumer movement started in the 1960s and continued to the late 1970s; it gave new life to consumer education. In 1962, President Kennedy gave the American public a Consumer Bill of Rights and established the Consumer Advisory Council. Later President Johnson appointed a Special Assistant for Consumer Affairs. The 1960s witnessed a host of consumer protection legislation. Consumer education flourished as "educators and the public recognized consumer education as being important for students at *all* levels" (Royer and Nolf, 1980, p. 31). In 1967, Illinois became the first state to mandate consumer education. The law stated that students in grades eight through twelve should be taught and be required to study courses that include instruction in consumer education. The state of Hawaii followed in 1970.

In 1970 the President's Committee on Consumer Interests published its *Suggested Guidelines for Consumer Education, K–12,* thus recognizing officially that consumer education should begin in early childhood along with the first formal education of the child. In the foreward of this landmark document, Mrs. Virginia Knauer, Special Assistant to the President for Consumer Affairs and also Chairman of the President's Committee on Consumer Interests that produced the document, made these statements emphasizing the importance of consumer education to children (emphasis added):

"Every effort should be made to help our *young* citizens become alert, responsive, and responsible consumers" (p. 111).

"Consumer Education is not merely a rhetorical exercise in buymanship. It is a continuing, *lifetime* learning experience" (p. 111).

"Consumer Education provides our *youth* with a useful frame of reference not only for the future but also for the sometimes difficult and perplexing *present*" (p. 111).

The President's Committee on Consumer Interests also recognized the need for a systematic approach to consumer education. In an opening paragraph to a section entitled "Systems Approach," the Committee states, "Possibly the most ambitious and far-reaching approach to consumer education is a system-wide commitment involving students, teachers, administrators, parents, business, consumer organizations, and other community interests" (p. 8). A systems approach to consumer education is not only recommended here, but it is suggested that without this approach, consumer education may be ineffective.

As of 1982, forty-one states plus the District of Columbia had a specific policy regarding consumer and/or economic education, and twenty-seven required it to begin at the kindergarten level. Thus it was really not until the 1970s that young children were viewed as needing consumer education.

Then, as now, the rationale for the requirement varied. The main purpose of the early childhood requirement appeared to be that consumer education is a life-long process and should begin as early as possible if adult consumer behavior is to be effective. Another purpose, one that is important to this discussion, is that children need instruction in consumer education because they are consumers. This latter rationale for consumer education appears not to have much support across the education community. This seems ironic in view of the many people and organizations concerned with children acting as consumers and being treated as consumers by business.

The Subject Matter of Consumer Education

The one sure thing that proponents of consumer education *disagree* about is what constitutes consumer education. The disagreement is due in part to the different perspectives of those concerned with consumer education, to the lack of maturity of the subject matter even though it has been around for at least one-half century, and to the complicated nature of consumer education. In particular consumer educationists have two perspectives—the economic perspective and the life goals perspective—and these will be considered in a subsequent discussion of who should teach consumer education. Although the two perspectives often treat similar materials, they differ substantially in application.

The primary objective of consumer education is to produce an effective consumer, but therein lies the problem. What is an effective consumer? Is it one who gets the most for his or her money, one who gets the most satisfaction of his or her needs in the marketplace, or one who is most skilled in buymanship? There are other options in addition to these, but the point here is to emphasize the disparity of viewpoints regarding even the fundamental nature of consumer education.

To determine the appropriate subject matter of consumer education, a definition of consumer education is needed. Naturally, there is disparity here, too, but a review of definitions in the literature revealed surprising agreement. The definition most generally agreed upon is similar to the following: "Consumer education is the preparation of the individual in the skills, concepts, and understandings that are required for every day living to achieve, within the framework of his own values, maximum satisfaction and utilization of his resources" (Schoenfeld, 1968, p. 6).

This definition gives recognition to what one has to learn to be an effective consumer: "skills, concepts and understandings." It recognizes the relevance of the material: it must relate to "every day living." It recognizes that effectiveness as a consumer is an individual matter: "within the framework of his own values." It takes a behavioral and an economic approach by recognizing that an effective consumer maximizes satisfaction and maximizes resource utilization. This definition also underlines the multiple nature of consumer education.

Each state that requires or encourages the teaching of consumer education provides curriculum guides at the various grade levels. These guides supply a range of topics to be treated under the banner of consumer education. In addition, there have been several suggestions in the literature about what the subject matter of consumer education should be. One of the most thorough of these, in good agreement with the above definition of consumer education, is a set of concepts by Stampfl, Moschis, and Lawton (1978). These authors determined the appropriateness of suggested subject matter for each unit by subjecting them to three criteria. These criteria were: (1) fundamentalness—is it necessary for explaining how the marketplace works; (2) accessibility—is it understandable to the youngest consumers; (3) relevance—does it serve in supporting an increasingly sophisticated understanding of the marketplace as the child grows older (p. 16). The procedure of these investigators gives their suggested subject matter an air of validity not always obvious in other recommended guides.

The Stampfl, Moschis, and Lawton study suggested a set of topics for consumer education; they call them building blocks. They are listed in the first column in table 9-1. Shown additionally in the second and third columns are the concepts translated into everyday language of preschool children and of adults, respectively. An important feature of this subject matter is that it treats the child as a consumer now, not just as a person who will become a consumer. Often consumer education in the classroom is put in terms of "When you grow up" or "When you start making purchases." This latter kind of education does little to make the child effective as a current consumer who is watching television advertisements, getting ideas for new products, and buying or requesting them.

It is not suggested that the list of topics in table 9-1 is complete or ideal. It is an appropriate list and fairly thorough, but at least three topics are omitted that might strengthen it. The subject of social influence on wants and purchases should be given emphasis. Also, the influence of advertising and other kinds of promotion on children's desires should be listed. Finally, it would be logical to include the idea of obtaining recourse for faulty products and services. All of these topics are easily accommodated as subtopics to some of those already listed.

Because of diverse perspectives, subject matter recommendations for consumer education differ. How can we decide which is correct? How can we decide when coverage is adequate? A model that shows the general topical areas of consumer education would help answer these questions and keep educators from being misled by the biases of others. Figure 9-1 presents such a model. Although it is only suggestive, the model attempts to depict all those

Table 9-1
The Building Blocks of Consumer Education

Consumer Education Building Block Concepts (Learning Properties)	*Marketplace Perceptions*	
	Preschool Child	*Adult Consumer*

1. a. purchasing power
   b. money as exchange
      medium
   c. budget constraints
	1. If I have some
	   money . . .
		1. When I can *afford*
		   it . . .

2. a. retailer
   b. distribution system
   c. store types
	2. I go to the *store* . . .	2. I go to the *store* . . .

3. a. information gathering
   b. also item 7 below
	3. And I *look* at goods
	   in the store.
		3. And I *shop to find
		   out* which . . .

4. a. merchandise
      assortments
   b. product lines
   c. brands
	4. I look at the *different
	   kinds* of a product or
	   different products. . .
		4. *products and brands*
		   are carried . . .

5. a. needs, wants, desires
   b. need recognition as
      first stage in the
      consumer decision
      process
   c. buying motives—
      rational vs. emotional
   d. preferences and tastes
	5. I think I *want or
	   need*
		5. that may *satisfy my
		   needs*

6. a. price system
   b. resource allocation
	6. I then find out *how
	   much of my money I
	   have to give* so I can
	   keep each of the
	   things I want.
		6. I check *prices* and
		   determine the cost of
		   each item.

7. a. search for and
      evaluation of
      alternatives as the
      second and third
      stage in the consumer
      decision process
	7. If many of the things
	   I see would make me
	   happy, *I think about
	   which one I like best
	   or need most.*
		7. I then *compare* the
		   important
		   characteristics of
		   each item.

8. a. purchase decision as
      the fourth stage in the
      consumer decision
      process
	8. I then *pick that one.*	8. I then *choose the
		   item* I think is best
		   for the money, all
		   things considered.

9. a. private property
   b. salesman or clerk
   c. store owner
	9. I take it to *the person
	   I must give my
	   money to.*
		9. I go to the checkout
		   counter and prepare
		   to *pay the person* for
		   the product.

Table 9–1 continued

Consumer Education Building Block Concepts (Learning Properties)	Marketplace Perceptions	
	Preschool Child	Adult Consumer
10. a. purchase transaction b. exchange process c. buying or paying for a product d. transfer of ownership	10. I *give this person a piece of money and this person gives me the thing I want in a bag*. It is now *mine* to take home.	10. I usually *give the clerk a currency* larger than the price and the clerk *gives me*, in return, *the product* in a bag . . .
11. a. making change b. money denominations	11. This person also *gives me back money* left over from my piece of money.	11. and *change*.

Source: Ronald W. Stampfl, George Moschis, and Joseph T. Lawton (1978), "Consumer Education and the Preschool Child," *Journal of Consumer Affairs*, 12 (Summer), p. 13. Reprinted with permission.

general subject areas that normally would be taught in consumer education. It does not rank each area according to importance. This should be a function of the instructor in relationship to a particular audience.

The model consists of four essential parts: consumer characteristics, consumer behavior, consumer objects, and consumer environment. In effect, it says that consumers are individuals with certain characteristics that affect their consumer behavior as performed toward certain consumer objects within a particular environment. For each of these four parts, a curriculum guide can be developed that itemizes the specific topics to be covered within each part and the time to be devoted to each topic depending on the students and the goals of the instructor. Some topics are inherently more complex than others, some have more immediate impact as compared to long-range impact on children's learning of consumer education matter, and some topics are inherently more interesting to either the teachers or students.

The model in figure 9-1 presents the essential components of the subject matter of consumer education. Not teaching one of the components would provide a very incomplete experience for children. However, it is just a model on which to "hang things" and does not depict the "things" appropriate for each component. Also, the topics change over time; the components do not. For example, based on the events of the past decade, much more emphasis today would be given to single-person households, the impact of space technology, and the international aspects of business than before. Therefore, no attempt is made here to itemize all the topics that might be covered under each component. These topics can be gleaned from a wide search of the consumer education literature or brain-storming sessions among an appropriate group of experts on the subject.

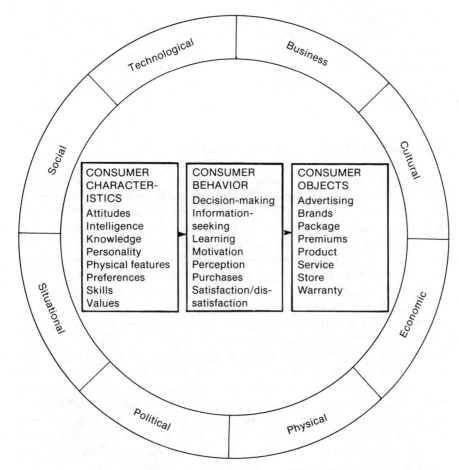

The figure contains, from left to right within the circle:

CONSUMER CHARACTER-ISTICS	CONSUMER BEHAVIOR	CONSUMER OBJECTS
Attitudes	Decision-making	Advertising
Intelligence	Information-	Brands
Knowledge	seeking	Package
Personality	Learning	Premiums
Physical features	Motivation	Product
Preferences	Perception	Service
Skills	Purchases	Store
Values	Satisfaction/dis-	Warranty
	satisfaction	

The surrounding circle is labeled: Technological, Business, Cultural, Economic, Physical, Political, Situational, Social.

Figure 9-1. A Model for Determining the Subject Matter for Consumer Education

What is not included in the model are such viewpoints as "Business consists of unscrupulous people out to make a buck," "Advertising makes you buy things you don't need," "Most consumers are materialistic," and "Most consumers make purchases on the basis of emotion rather than rationality." There is a tendency among some untrained consumer educators in primary and secondary schools to point to business as the enemy and many consumers as irrational and to present consumerism or the consumer movement as the answer to both. These are value judgements, and the subject matter of consumer education should be taught without them. In fact, dwelling on consumerism (which is not included in figure 9-1) probably has very little benefit and tends to create an "us versus them" climate. Consumer education materials should be presented with a cooperative spirit toward the business-consumer relationship. Why should children grow up thinking that the main source of satisfaction of most of their needs is actually an adversary? It appears that around 20 percent of consumers today do not want to be consumers at all (McNeal and McKee, 1985). We should want to decrease rather than increase this number.

Who Should Teach Consumer Education

It was suggested at the beginning of this chapter that the David-Goliath relationship of the child consumer to business could be overcome with systematic consumer education. What should be taught under the banner of consumer education was reviewed above, with the emphasis on teaching everything related to being a consumer rather than a limited number of important concepts. No mention was made of who does the teaching or who should do the teaching. Let us now treat this aspect of consumer education while stressing again the teaching of the entire spectrum in a systematic way.

Some state laws require the teaching of consumer education in public schools, and it is difficult to disagree with such mandates. These laws are oblivious, however, to consumer education taught by persons not associated with schools. Legislators do not, for example, suggest that the schools should teach certain aspects of consumer education while other aspects are taught elsewhere, yet from a systems standpoint, this might make sense. We have already shown that consumer education is a very broad topic, and it therefore may be unrealistic to expect educational institutions to teach it all. This may be asking far too much of a typical elementary school teacher. In fact, reality prevails, and teachers teach whatever they are capable of teaching; therefore, by definition, they may omit part of the children's needed consumer education, in some cases a very large part.

There are two other institutions in addition to education that can and do teach our children consumer education; these are the family and business. They should be viewed as important necessary sources in systematic consumer education. It is also true that our national government has been a participant in consumer education, although neither a very willing or very dependable participant. It often has assumed some responsibility for consumer education simply because this responsibility was not shouldered by the appropriate institutions. We will assume here that the federal government's role in consumer education is that of fatherly coordinator, as it is for the nation's education in general, and that the primary responsibility is that of the three institutions already noted, education, family, and business. Let us examine the role of each of these in a systematic consumer education program.

The Family as Consumer Educator

In a novel program intended to teach basic economic concepts to kindergarten children, Kourilsky (1977) found that its effectiveness was due in great part to the participation of the family and to discussions between the children and their parents and older siblings. In another very well known study by Ward, Wackman, and Wartella at about the same time (1977A), however, it was found that very few parents were actively contributing to their children's consumer education. An explanation for the differences in these two findings may be that the children in the Kourilsky study were in a formal consumer education program at school that encouraged the parents to get involved in their children's consumer education. This is a good example of systematic consumer education in which education institution and family are both contributing synergistically to the child's learning of consumer education concepts.

The home environment ordinarily is a very logical place for teaching consumer education to children. The children have a trusting attachment to their parents because since birth the children have been dependent upon their parents for all their need satisfaction. As observed in chapter 2, a great variety of consumer education does take place in the home. Parents demonstrate use of products to their children, provide evaluations of advertisements they see, suggest to them basic budgeting procedures, and actually take them to a variety of shopping environments. In pounds and ounces, this amounts to a lot of consumer education.

Most of the consumer education in the family is not formalized, however, but takes place mainly through incidental learning and may lead investigators to conclude erroneously that practically no consumer education occurs in the home. The way in which consumer concepts are learned by children does not invalidate what is learned or make it less important, and the mere fact that what is taught is taught by caring parents means that the children have an excellent learning environment. The fact is, parents, for the most part, do not formalize any education in the home. As was observed in chapter 2,

> We know that the spare bedroom is rarely turned into a classroom for teaching marketplace behavior, or medicine, or marriage. We know that the children are not graded on the bargains they bring home or the money they save by comparison shopping, and we know there are not pop quizzes on Saturday morning television advertisements. However, as former children and present parents, we know that successful consumer behavior on the part of our children is a major concern long before we become concerned with teaching children about sexual matters or getting their first job.

It is regrettable, however, that the consumer education that transpires in the home is not more formalized. It would then be easier to integrate it with the consumer education taught in school or by business. For systematic consumer education to work, there must be teaching assignments of sorts that capitalize on the strengths of the teachers while attempting to limit duplication, although repetition enhances learning. When the teaching is done informally and indirectly, as it is in the home, it is difficult to account for it. The Kourilsky experiment mentioned above demonstrated the teaching assignments that could be given to parents, which parents often assume indirectly anyhow. The concepts that the school teaches become topics of conversation and demonstration for the parent. In effect, classroom teachers plant the concepts; parents water and nourish them. For such a process to work, a formal working relationship between parents and teachers would be necessary. Perhaps the development of this consumer education relationship could be a service opportunity for Parent Teacher Associations across the nation.

Although it may seem unrealistic to expect parents (and perhaps older siblings, too) to work formally with elementary school teachers and it is probably equally unrealistic to assume that most elementary school teachers would work formally with parents, the alternative is what we have now—very little formal consumer education for a person who is just beginning the process of being a consumer in a marketplace made up of magic marketers. For all those concerned parents and consumer protectionists, here is a chance to accomplish some long-term good by attempting to implement this relationship in consumer education.

Business as Consumer Educator

To suggest that parents be consumer educators to children is one thing—but *business!* To consumer protectionists, this surely must sound like putting the foxes in charge of guarding the chicken house. In addition to consumers, however, who could benefit more from consumer education than business? Consumer education theoretically means satisfied customers, and next to profits there is nothing that business loves more.

Business has a legitimate contribution to make to children's consumer education. Business knows more about its products and services than anyone, and it has at its disposal some of the most powerful educational tools ever invented—its communication mix of advertising, selling, packaging, sales promotion, and publicity. Logically, its teaching assignment would be the nature, use, and benefits of its products and services. These are the very topics that teachers and parents often know so little about, yet feel compelled to explain to children. The synergism is apparent.

What products and services should business educate children about? Certainly, all of those targeted to children. These would include cereals, snacks, candies, soft drinks, frozen desserts, toys, games, and crafts. Part of the consumer education should be aimed at parents when it would be more appropriate, such as nutrition information about snack foods or uses and care of some toys.

Most product and service education for children logically would be the responsibility of their producers. Retailers probably should be involved at least in the education about services because they ordinarily provide them. Retailers also could assume the responsibility for educating children about gift decisions and gift purchases when these items are for adults and not ordinarily targeted to children. The stores that seek this business from children should be responsible for the related consumer education.

Retailers, like parents, should help children understand some of the concepts taught in the classroom, such as counting money, calculating sales taxes, and comparing products. Retailers could also post information where appropriate for parents and children. For example, fast food restaurants could post nutritional information about its main products, such as sandwiches, chicken, fish, and beverages. Retailers should offer their store environments as laboratories to parents and teachers for demonstrating consumer education concepts taught in the classroom. Parents already use the stores for this purpose in an informal manner, and retailers often invite elementary classes to take field trips to their stores. These activities only need more structure.

Of course, business is already practicing consumer education, just as parents are. For example, it already provides some useful information in its advertising, on its packages, and with its product use directions. It simply needs to do more and do it systematically, along with parents and schools. Business already spends over $300 billion annually on its communication mix. All business has to do is re-examine the information segment of its communications mix and make that part fit systematically with the overall consumer education requirements, and it is in the consumer education business (McNeal, 1978). It will probably not have to spend a penny more than it is spending now, yet it will serve children so much better. Consumer education can thus be a wonderful way for business to compete.

Of course, this means that business will have to be honest, open, and informative. For instance, it will have to produce many more two-sided rather than one-sided advertising messages. What does it have to lose by competing on the basis of consumer education? Only its bad image of not being honest, open, and informative enough.

Schools as Consumer Educators

The school seems to be the most appropriate institution for teaching consumer education to children. The definition of consumer education presented earlier states that "consumer education is the preparation of the individual in the skills, concepts and understandings. . . ." The classroom setting is ideal for teaching the "concepts and understandings" and for teaching about "skills." The actual learning of the skills is best accomplished through practice in the home and marketplace.

Currently, consumer education is taught to some extent in kindergarten and the first to sixth elementary grades in most states, but its effectiveness in many cases is in question. Let us summarize these reasons.

Subject Matter Disagreement. There are major disagreements among consumer educators about what they should be teaching. Although such models of the subject matter of consumer education as the one presented in figure 9-1 are available, they are often ignored in favor of the biases or weaknesses of the teacher or their superiors.

Image Problem. Consumer education as a teaching field has an image problem among teachers and administrators. It is not viewed by some as scholarly or substantive enough. Sometimes its title is changed to deal with its image. The Michigan Consumer Education Center (1982) reports that the title of consumer economics is often used to "upgrade the negative perception held by some persons that consumer education has insufficient intellectual content or rigor . . ." (p. 4). This image problem may result in consumer education being minimized or overtheorized.

Antibusiness Attitudes. There is all too often an antibusiness atmosphere among consumer education teachers; the classroom approach to consumer education consequently may have an "us versus them" flavor. The essential reason for this attitude has already been described in other chapters. Many people dislike the notion of business with its expertness in marketing selling to children with their vulnerability in consuming. Another reason is the great amount of antibusiness consumer education literature. *Hucksters in the Classroom,* by Harty (1979), is a particularly radical example of how to arouse this antibusiness feeling among consumer educators. A consequence of this negative attitude is the unwillingness of some teachers to work with members of the business community or to use business-produced materials in their classrooms. Such an attitude naturally prevents a systematic approach to consumer education.

Fitting It In. The classroom is already overflowing with topics to teach. Many parents complain that not enough of the basics—"reading, writing and 'rithmetic"—are being taught. It is difficult to find room to fit in units of consumer education. There is also a tendency to teach consumer education as part of another subject, rather than as a separate subject. There often is the question of whether it needs to be taught at every grade level, particularly as compared to some other subjects. This often results in consumer education receiving stepchild treatment or not being fitted in at all.

Preparation for Adulthood. Very commonly and very logically, consumer education is perceived in the school system as preparation for adulthood, but it is not seen as preparation for childhood. The same teachers who dislike the idea of business selling to children often fail to see children as bona fide consumers in need of consumer education. These teachers tend not to see the youngsters as part of the consumer decision-making activity in the family or do not know that consumer education of the child can contribute to the entire family's consumer satisfaction (Kourilsky and Murray, 1981). This kind of thinking often results in consumer education not being taught in kindergarten or the early grades; this delays the formal preparation of children as consumers.

The above reasons for questioning the effectiveness of consumer education at the level of kindergarten through grade six do not address the professional preparation of the teachers assigned to teach consumer education or the resources allocated to its teaching. Because the subject matter of consumer education that is actually taught is so varied, it is difficult to assess the professional preparation of consumer education teachers. For example, if a school integrates consumer education into a math course, a teacher may be considered prepared if she or he is qualified in math and simply follows a curriculum guide in consumer education. Where separate units of consumer education are taught, a teacher may be qualified with course work or in-service work in economics or home economics, depending on the school's viewpoint. Also, it is implicit in some of the thinking of consumer education teachers and administrators that a teacher is qualified by virtue of being an adult. This experience-is-the-best-teacher kind of thinking is flawed because it tends to disregard tested principles and concepts. It is unusual to find a broadly trained and qualified consumer education teacher at the elementary school level. Royer and Nolf (1980, p. 51) observe that "most teachers of economic education at the K-12 level have had no more than one introductory economics course at the college level, and many consumer education teachers have not had even that much training." One course hardly makes a consumer education teacher, so it does seem safe to conclude that teacher preparation in consumer education is inadequate. When one looks closely at the broad scope of consumer education as shown in figure 9-1, it is difficult to imagine this amount of material being taught to a consumer education teacher in one or even two courses. The subject matter of the consumer's environment alone seems to beg for specialized courses in macroeconomics and microeconomics. It also seems unlikely that consumer characteristics and consumer behavior could be covered in less than one course.

It might be expected that in those states that mandate consumer education teachers are properly prepared for teaching it. This is not necessarily the case. Royer and Nolf (1980, p. 51) note that "states which mandate consumer and/or economic education rarely provide the funds necessary for pre-service or in-service teacher training.

Teaching resources for children's consumer education are in plentiful supply. Various agencies in all the states produce a wide range of instructional materials. There are also a few textbooks for elementary grades. Teachers often develop their own materials to suit their viewpoints and their students. Finally, business, usually retailers, provides consumer materials for the class-room and field trips for the children. These materials may be controversial because it is sometimes difficult to separate their promotional intent from their educational benefits. This is the concern of Harty (1979).

When Should Consumer Education Be Taught

Definitions of consumer education do not say who is being prepared to be consumers nor indicate when preparation is complete. None of the literature describes a certified consumer or tells us the length and requirements of a consumer education program that will produce the complete consumer.

The assumption, in general, among consumer educators is that consumer education is preparation for adulthood. Further, it is generally assumed that consumer education will occur to a small extent among chldren in elemen-tary school, but serious preparation should take place at high school age. These assumptions are understandable because most critical purchasing be-havior is among adults. Chapters 3 and 4 provide ample evidence, however, that children are performing as consumers as early as age four or five and are seriously involved with it by ages eight or nine. Consumer education is defi-nitely needed during these formative years of consumership. Otherwise, the children may put into practice ineffective and incorrect consumer behavior patterns. We certainly could also theorize that young consumers without consumer education are likely to achieve less satisfaction in the marketplace.

Consumer education at school should commence with kindergarten or at least during the first grade. It should have and most likely will have started in the home by this time, although in ad hoc form. Business is already targeting advertising to this age group; if this advertising is also educational, the chil-dren can, in total, be learning a great deal about being a consumer. Naturally, the results of all of this consumer education can be insignificant if it does not take place in systematic fashion.

Logically, there is the question of the amount of consumer education children can learn at ages five, six, or seven. Because consumer education uncommonly takes place at this age level, there is not much literature to tell us of its effectiveness or ineffectiveness. Two studies previously cited do present some exciting evidence of young children's ability and willingness to learn consumer matters. Kourilsky (1977) developed an economic education program that introduces economic concepts to children in the primary grades. Called the Kinder-Economy, it was designed to be administered thirty minutes a day for a semester. With a group of five- and six-year-old children, Kourilsky achieved good success in teaching the following nine topics: scarcity/economic problems; decision making and cost-benefit analysis; production of goods; specialization in work; distribution of goods; consumption and savings; demand/supply concepts; business operations; and money use and bartering. Not all the topics were equally mastered by the children. The topics of scarcity and economic problems, decision making, production, and business operations had high mastery scores; the concepts of distribution and specialization received much lower scores, suggesting difficulty with these two topics or how they were taught. The topics were learned at least as well by the children as they were by teachers who were first taught them.

Stampfl, Moschis, and Lawton (1978) conducted a study among four-, five-, and six-year-old children to determine their ability to learn the eleven concepts listed in table 9-1 and also to determine the best way to teach them. The eleven "building blocks of consumer education" were taught in both a structured and an unstructured classroom setting. The results showed learning from both methods, although clearly the structured approach was superior. The different results obtained from the two different teaching methods does suggest that consumer education of young children can better be accomplished through a formal, expository teaching style as compared to an informal, sociodramatic method. This finding suggests also that learning to be a consumer is complex for children and requires the teaching of a considerable amount of knowledge as well as skill. Another key to success that was noted by these investigators is that the material must be translated into an appropriate vocabulary level (p. 26).

These two studies, conducted by well-qualified investigators utilizing sound methodological procedures, suggest that very young children can learn the concepts of consuming and apparently do so with eagerness. What is needed now is to convince the appropriate legislators and education officials that consumer education should be taught to children for the purpose of making children, not just adults, effective consumers. If systematically taught, consumer education at a particular level will be preparation for upcoming consumer behavior. Thus, consumer education taught each year readies the young consumer for being a consumer next year, as well as for being a student of consumer education next year. As the cumulative effect occurs over time, the individual will always be prepared to be a consumer at any point in time right into adulthood. This seems like a much more logical and useful approach to consumer education than perceiving it as mainly preparation for adults. Consumer education systematically taught in this manner is for consumers at all ages.

Such a proposed program is not without its problems—and certainly its critics. One major problem is training of elementary school teachers in systematic consumer education, but the greatest problem is gaining general acceptance of the idea of consumer education for children.

Implications and Conclusions

It is amazing how much consumer behavior children learn without formal consumer education. They obtain it mainly through incidental learning in their interactions with parents, retailers, and media, mainly television.

The amount of consumer behavior that children do learn on their own could be used as evidence against a systematic consumer education program such as that proposed here. Why, someone might ask, formalize and systematize consumer education for children when they are already learning it incidentally? One critic of consumer education suggested, for example, that the public might be better off if we took the money we already spend on consumer education and spend it in other ways (Seitz, 1972). Such a suggestion probably has some merit in light of much of the current consumer education taught to children, which is often haphazard, ad hoc, and biased, but not where it is systematized.

There is much that children do not know about being consumers, and what they don't know can hurt them. Just consider one product, ready-to-eat cereal, that is of concern to many investigators in the field of children's consumer behavior. Research and discussions noted in previous pages that many children under eight do not know:

Why cereal companies advertise

What criteria to use for evaluating the product

What the significance of the sugar content is

How nutritional the cereal is

How many cereal products are the same

How many cereals are made by the same company and why

What the cost is of a premium that accompanies the cereal

When a cereal advertisement is deceptive

When a cereal box is deceptive

What the unit cost of a cereal is compared to another

There are many other products that children buy daily on their own, such as candy, soft drinks, and ice cream, about which they know little except that they taste good. Beyond the product level, the typical seven year old usually does not understand the motives of the retailer or advertiser, the nature of the marketing system in which a product is sold, or all the choices he or she has on spending money, and they often do not know much about managing that money. There are substantial consumer knowledge and many skills to be gained by the child from formal consumer education.

Consumer education has other potential benefits in addition to just the learning of consumer know-how and related topics by children. Overall consumer satisfaction for the child should increase; this benefit grows as the child matures into an adolescent and then an adult. Better informed young consumers should stimulate honest competition, and those competitors that practice deception are less likely to survive unless they change their tactics. More knowledgeable child consumers should permit more effective marketing research among them and that, in turn, should produce more effective marketing. Finally, if children can become more effective, wiser consumers, the fighting that takes place between business and consumer protectionists about children as consumers should lessen. Possibly there even may be less need for legislation or regulation related to business/child relationships. Perhaps consumer education could even reduce problems between parents and their insatiable children.

Before all of these benefits can accrue, systematic consumer education must occur. To some pessimists this may be just wishful thinking. Certainly there are many forces working against it, but none appear impervious to change. The critical problem is inherent in the systems approach to consumer education; this means letting each party—school, family, and business—do what it does best while someone coordinates. It also means deciding what constitutes an entire program of consumer education and formally making assignments to the principals involved. Questions immediately arise. Who will decide the content of the program? Who will coordinate it? How can we trust business to educate without promoting its goods and services? Can we get parents to be active and dependable participants?

Some of these questions arise simply because of selfishness. The mere fact that the subject matter of consumer education or even its name is not settled after fifty years of teaching it attests to selfishness. The fact that some teachers do not want to teach consumer education unless it is termed economic education is another example. It is amazing how concern for children's welfare declines when it comes to the doing and the doing does not fit our views. There is little actual risk in taking a curriculum guide for elementary consumer education that has been judged successful by a particular state's education department and using it for subject matter. The greatest risk surely is that the children will not be taught enough, and that can be corrected.

As for coordination, it seems sensible in terms of the players to select an agent of the federal government or to create a subagency, if necessary, for this major task. The coodinator needs some clout in order to effect a working relationship between business and education while attempting to satisfy consumer advocates. Why not the federal government, which could also help with start-up financing?

Many businesses now commonly have a consumer affairs department in their organization whose members are skilled in putting the consumer's interest and views into such marketing activities as advertising and packaging. It is true, as Fornell (1981, p. 191) observes, that these consumer affairs departments often actually have "little influence in such matters as advertising, product quality, pricing and marketing" simply because many firms are not really as consumer-oriented as they claim to be. If active consumer affairs departments can be enrolled as partners in consumer education programs, however, their success and the applause they will receive from the public are likely to awaken those in other businesses to the benefits of getting into the consumer education business. Those many businesses that seek excellence also thrive on competition, and the kind of competition does not matter, whether price, promotion, or consumer education. We can still recall the oil embargo days of the 1970s when many businesses competed on the basis of demarketing of energy and energy-using products. Competing under the banner of consumer education may actually involve some demarketing efforts, but whatever the base of competition, well-managed businesses are up to it.

As for those consumer advocates and consumer educators who do not trust business to be objective and fair in its consumer education of children, they must reach some accord with business, otherwise systematic consumer education will not work. There is no doubt that business often has presented promotional messages to elementary school children under the guise of consumer education, and this is unpardonable. It is also true that business has provided some fine consumer education materials to elementary school classrooms that were unbiased, very valuable, and unavailable from any other source. Sometimes what appears to be promotional may not be. It is difficult, for example, for a fast food chain to present the facts about salt in hamburgers and french fries without talking about hamburgers and french fries. It appears that for systematic consumer education to function, both consumer advocate and business will have to be more objective. Consumer advocates must modify their antibusiness attitudes; business must give them reason to by acting professionally and ethically in all its consumer education activities.

Getting parents to assist their children with consumer education homework as they do arithmetic or spelling may take some doing. The literature indicates that many parents will like the idea of consumer education in the classroom and its application and confirmation in the home, but that some lower and upper middle social class parents, particularly, will feel it is unnecessary. Some marketing principles applied to consumer education may be useful in overcoming parent apathy in consumer education. It is quite possible that many parents, particularly those who are not educated, may benefit from the consumer education of their children by learning more effective consumer behavior themselves. Although this is not the expected outcome of systematic consumer education, it is still a good outcome. A greater worry is that some uneducated parents may not understand how to work with their children in the area of consumer education and many actually teach them improper consumer behavior patterns.

Finally, the elementary classroom teacher will probably have to make the most adjustments in the implementation of systematic consumer education. Working with business may not be desirable; working with parents is already a problem at times, and it could be more so with the topic of consumer education than, say, spelling. Being part of a system outside of the school system may not be acceptable to the more independent educator. Most teachers will have to obtain some preparation in consumer education, probably over a period of several summers. This could be viewed as interference, particularly if consumer education is viewed as an unsophisticated area of study. Finally, the teacher, as well as the school administration, will have to wrestle with making room for consumer education instruction in an already-crowded curriculum.

All this in the name of consumer education for children! It may not make sense to many, but some choices must be made. Do we let things continue as they are or do we educate in order to help our children as consumers? Perhaps it would be simpler if we just did not permit our children to be consumers. This is a possibility that is rarely mentioned but will be considered in the next and final chapter.

10

Should Children Be Consumers?

Potentially, children constitute the most lucrative market there is for many businesses because the youngsters are actually three markets in one, not "just one minor market" as a myopic hamburger merchant once described them. They are a current market of five to twelve year olds that spend $4.2 billion a year of their own money on their own desires. This spending behavior makes them much more than just a blip on the sales charts of the $13 billion toy industry, for example, where children spend well over $1 billion annually. They independently choose and purchase many products from the giant snack industry, also, including such favorites as Kool-Aid, Dr. Pepper, Fritos Doritos, and Reeses Pieces.

Children also constitute a market of influentials who cause many billions of dollars of purchases among their parents. Marketers of ready-to-eat cereals, fast foods, video games, and many other products and services compete vigorously for this dimension of the children's market. For example, according to research, most of the toys that parents buy their children for Christmas are toys that the children have seen advertised on television and have requested from their parents. In 1985, Kellogg's Frosted Flakes, a sweetened cereal, edged out General Mills' Cheerios as the long-time number two selling cereal. Tony the Tiger's sugar-coated corn flakes won out over those little toasted oat doughnuts that "contain only one gram of sugar per serving" because Tony told children for years about how gr-r-reat his cereal was and asked children to make sure moms served it as part of a nourishing breakfast. The final result was that not only did the kids ask for it and get it, but the parents learned to love it, too; they became willing to admit openly that they, like their children, also ate presweetened cereals.

Children are also a future market for most goods and services. As they become adults and mothers and fathers, marketers hope that they will have developed preferences for their particular products rather than those of competitors. Consequently, many marketers try to develop awareness of and desire for their brands of products among children, hoping that when the children are grown, the brands will be important to them. In the 1960s, for example, there appeared a *Grocery Store Coloring Book* for children that sold for 19 cents. It pictured for children many aspects of grocery stores, their variety of products, and how much fun it was to shop in them. Scattered throughout the coloring book was one brand name, Skinner, and if one looked closely on the last page one would discover that the coloring book was a product of Bozell and Jacobs, an advertising agency, and Skinner Macaroni Company. This coloring book was obviously an effort to create brand recognition among children. In 1981, Golden Book came out with a *Reading Fun* book for children that is intended to help teach children to learn to read by "emphasizing word recognition in appealing visual contexts." Throughout the 99-cent book, children learn about all kinds of objects, such as school buses, police cars, restaurants, toys, animals, and many others, with one or more pictures of each. On page five, a restaurant and a diner are shown; additionally, a picture of a McDonald's restaurant complete with golden arches is shown, the only brand name on sixty-four pages. It appears that this was one small effort on the part of McDonald's to get its brand name appropriately presented to children in order to encourage the development of brand awareness among the children now and hopefully product desire in the future.

Negative Outcomes of Viewing Children as Consumers

Regardless of which dimension of the children's market business pursues (diverse consumer product firms such as General Foods and General Mills might pursue all three), there are questions, problems, and repercussions that arise. If marketers view children as a current market and merchandise specifically to them, such as advertising candy bars on children's television programming and displaying them in convenience stores and supermarkets at children's eye level, serious questions arise, for example, about children's ability to understand fully the advertising messages and their intent, the impact of candy on their teeth, and why candy bars often are displayed three feet from the floor rather than four or five feet.

If marketers appeal to children as a future market, for example, by distributing free book covers to them at school with the companies' brand names emblazoned on the fronts and backs of the covers, a problem in ethics may be envisioned. Is the school saving money or is it acting as a partner with the brand name owner in the exploitation of the children as consumers?

If business advertises toys or fast foods, for instance, to children as a market of influentials and directly or indirectly encourages the children to pressure their parents to buy these products, certain repercussions often result. Parents may feel strongly pressured to buy these products; they may not want to buy them, however, because of their cost or because they do not want their children to have them. Consequently, arguments and disagreements may result between parents and children as a result of these marketing efforts to the children.

In order to deal with the questions and problems that are caused by children acting as consumers and being treated by marketers as consumers, reactions by various segments of the public have resulted in organization, regulation, and education.

Organization

Concerned citizens have united and formed organizations to cope with some of the issues resulting from the interactions between marketers and children. For example, Action for Children's Television (ACT) came about to challenge television advertising to children. Other organizations already in existence have given consideration to related problems; for example, the National Association of Broadcasters and the Better Business Bureau have devoted attention to format, procedures, and taste in television advertising to children.

Regulation

Some problems resulting from the pursuit of children as consumers by marketers have been viewed as severe enough to require regulation. For example, in the 1960s Congress passed the Child Protection Act of 1966 and the Child Protection and Toy Safety Act of 1969, and in the 1970s the Federal Trade Commission attempted to ban most advertising to children.

Education

Others have accepted the fact that children are consumers and have recommended and installed education in schools to help the children be effective in the consumer role. In several states this education has been legislated.

When one steps back and looks at all these counteractive and counterbalancing efforts, they do not appear to have been very effective in their various goals—to make children better consumers, to make business more responsive to children and their limited consumer skills and knowledge, or even to put business out of the business of advertising to children. These efforts also have not been without their critics. Some members of the business community, some regulatory agency members, and some legislators have been critical of the "meddling" of consumer organizations in the free enterprise system. Certainly, some of the consumer organizations have been critical of some of the regulation, usually because it did not go far enough or did not treat a particular

problem as expected. Consumer educators have even fought among themselves, usually over the matter of consumer education, and many educators in
other fields have been critical of consumer education, particularly in regard to
its lack of sophistication.

Thus, we have an enormous amount of business effort and energy aimed
at children as consumers that has been judged by various segments of society
as inappropriate, unethical, unfair, or simply wrong. These various segments of
society have initiated organizations, regulations, and education in order to
respond to business's pursuit of children as consumers that in turn have been
criticized as unnecessary, ineffective, or simply wrong.

So much cost and cussing, trials and tribulations, lobbying and lambasting,
and for what! Has it really been worth it to anyone? Have children been made
happier or businesses richer? Have consumer advocates won a moral victory
or consumer educators a moral purpose? The plain fact of the matter is that
nobody has stepped forward and claimed success, although business does
appear to be displaying a bit of a smirk on its face.

Maybe Children Should not be Permitted to be Consumers

What if children were not permitted to participate in the consumer role until,
say, age ten? That is, assume that children could not buy anything and could
not be the target of any marketing efforts such as advertising, packaging, and
premiums. We already have such a model in the case of alcoholic beverages.
Alcoholic beverages cannot be marketed to children; children cannot buy
them. Why not a lot of other products? What would be wrong with this? What
ills would this produce? How many actual dollars in sales would business lose?
How many fewer toys and snack items would children have? How many less
advertising dollars would the television networks receive? Would there be a
noticeable decline in the gross national product?

Probably after a period of adjustment for all parties involved, children,
parents, protectionists, and businesses, there would be only one noticeable
change. All the advertising previously aimed at children would be aimed at
parents. Instead of advertising asking children to buy, or asking children to ask
their parents to buy, the advertising would ask parents to buy for their children. Instead of saying to children, for example, "Crunches. You'll love 'em.
Have some for breakfast tomorrow," the ad might say, "Mom, your children
will love Crunches. Serve them some tomorrow." Knowing marketers, they
might add a line designed to create just a slight bit of guilt, such as, "If you love
your children, you'll serve them Crunches." The net result would be that the
children would eat Crunches just as they always have, and the Crunches
producer would still make a bundle. Of course, the advertisers of Crunches

would still be doing the same amount of billings, and the networks would still be getting their respective shares. Presumably consumer advocates would be much happier. Regulators would rest easier, too. Consumer educators could still prepare children for being consumers when they reach adolescence and adulthood. In fact, the burden on consumer educators of trying to help children be effective consumers as children would be lifted (if the burden was ever felt).

Millions of dollars would be saved and millions of headaches would be prevented or relieved if children were not consumers. The dollars saved would be mainly those spent by consumer advocates for the welfare of children, those spent by government for developing and implementing regulations designed to protect children from unfair and deceptive business practices, and those spent by business for legal fees protecting itself from consumer advocates and government. The headaches saved should be apparent. They are the headaches of parents and children who fight over the children's request for an advertised product, the headaches of consumer advocates who cannot get anything done to regulate the advertising, the headaches of regulators who refuse the requests of the advocates, and of course the headaches of the business people who are just trying to make a buck off of kids and get criticized for doing so.

What about the children as *un*consumers? It is likely that they would still have all the products they want and have now. Their consumer socialization— their learning to be consumers—however, would be substantially slowed because actual practice, which is a great teacher, would not be possible. They still would receive some consumer education in school and from parents, but the ability to implement it except through play or fantasy would be eliminated. Of course, in theory the necessity for trying out consumer behavior ideas actually would be less important until several years later. The children, like those in Quebec for example, would be denied the information that they ordinarily receive from advertising. The information that would be missed mainly would be that related to new products and services.

There is something else that children would lose. They would lose the joy of being a consumer. Children receive a double-barreled set of satisfactions from going to the store and buying a snack or toy they saw advertised. They receive the satisfaction that the product provides; in addition, they receive the satisfaction that a shopping trip can produce—the stimulation from the shopping atmosphere and the opportunity to do something that is adult-like.

This new unconsumer system for children, if it were to occur, would present some potential problems for parents, businesses, and even regulators, as well as for children. Because children would not see as much advertising for new products, they might make fewer product requests in the home, but probably they would make more in the store if they were permitted to accompany their parents on shopping trips. There would be other problems in the store. Parents would have to keep their children from purchasing on their own and perhaps even from handling merchandise. Of course, this would give parents more control over what children choose for snacks. Overall, there likely would be more interaction between children and parents in the store, which would be beneficial to the children but perhaps more annoying to the parents. Parents would not be permitted to let their children shop or even browse alone. Children could not be sent to the nearby convenience store for bread and milk until age ten, which means that the parents would lose some assistance with household duties.

Stores probably would not lose any substantial sales dollars, and those that prefer not to serve children, and there are many, would like the new system better. However, store personnel would have to do more policing in order to make sure that goods are not sold to children who are under age. They might be required to check identification, for example. Some changes in merchandising and display would be necessary for those stores already serving children. Shelves near the floor might be used for storage instead of for display to children, and eye-level fixtures for children would probably be phased out.

Regulators would have to pass the laws necessary to disenfranchise children as consumers; assuming that is done, the problem would be enforcement. Television advertisements could not contain "kiddy-talk" or stimuli that could be considered attention-getting to children. Enforcement of regulations that forbid selling to children by stores might be troublesome and expensive to implement.

Manufacturers of toys and snacks would have to find other television time slots for their advertisements. They would need time slots where viewers are mainly parents. They would have to get used to selling children's items to adults. They do this to some degree now, but they would have to develop more skill in this type of advertising. They might decide to take some of their television advertising dollars and put them into other media, such as household magazines and newspapers, as tobacco producers did when cigarette advertising was banned from television. Packaging would have to be adult-oriented, and premiums, like advertisements, would have to be aimed at parents.

But Being a Consumer is a Right

In sum, if children were not permitted to be consumers until age ten, it probably would not matter much in the long run to anyone except the children. The children might lose some programming choice in television, but mainly they would lose the privilege of being a consumer, the opportunity to become socialized in the consumer role through practice until age ten, and the fun and pleasure that comes with being a consumer. Business would be denied the current channels to children, but would gain about the same sales through parents. Television broadcasters would have to make some major adjustments, mainly of a reprogramming nature, but they could do this over time. Parents would have more control over children—over what they watch on television and over their snacking habits and, of course, over all products purchased by their youngsters. Consumer advocates should be pleased—but would they be? One might guess that there actually would be a groundswell of resentment among many consumer advocates against the disenfranchisement of children as consumers on the basis that being a consumer is a right, not a privilege. They would, ironically, be warmly supported by business in their opposition to the unconsumer movement. Consumer advocates would contend that they have never intended to deny the rights of children as consumers, only to protect them, and they would be essentially correct.

Being a consumer in our nation is a right. Being a marketer is a privilege. It is the marketer that must be licensed, not the consumer. Because children, at least children under eight, can be a problem as consumers, however, some might want to limit their consumer activities. However, this is wrong. Children have a right to be consumers in spite of some inadequacies—their limited abilities, their limited knowledge, and their clumsiness. If business chooses children as a target market, whether current, future, or influential, it assumes the responsibility in general for acknowledging their inabilities. This does not mean that business is charged with correcting children's inabilities. It simply means that business has to build children's relative shortcomings into its marketing strategy, just as it does for any market. Before any business firm undertakes marketing efforts aimed at a particular target market, it conducts research in order to define the major characteristics of the members of the market. For instance, if their income or education level is lower than average, these factors must be taken into account before actual marketing efforts are put into effect. In the case of children, much of the marketing research already has been done regarding their major characteristics, as is noted within the pages of this book, but it appears that business too often ignores these findings.

If a Business Wants to Pursue Children as a Market

After a quarter-century of marketing to children, during which time there has been much criticism by consumer advocates and even substantial regulation invoked, business ought to have developed some assumptions about this market that underlie all marketing efforts aimed at its members. That is, if business wants to pursue this market without eventually provoking regulatory actions that will put the market off limits to its marketing efforts, as has been done in Quebec, it must establish and be guided by a few fundamental assumptions. Let us review these assumptions.

Assume that Children Are Gullible

Webster's dictionary describes a gullible person as one who is easily deceived. Children generally are easily deceived, although their gullibility gradually decreases with age. If marketers assume gullibility, they are less likely to incur the wrath of consumer protectionists or to be charged with deception by regulators. By assuming gullibility, marketers are less likely to be misunderstood by children in their advertising, packaging, and other promotion efforts. When these promotion efforts are aimed at children, they are more likely to speak the children's language and not speak over their heads. The simplest way to implement the gullibility assumption is to pretest all products and promotion efforts on a sample of children who are similar to those in the target market.

Assume Children Possess Limited Understanding of Business Operations

One of the reasons that children can be deceived by advertising is that many of them do not understand its purpose, just as many children do not comprehend the profit motive of business or its setting of sales quotas and market share goals. Rubin (1974, p. 415), for example, reported that when children were asked the purpose of a television commercial, some of the responses included "for fun," "for children," "for cartoons," and "I don't know."

Looking at some of the pizazz-packed advertising aimed at children, the elaborate packaging that surrounds many children's products, and the attractive display of such children's products as toys, one might think that business believes that children do know the intent and nature of business practice. These promotion efforts convey the notion that the recipients of them are experienced consumers. Also, within all this marketing fanfare, one rarely can find any warranties or any cautions aimed at the children. For example, marketers rarely say to children, "If you made a mistake in your purchase, or if your parents disapprove of it, just return it for a full refund." It is a rare advertisement that tells children, "If your parents say no to your request for the product, listen to them."

Children do not understand, nor according to chapter 6 are they very concerned about, how business prices its products and services. They do not understand and often forget the sales taxes on the price of the purchases they make in stores. Advertisements for children's goods rarely mention price; this may fit well with children's lack of knowledge and involvement in price, but certainly works against children learning about it. Consider cereal, for example. Children rarely know the price of a box of their favorite cereal or the value of a bowl of it, and business does not inform them of this price or how it was derived. Price scanning at the check-out counter has virtually eliminated the price from the package, which only makes it more difficult for children to learn product prices and their relationships. Children are usually unaware of the concept of competition, also, and therefore cannot appreciate how it tends to keep prices of their favorite products in check.

The business community is often involved in consumer education; due to its central role in the consumer behavior process, it should be. It should provide teaching materials to kindergarten and elementary school classrooms that explain in easy-to-understand form the intent and nature of business operations. Business does a fantastic job of getting and keeping children's interest through television advertising. Why not use this same talent to produce equally interesting public service announcements aimed at young children that inform them of the purposes of advertising, selling, displaying, premiums, and promotional packaging. Understanding of these activities will help alleviate children's gullibility and make them more effective consumers.

Assume that Children Possess Limited Dexterity

Children naturally have limited dexterity when compared to adults. They usually are more flexible than adults, and when it comes to climbing, twisting, and turning, they are the envy of adults, but they are less dexterous. Yet, marketers often treat children as being on par with adults in dexterity. All those brands of sweetened cereal that children just love and parents often despise but buy for their children anyhow are packaged just like adult cereals. As observed in chapter 7, these packages, and packages for many other children oriented products, are typically difficult for children to open and close properly. The problem seems to be that these packages are designed by adults; as is too often the case with the packaging industry, the consumer is virtually ignored. Parents do take notice of children's handling of packages, and they have many occasions to get upset with their children when the youngsters tear apart a cereal box while attempting to open it or fail to close its inner wrapper properly. Cereal producers and their package suppliers could easily get together and design a user-friendly cereal package, one that works well in the small, less experienced hands of children, but they choose not to for unknown reasons. Perhaps the Zip-Loc concept that has become so accepted by households for bagging lunches and leftovers would be a useful model for children's cereals, as well as other perishables that children eat, such as potato chips, corn chips, and pretzels.

Retailers who want children in their stores also need to be tolerant of the less dexterous youngster. For instance, it takes a while to learn to stop a shopping cart once it gets rolling or to turn it slightly to one side in order to avoid a head-on collision. Children should not be expected to shop on their tiptoes; if merchandise is intended for children, it should be displayed at or below their eye level.

Assume Limited Mastery of the Language

Children cannot understand everything that is said in commercials aimed at them, read all the information provided on packages of products targeted for them, or comprehend all the words used by salespeople in stores that welcome them. It should not be this way, but it is. It is, because marketing is an adult world, and even though it subscribes to a consumer orientation, it has not discovered yet how to adequately serve children as consumers.

Children learn the language fast, but study after study shows that those under age eight often cannot understand separators and disclaimers in television commercials, yet these studies also demonstrate that the wording in the separators and disclaimers can be modified so that children can understand them. Clearly, then, many advertisers are not assuming limited mastery of the language among these youngsters, and this appears no less true of other marketing communication efforts, such as packaging, premiums, and in-store selling.

The main cause of children's gullibility is their limited mastery of the language; therefore, they are deceived easily by various marketing communications. It also causes confusion and discomfort in shopping and mistakes in purchases and purchase requests to parents. We cannot improve the language skills of the young child very much. Consumer educators can sometimes help by teaching young children marketing jargon, which is really the language of those marketers who mistakenly refuse to adapt to their markets, such as the wording used in advertising disclaimers and separators. In the main, however, it is up to marketers to take into consideration the language limitation of children if they want to serve children fairly. There is a simple and obvious rule for marketers who target children as markets: speak the language of those you are talking to. If marketers have difficulty doing this, and apparently some do, conferring with elementary school teachers can solve the problem.

Assume that Children Have Critical and Caring Parents.

There is probably no greater inciter of consumer protectionists' wrath than the pressure that marketers cause to be put on parents by their children. This pressure mainly comes from advertising that suggests that children ask their parents for the advertised product or from advertising of a desirable product that costs more than the children can afford out of their own income, so that they must request it from their parents. The pressure also stems from premium offers on packages, mainly cereal boxes, that require money and/or the purchase of several more boxes of the cereal. Finally, some pressure is caused by certain displays of products in stores when children accompany their parents on shopping trips. These displays, sometimes found at the checkout counter where a long wait is often required, simply entice the children to make purchase requests to their parents.

All too often the product itself or its package is an irritant to parents, which means problems between parent and child. It may be a sticky, gooey candy bar, a crumbly cookie, a dripping ice cream bar, or a toy or game that is not easily returned to its box after play. These products cause children to make a mess, and many times these products are ones that the children pressured the parents to buy as a result of some marketing effort. This is tantamount to adding insult to injury.

Whether it is the premiums, displays, or advertisements encouraging children to make purchase requests to parents or products that cause the children to make a mess, the results can be conflicts, arguments, and downright ugliness between parent and child. It is apparent in most cases that the marketer expects these purchase requests to be made to parents; although he may not intend the conflicts that arise, he knows they are likely. Thus, the marketer tends to assume a parent made of putty and money, more so than a critical and caring parent. While this assumption is often more correct than not, all parties would be far better off if the marketer assumed a critical and caring parent. The result would be less high pressure promotion aimed at children and fewer unsatisfactory children's products and packages and consequently less parent-child conflict. Children and parents would be happier, parents would be less apprehensive about marketers' activities, and therefore both parents and children would be more responsive markets for what would amount to family-approved products and services.

By assuming critical and caring parents, marketers would be required to consider the responses of children *and* parents to new children's products, their packages, advertising, and other accompanying promotion. After twenty-five years of marketing to children, the problems and complaints make it apparent that these marketers have not given much consideration to the entire family before offering a new product or starting up a new promotion campaign. Why they have not is less apparent because marketers try to be consumer oriented. It is time now that all businesses that target children as a market should family-test their entire marketing mix—product, package, advertising, premiums, and price—before market entry. Further, each time there is a change in the mix, the new additions also should be family-tested. In family-testing a marketing mix, the firm would, in appropriate ways, subject each element of the mix to a sample of target children and their parents for acceptance and approval.

The family-tested, family-approved concept should be extended from the factory to the store. Manufacturers usually have little control over the retailers of their goods, but a program such as that suggested in chapter 4 could be implemented to complement the family-tested concept at the manufacturing level. What was suggested in chapter 4 was the designation of those stores that welcome children as consumers as child-centered stores. A "Child Centered" sign on the door and in advertisements would indicate to children and parents alike that the store welcomes children, provides appropriate safeguards for their welfare, and actually wishes to make a positive contribution to their consumer socialization. The child-centered store concept recognizes that many retailers do not want to serve children, whereas others do. It recognizes that children sometimes need help with their purchases and perhaps need special return services. It guarantees to parents that children will not be subjected to abuse by salespeople or to undesirable products.

The combination of a family-tested product and marketing mix from the manufacturer and a child-centered store in which to offer the product would assure parents and consumer protectionists and regulators that children are a special market and are being treated that way by the business community. Naturally, some businesses will object regardless of what mechanism was set up to institute and guide the family-tested, child-centered concept. It might be appropriate for those businesses that strongly disagree with these concepts to be given a choice: market their products to parents or to children. If they choose to market to children, however, they must family-test their offerings.

The plain fact of the matter is that something needs to be done to improve the marketing-child consumer relationship. It is a good thing for marketers— it means sales and profits now, and even greater sales and profits in the future. It is a good thing for children—it provides enormous input to their consumer socialization process while providing them with current satisfaction from products and from the purchase of them. Children, particularly those under eight, are vulnerable to abuses by marketers, however, and marketers have been shown to be abusive to children far too many times. If a mechanism can be introduced into the system that will improve it for all parties, it should be done. Concepts like those two suggested here would move in this direction.

All consumers should be viewed as special by marketers if those marketers are to fully satisfy them. Children should be viewed as superspecial consumers deserving of superspecial treatment by the marketing system. This is necessary only for a short time, while the children are becoming fully qualified consumers, and it will guarantee happier and more effective customers for all marketers for all time.

References

Abel, John D. (1969), "Television and Children: A Selective Bibliography of Use and Effects," *Journal of Broadcasting,* 8 (Winter), 101-105.

Adler, Richard P., Gerald S. Lesser, Laurence Meringoff, Thomas S. Robertson, John R. Rossiter, & Scott Ward (1980), *The Effects of Television Advertising on Children,* Lexington, MA: Lexington Books.

Advertising Age (1974A), "Ad Industry Readies Fight on TV Ad Ban of Premiums" (July 8), 2, 64.

———— (1974B), "FTC Seeking Data for TV Premium Compromise" (September 16), 86.

———— (1978A), "FTC Staff Report on TV Advertising to Children" (February 27), 73-77.

———— (1978B), "Report by FTC's Staff Recommends Major Strictures on Children's TV Ads" (February 27), 1, 95.

———— (1979), "Study Finds Kids are Getting the Message" (June 4), 44.

———— (1983), "FCC Outlines TV Deregulation Plan" (July 4), 3.

———— (1985), "Viewpoint: Editorial—A TV License to Steal from Kids" (April 8), 18.

Aldous, J., & J.M. McLeod (1974), "Commentaries on Ward, 'Consumer Socialization'," *Journal of Consumer Research,* 1 (September), 15-17.

Allport, Gordon W. (1961), *Pattern and Growth in Personality,* New York: Holt, Rinehart and Winston, Inc.

Alsop, Ronald (1985), "Comic Publishers Woo Kids with Top Dog and the Pope," *Wall Street Journal* (October 10), 33.

Anderson, Carol, & James U. McNeal (1981), "The Education of the Young Consumer," in Thomas R. Baird et al., *Developments in Marketing Science,* 4, Muncie, Indiana: Ball State University, 298.

Atkin, Charles (1975), *Effects of Television Advertising on Children—First Year Experimental Evidence,* East Lansing, MI: Michigan State University.

———— (1976), "Children's Social Learning from Television Advertising: Research Evidence on Observational Modeling of Product Consumption," *Advances in Consumer Research,* 3, 513-519.

———— (1978), "Observation of Parent-Child Interaction in Supermarket Decision-Making," *Journal of Marketing,* 42 (October), 41-45.

———— & Gary Heald (1977), "The Content of Children's Toy and Food Commercials," *Journal of Communication,* 27 (Winter), 107-114.

Bacot, Eugene, & Richard Gordon (1980), "Children Shrewd Critics of Ads: U.K. Study," *Advertising Age* (February 27), 28.

Bandura, Albert (1962), "Social Learning through Imitation," in Marshall R. Jones, ed., *Nebraska Symposium on Motivation,* Lincoln: University of Nebraska Press.

Banks, Seymour (1975), "Public Policy on Ads to Children," *Journal of Advertising Research,* 15 (August), 7-15.

—— (1980), "Children's Television Viewing Behavior," *Journal of Marketing,* 44 (Spring), 48.

Barcus, F. Earl (1962), "Advertising in the Sunday Comics," *Journalism Quarterly,* 39 (Spring), 196-202.

Barnard, James D., Edward R. Christophersen, & Montrose M. Wolf (1977), "Teaching Children Appropriate Shopping Behavior Through Parent Training in the Supermarket Setting," *Journal of Applied Behavior Analysis,* 10 (Spring), 49-59.

Barry, Thomas E. (1978), "Children's Television Advertising: The Attitudes and Opinions of Elementary School Guidance Counselors," *Journal of Advertising,* 7 (Fall), 9-16.

—— (1980), "A Framework for Ascertaining Deception in Children's Advertising," *Journal of Advertising,* 9, 11-18.

—— & Richard W. Hansen (1973), "How Race Affects Children's TV Commercials," *Journal of Advertising Research,* 13 (October), 63-67.

—— & Anees A. Sheikh (1977), "Race As a Dimension in Children's TV Advertising: The Need for More Research," *Journal of Advertising,* 6, 5-10.

Bearden, William O., Jesse E. Teel, & Robert R. Wright (1979), "Family Income Effects on Measurement of Children's Attitudes Toward Television Commercials," *Journal of Consumer Research,* 6 (December), 308-11.

Belk, Russel W., Kenneth D. Bahn, and Robert N. Mayer (1982), "Developmental Recognition of Consumption Symbolism," *Journal of Consumer Research,* 9 (June), 4-17.

——, Robert Mayer, & Amy Driscoll (1984), "Children's Recognition of Consumption Symbolism in Children's Products," *Journal of Consumer Research,* 10 (March), 386-397.

Bellur, Venkatakrishna V. (1979), "The Member Speaks—TV Not Top Influence on Children's Buying," *Marketing News* (June 15), 4.

Berelson, Barnard, & Gary A. Steiner (1964), *Human Behavior: An Inventory of Scientific Findings,* New York: Harcourt, Brace and World, Inc.

Berey, Lewis A., & Richard W. Pollay (1968), "The Influencing Role of the Child in Family Decisions," *Journal of Marketing Research,* 5 (February), 70-72.

Berger, Peter L., & Brigette Berger (1979), "Becoming a Member of Society," in Peter I. Rose, ed., *Socialization and the Life Cycle,* New York: St. Martin's Press.

Berkowitz, Leonard (1964), *The Development of Motives and Values in the Child,* New York: Basic Books.

Beuf, Ann H. (1976), "Television Commercials as Socializing Agents," *Advances in Consumer Research,* 3, 528-530.

Bever, T.B., M.L. Smith, B. Bengen, & T.G. Johnson (1975), " 'Young Viewers' Troubling Response to TV Ads," *Harvard Business Review,* 53 (Nov.-Dec.), 109-21.

Beverage Industry (1980), "Monarch Targets Under-12 Market with Monster Ads," 69 (July), 2, 29.

Bjorklund, G., & R. Bjorklund (1978), "An Exploratory Study of Toddlers' Satisfaction with Their Toy Environment," *Advances in Consumer Research,* 6, 400-06.

Bohuslav, Bethany, Mary Frances Egan, & Joyce Morgan (1985), "Content Analysis of Children's Saturday Morning Television Advertising," College Station: Texas A&M University, Department of Marketing, A Working Paper.

Brackin, Ronn (1982), "Look-alikes," *Moody Monthly* (October), 78-80.

Breckenridge, Marian E. (1959), "Food Attitudes of Children," *Journal of the American Dietetic Association,* 35 (July), 704-709.

Brim, Orville G. (1966), "Socialization through the Life Cycle," in O. Brim and S. Wheeler, eds., *Socialization After Childhood,* New York: John Wiley & Sons, Inc.

Brown, Ray, ed. (1976), *Children and Television,* Beverly Hills, CA: Sage Publishing Co., Inc.

Brown, Wilson (1979), "The Family and Consumer Decision Making: A Cultural View," *Academy of Marketing Science Journal,* 7 (Fall), 335-345.

Bruner, Jerome S., & Cecile C. Goodman (1947), "Value and Need Organizing Factors in Perception," *Journal of Abnormal and Social Psychology,* 42 (January), 33-44.

Bryan-College Station Eagle (1985), "Packaging Costs Consumers," (May 12), 4D.

Bryant, W. Keith, & Jennifer L. Gerner (1981), "Television Use by Adults and Children: A Multivariate Analysis," *Journal of Consumer Research,* 7 (September), 154-161.

Burr, Pat L., & Richard M. Burr (1976), "Television Advertising to Children: What Parents are Saying About Government Control," *Journal of Advertising Research,* 16 (April), 37-41.

—————— & Richard M. Burr (1977A), "Product Recognition and Premium Appeal," *Journal of Communication,* 27 (Winter), 115-117.

—————— & R.M. Burr (1977B), "Parental Responses to Child Marketing," *Journal of Advertising Research,* 17 (December), 17-20.

Burton, Grace M. (1975), "Consciousness-Raising for Young Consumers," *Children Today,* 22 (November-December), 18-22.

Bush, Alan J., Joseph F. Hair, Jr., & Robert P. Bush (1983), "A Content Analysis of Animation in Television Advertising," *Journal of Advertising,* 12, (4), 20-41.

Business Week (1967), "Do Boy Scouts Rate a Badge for Retailing?," (August 12), 72-74.

—————— (1968A), "Grooving Shoe Sales to a Young Market" (April 27), 78-81.

—————— (1968B), "Secret Shop for Little Spenders" (December 21), 52-54.

—————— (1969), "Where Shopping is Child's Play" (March 8), 88-90.

—————— (1971), "The Toy Battle is No Game" (February 27), 38.

—————— (1975), "National Lampoon's Line into the Youth Market" (November 3), 50.

—————— (1976), "How the Changing Age Mix Changes Markets" (January 12), 74-78.

Butter, Eliot J., Paula Popovich, Robert Stockhouse, & Roger Garner (1981), "Discrimination of Television Programs and Commercials by Preschool Children," *Journal of Advertising Research,* 21 (April), 53-56.

Bymers, Gwen J. (1983), "On Being Consumer Educators in the 1980's." *The Journal of Consumer Affairs,* 11 (Winter), 63-79.

Cagley, James W. (1974), "Children's Preferences of Selected Print Appeals," *Journal of Advertising,* 3, 34-39.

Calder, Bobby J., Thomas S. Robertson, & John R. Rossiter (1975), "Children's Consumer Information Processing," *Communication Research,* 2 (July), 307-316.

——, T.S. Robertson, & J.R. Rossiter (1976), "Cognitive Response to Advertising: The Research of Child to Adult Models," *Advances in Consumer Research,* 3, 536-37.

Capon, Noel, & Deanna Kuhn (1980), "A Developmental Study of Consumer Information-Processing Strategies," *Journal of Consumer Research,* 7 (December), 225-233.

Caron, Andre, & Scott Ward (1975), "Gift Decisions by Kids and Parents," *Journal of Advertising Research,* 15 (August), 15-20.

Cattin, P., & S.C. Jain (1979), "Content Analysis of Children's Commercials," in Neil Beckwith et al., eds., *Educators's Conference Proceedings,* Chicago: American Marketing Association, 639-644.

Chestnut, Robert W. (1979), "Television Advertising and Young Children: Piaget Reconsidered," *Current Issues and Research in Advertising,* Ann Arbor: The University of Michigan, 5-15.

Children's Advertising Review Unit (1977), *Children's Advertising Guidelines,* New York: National Advertising Division, Council of Better Business Bureaus, Inc.

Choate, Robert (1973), "The Selling of the Child," in William T. Kelley, ed., *New Consumerism: Selected Readings,* Columbus, Ohio: Grid, Inc., 547-562.

Clancy-Hepburn, Katherine, A.A. Hickey, & G. Nevill (1974), "Children's Behavior Responses to TV Food Advertisements," *Journal of Nutrition Education,* 93-96.

Clarke, T.K. (1984), "Situational Factors Affecting Preschoolers' Responses to Advertising," *Journal of the Academy of Marketing Science,* 12 (Fall), 25-40.

Cleaver, Joanne Y. (1985), "Brand Names Rattle Retail Shelves," *Advertising Age* (February 4), 28-29.

Cohen, Stanley E. (1977), "FTC Lifts Curtain on New Approach to Judging Kids' Ads," *Advertising Age* (October 24), 1.

—— (1978), "Children Need Help from Ad Council," *Advertising Age* (April 17),10.

Coleman, Richard P. (1983), "The Continuing Significance of Social Class to Marketing," *Journal of Consumer Research,* 10 (December), 265-280.

Collins, W. Andrew (1975), "The Developing Child as Viewer," *Journal of Communication,* 25 (Autumn), 35-44.

Colvin, Geoffrey (1983), "Children are Getting Hard to Find," *Fortune* (May 2), 125.

Cosmas, Stephen C., & Niki Yannopoulos (1981), "Advertising Directed to Children: A Look at the Mother's Point of View," *Journal of the Academy of Marketing Science,* 9 (Summer), 174-89.

Coulson, John S. (1966), "Buying Decisions Within the Family and the Consumer-Brand Relationship," in J. Newman, ed., *On Knowing the Consumer,* NY: John Wiley & Sons, Inc.

Culley, James D. (1974), "Perceptions of Children's Television Advertising: An Empirical Investigation of Beliefs and Attitudes of Consumer, Industry and Government Respondents," *Proceedings: American Academy of Advertising,* 144-153.

——, William Lazer, & Charles K. Atkin (1976), "The Experts Look at Children's Television," *Journal of Broadcasting,* 20 (Winter), 3-21.

Davis, Clara M. (1931), "Self-Selection of Diets," *The Trained Nurse and Hospital Review,* 86, 629-634.

Davis, Harry L. (1976), "Decision Making Within the Household," *Journal of Consumer Research,* 2 (March), 241-60.

DeLozier, M. Wayne (1976), *The Marketing Communications Process,* New York: McGraw-Hill Book Company.

Demuth, Christopher (1979), "Hands Off Children's TV," *Advertising Age* (May 7), 65.

Denzin, Norman K. (1977), *Childhood Socialization,* San Francisco, CA: Jossey Bass, Inc.

Dommermuth, William P. (1985), *Promotion: Analysis, Creativity and Strategy,* Boston: Kent Publishing Company.

Donohue, Thomas R. (1975), "Effects of Commercials on Black Children," *Journal of Advertising Research,* 15 (December), 41-47.

——— (1978), "Children's Understanding of the Intent and Purpose of Specific Adult and Child-Oriented Commercials," *Journal of Marketing,* 42 (October), 34-40.

———, L.L. Henke, & W.A. Donohue (1980), "Do Kids Know What TV Commercials Intend?" *Journal of Advertising Research,* 20 (October), 51-59.

———, T.P. Meyer, & L.L. Henke (1978), "Black and White Children: Perceptions of TV Commercials," *Journal of Marketing,* 42 (October), 34-40.

Doolittle, John, & Robert Pepper (1975), "Children's TV Ad Content: 1974," *Journal of Broadcasting,* 19 (Spring), 131-142.

Duke, Judith S. (1979), *Children's Books and Magazines: A Market Study,* White Plains, NY: Knowledge Industry Publications, Inc.

Elias, Mary (1974), "How to Win Friends and Influence Kids on Television," *Human Behavior* (April), 16-23.

Elkin, Frederick, & Gerald Handel (1972), *The Child and Society,* New York: Random House.

Enis, Ben M., Dale Spencer, & Don R. Webb (1980), "Television Advertising and Children: Regulative vs. Competitive Perspectives," *Journal of Advertising,* 9 (1), 19-26.

Faber, Ronald, & Scott Ward (1977), "Children's Understanding of Using Products Safely," *Journal of Marketing,* 41 (October), 39-46.

Faison, Edward W.J. (1977), "The Neglected Variety Drive: A Useful Concept in Consumer Behavior," *Journal of Consumer Research,* 4 (December), 172-175.

Feldman, Laurence P. (1980), *Consumer Protection: Problems and Prospects,* second edition, St. Paul: West Publishing Company.

Feldman, Shel, & Abraham Wolf (1974), "What's Wrong With Children's Commercials?" *Journal of Advertising Research,* 14 (February), 39-43.

———, Abraham Wolf, & Doris Warmouth (1977), "Parental Concern about Child-Directed Commercials," *Journal of Communication,* 27 (Winter), 125-137.

Ferguson, Clara P. (1975), *Preadolescent Children's Attitude Toward Television Commercials,* Austin: Bureau of Business Research, University of Texas.

Fornell, Claes (1981), "Increasing the Organizational Influence of Corporate Consumer Affairs Departments," *The Journal of Consumer Affairs,* 15 (Winter), 191- 213.

Fowles, Barbara R. (1976), "Moppets in the Market Place: Evaluating Children's Responses to Television Advertising," *Advances in Consumer Research,* 3, 520-22.

Franz, Julie (1986), "General Mills Pours Out 3rd Cereal," *Advertising Age* (March 17), 3, 104.

Frazer, Charles F., & L.N. Reid (1979), "Studying the Child/Television Advertising Relationship: A Symbolic Interactionist Approach," *Journal of Advertising,* 8, 13-19.

Freeman, Alan (1985), "Quebec Law Protecting Kids from Ads Rankles Companies," *Wall Street Journal* (December 19), 23.

Frideres, James S. (1973), "Advertising, Buying Patterns and Children," *Journal of Advertising Research,* 13 (February), 34-36.

Gallese, Liz Roman (1974), "Consumers' Advocate Better Children's TV, Get Some Concessions," *Wall Street Journal* (August 5), 1, 21.

Galst, Joann P., & M.A. White (1976), "The Unhealthy Persuader: The Reinforcing Value of Television and Children's Purchase-Influencing Attempts at the Supermarket," *Child Development,* 47 (December), 1089-96.

Gavian, R.W., & L.C. Nanassy (1955), "Economic Competence as a Goal of Elementary School Education," *Elementary School Journal,* 55 (January), 270-73.

Gene Reilly Group, Inc. (1973), *The Assumption by the Child of the Role of Consumer,* Darien, CN: The Gene Reilly Group, Inc.

Gesell, Arnold, & Frances L. Ilg (1954), *The Child from Five to Ten,* New York: Harper and Brothers.

Giges, Nancy (1985), "Cereal Boxes Won't Limit GF Promos," *Advertising Age* (March 11), 87.

Goldberg, Marvin E., & Gerald J. Gorn (1974), "Children's Reactions to Television Advertising: An Experimental Approach," *Journal of Consumer Research,* 1 (September), 69-75.

———— & G.J. Gorn (1978), "Some Unintended Consequences of TV Advertising to Children," *Journal of Consumer Research,* 5 (June), 22-29.

————, G.J. Gorn, & Wendy Gibson (1977), "The Effects of TV Messages for High and Low Nutritional Foods on Children's Snack and Breakfast Food Choices," *Advances in Consumer Research,* 5, 540-45.

————, G.J. Gorn, & Wendy Gibson (1978), "TV Messages for Snack and Breakfast Foods: Do They Influence Children's Preferences?" *Journal of Consumer Research,* 5 (September), 73-81.

Goldsen, Rose K. (1978), "Why Television Advertising is Deceptive and Unfair," *Et Cetera* (Winter), 354-75.

Gorn, Gerald J., & Renee Florsheim (1985), "The Effects of Commercials for Adult Products on Children," *Journal of Consumer Research,* 11 (March), 962-967.

———— & M.E. Goldberg (1977), "The Impact of Television Advertising on Children from Low Income Families," *Journal of Consumer Research,* 4 (September), 86-88.

———— & M.E. Goldberg (1980), "Children's Responses to Repetitive Television Commercials," *Journal of Consumer Research,* 6 (March), 421-24.

———— & M.E. Goldberg (1982), "Behavioral Evidence of the Effects of Televised Food Messages on Children," *Journal of Consumer Research,* 9 (September), 200-05.

Granbois, D. (1978), "Wives, Husbands, and Children: Three Studies of Consumer Roles," *Advances in Consumer Research,* 6 (October), 377-80.

Greenberg, Bradley S., & Bryan Reeves (1976), "Children and the Perceived Reality of Television," *Journal of Social Issues,* 32, 86-97.

Griffin, Emilie (1976), "What's Fair to Children? The Policy Need for New Research on Children's Perceptions of Advertising Content," *Journal of Advertising,* 5, 14-18.

Grocery Store Coloring Book (1955), Dallas, TX: Bozell and Jacobs Inc. and Skinner Macaroni Co.

Grossbart, Sanford L., & Lawrence A. Crosby (1984), "Understanding the Bases of Parental Concern and Reaction to Children's Food Advertising," *Journal of Marketing,* 48 (Summer), 79-92.

Grubb, Edward L., & Harrison L. Grathwohl (1967), "Consumer Self-Concept, Symbolism and Market Behavior: A Theoretical Approach," *Journal of Marketing,* 31 (October), 22-27.

Gruenberg, S.M., & H.S. Krech (1955), *Pennies in Their Pockets: Helping Children Manage Money,* Chicago: Science Research Associates.

―――― & H.S. Krech (1958), "Young Financier: The Child with an Allowance," *National Parent-Teacher,* 53 (October), 7-9.

Guber, Selina (1986), "Today's Youth's Have a Lot of Money to Spend," *Marketing News* (January 3), 59, 68.

Guest, L.P. (1942), "The Genesis of Brand Awareness," *Journal of Applied Psychology,* 26 (6), 800-808.

―――― (1955), "Brand Loyalty―Twelve Years Later," *Journal of Applied Psychology,* 39 (6), 405-408.

Gussow, Joan (1972), "Counternutritional Messages of TV Ads Aimed at Children," *Journal of Nutritional Education,* 4 (Spring), 48-52.

Haley, Elizabeth G., & N.J. Henrickson (1974), "Children's Preferences for Clothing and Hair Styles," *Home Economics Research Journal,* 2, 176-93.

Hallaq, John H. (1977), "Children's Reaction to Premiums: An Experimental Approach," in Barnett Greenberg and Danny Bellenger, eds., *Contemporary Marketing Thought,* Chicago: American Marketing Association, 65-67.

Harris, Lauren (1977), "The Effects of Relative Novelty on Children's Choice Behavior," *Journal of Experimental Child Psychology,* 2 (September), 297-305.

Harty, Sheila (1979), *Hucksters in the Classroom: A Review of Industry Propaganda in Schools,* Washington: Center for Study of Responsive Law.

Hawkins, Del I., & K.A. Coney (1974), "Peer Group Influences on Children's Product Preferences," *Journal of the Academy of Marketing Science,* 2 (Spring), 322-331.

Hendon, Donald W., A.F. McGann, & B.L. Hendon (1978), "Children's Age, Intelligence and Sex as Variables Mediating Reactions to TV Commercials: Repetition and Content Complexity Implications for Advertisers," *Journal of Advertising,* 3, 4-12.

Herrmann, Robert O. (1969), *The Consumer Behavior of Children and Teenagers: An Annotated Bibliography,* Chicago: American Marketing Association.

―――― (1982), "The Historical Development of the Content of Consumer Education: An Examination of Selected High School Texts, 1938-1978," *Journal of Consumer Affairs,* 16 (Winter), 195-223.

Heslop, Louise A., & A.B. Ryans (1980), "A Second Look at Children and the Advertising of Premiums," *Journal of Consumer Research,* 6 (March), 414-420.

Hess, Robert D., & Harriet Goldman (1962), "Parents' View of the Effect of Television on Their Children," *Child Development,* 33 (June), 411-426.

Higgins, Kevin T. (1985), "Research, Marketing Not Playthings for Toymakers," *Marketing News* (July 5), 1, 5.

Hise, Richard T. & James U. McNeal (1985), "Package Management," College Station: Texas A&M University, Marketing Department, A Working Paper.

Holbrook, Morris B., & Elizabeth C. Hirschman (1982), "The Experimental Aspects of Consumption: Consumer Fantasies, Feelings, and Fun," *Journal of Consumer Research,* 9 (September), 132-140.

Jacoby, Jacob, & D.B. Kyner (1973), "Brand Loyalty vs. Repeat Purchasing Behavior," *Journal of Marketing Research,* 10 (February), 1-9.

Jenkins, Gladys Gardner (1977), "Families, Mass Communications, and the Marketplace," *Childhood Education,* 54 (November-December), 67-70.

Jenkins, R.L. (1978), "The Influence of Children in Family Decision-Making: Parent's Perceptions," *Advances in Consumer Research,* 6, 413-18.

Jennings, Marianne M. (1984), "Kidvid 'Promercials' Raise Hackles of Parents, But Regulations Unlikely," *Marketing News* (February 17), 3.

Kassarjian, Harold H. (1977), "Content Analysis in Consumer Research," *Journal of Consumer Research,* 4 (June), 8-17.

Katz, Lilian G. (1973), "The Child: Consumer or Consumed?" *Childhood Education,* 49 (May), 394-97.

Kay, Herbert (1974), "Children's Responses to Advertising: Who's Really to Blame?" *Journal of Advertising,* 3, 26-30.

Keiser, Stephen K. (1975), "Awareness of Brands and Slogans," *Journal of Advertising Research,* 15 (August), 37-43.

Keyes, Ralph (1985), "Are Kids Too 'Old'?" *Family Weekly* (February 17), 4, 7.

Kotler, Philip (1973), "Atmospherics as a Marketing Tool," *Journal of Retailing,* 49 (Winter), 48-64.

Kourilsky, Marilyn (1977), "The Kinder-Economy: A Case Study of Kindergarten Pupils' Acquisition of Economic Concepts," *The Elementary School Journal,* 77 (January), 182-91.

——— & T. Murray (1981), "The Use of Economic Reasoning to Increase Satisfaction with Family Decision Making," *Journal of Consumer Research,* 8 (September), 183-188.

Kroger Food Foundation (1954), *A Study of "The Child" as a Consumer,* Cincinnati (mimeographed).

Kyner, David B., J. Jacoby, & R.W. Chestnut (1975), "Dissonance Resolution by Grade School Consumers," *Advances in Consumer Research,* 3, 134-137.

Langrehr, Frederick W., & J. Barry Mason (1977), "The Development and Implementation of the Concept of Consumer Education," *The Journal of Consumer Affairs,* 11 (Winter), 63-79.

——— (1979), "Consumer Education: Does It Change Students' Competencies and Attitudes?" *The Journal of Consumer Affairs,* 13 (Summer), 41-53.

Liebert, D.E., J.N. Sprafkin, R.M. Liebert, & E.A. Rubinstein (1977), "Effects of Television Commercial Disclaimers on the Product Expectations of Children," *Journal of Communication,* 27 (Winter), 118-124.

Liebert, R.M., J.M. Neale, & E.S. Davidson (1973), *The Early Window: Effects of Television on Children and Youth,* New York: Pergamon Press.

Lindquist, J.D. (1978), "Children's Attitudes Toward Advertising on Television and Radio and in Children's Magazines and Comic Books," *Advances in Consumer Research,* 6, 407-412.

Loughlin, Meagan, & R.J. Desmond (1981), "Social Interaction in Advertising Directed to Children," *Journal of Broadcasting,* 25 (Summer), 303-307.

Lourie, Reginald S., Emma M. Layman, & Francess K. Millican (1963), "Why Children Eat Things That Are Not Food," *Children,* 10 (August), 143-146.

Macklin, M. Carole (1983), "Do Children Understand TV Ads?" *Journal of Advertising Research,* 23 (February-March), 63-70.

_____ (1985), "Do Young Children Understand the Selling Intent of Commercials?" *Journal of Consumer Affairs,* 19 (Winter), 293-304.

Marich, Bob (1985), "Mattel's Barbie Grows Up," *Advertising Age* (March 18), 74.

Marketing News (1977), "The Older They Get, the Less They Believe TV Ads, Says Study of Kids" (April 8), 6.

_____ (1983), "Projective Research Techniques Extract Valuable Market Data From Children" (January 21), 19.

Marshall, Helen R. (1963), "Differences in Parent and Child Reports of the Child's Experiences in the Use of Money," *Journal of Educational Psychology,* 54 (March), 132-137.

_____ (1964), "The Relation of Giving Children an Allowance to Children's Money Knowledge and Responsibility and to Other Practices of Parents," *Journal of Genetic Psychology,* 104 (March), 35-51.

_____ & L. Magruder (1960), "Relations Between Parent Money Education Practices and Children's Knowledge and Use of Money," *Child Development,* 31 (June), 253-283.

Mazis, Michael B. (1979), "Can and Should the FTC Restrict Advertising to Children Workshop," *Advances in Consumer Research,* 6, 3-6.

McNeal, James U. (1964), *Children as Consumers,* Austin: University of Texas Bureau of Business Research.

_____ (1965), "An Exploratory Study of the Consumer Behavior of Children," in James U. McNeal, ed., *Dimensions of Consumer Behavior,* New York: Appleton-Century-Crofts.

_____ (1969), "The Child Consumer: A New Market," *Journal of Retailing,* 45 (Summer), 15-22.

_____ (1976), "Packaging for the Young Consumer: A Descriptive Study," *Akron Business and Economics Review,* 7 (Winter), 5-11.

_____ (1978), "Consumer Education as a Competitive Strategy," *Business Horizons,* 21 (February), 50-56.

_____ (1979), "Children as Consumers: A Review," *Journal of the Academy of Marketing Science,* 7 (Fall), 346-59.

_____ (1981), *Consumer Education in Texas High Schools 1970--1981,* College Station: Texas A&M University, Department of Marketing.

_____ (1982), *Consumer Behavior: An Integrative Approach,* Boston: Little, Brown & Company.

_____ (1984), "The Influence of Retailers on the Consumer Behavior of Children," College Station: Texas A&M University, Department of Marketing, A Working Paper.

_____ & S.W. McDaniel, eds. (1979), *Consumer Behavior: Classical and Contemporary Dimensions,* Boston: Little, Brown & Co.

_____ & S.W. McDaniel (1981), "Children's Perceptions of Retail Stores: An Exploratory Study," *Akron Business and Economics Review,* 12 (Fall), 39-42.

_____ , S.W. McDaniel, & Denise Smart (1983), "The Brand Repertoire: Its Content and Organization," in Patrick Murphy et al., eds., *1983 AMA Educators Conference Proceedings,* Chicago: American Marketing Association, 92-96.

———, & Daryle McKee (1985), "The Case of the Antishopper," in Robert Lusch et al., *1985 AMA Educators Conference Proceedings,* Chicago: American Marketing Association, 65-68.

Mehrotra, Sunil, & Sandra Torges (1977), "Determinants of Children's Influence on Mothers' Buying Behavior," *Advances in Consumer Research,* 4, 56-63.

Meyer, T.P., T.R. Donohue, & L.L. Henke (1978), "How Black Kids See TV Commercials," *Journal of Advertising Research,* 18 (October), 51-58.

Meyers, Janet (1985), "Bowlers Try to Lure Kids into Alley," *Advertising Age* (March 11), 76.

Michigan Consumer Education Center (1982), *Consumer and Economic Education: Recommendations for Policy Makers,* Ypsilanti, MI: Eastern Michigan University.

Miller, N., & T.D. Horn (1955), "Children's Concepts Regarding Debt," *Elementary School Journal,* 56 (March), 406-412.

Monroe, Will S. (1899), "The Money Sense of Children," *Pedagogical Seminary and Journal of Genetic Psychology,* 6, 152-158.

Moore, Roy L., & G.P. Moschis (1981), "The Role of Family Communication in Consumer Learning," *Journal of Communication,* 31 (Fall), 42-51.

Moschis, George P. (1978A), *Acquisition of the Consumer Role by Adolescents,* Atlanta: Georgia State University Publishing Services Division.

——— (1978B), "Consumer Socialization: A Theoretical and Empirical Analysis," *Journal of Marketing Research* (November), 599-609.

——— (1984), "Anticipatory Consumer Socialization," *Journal of the Academy of Marketing Science,* 12 (Fall), 109-123.

——— (1985), "The Role of Family Communication in Consumer Socialization of Children and Adolescents," *Journal of Consumer Research,* 11 (March), 898-913.

———, J.T. Lawton, & R.W. Stampfl (1980), "Preschool Children's Consumer Learning," *Home Economics Research Journal,* 9 (September), 64-71.

——— & R.L. Moore (1979), "Decision Making Among the Young: A Socialization Perspective," *Journal of Consumer Research,* 6 (September) 101-112.

Munn, Mark (1968), "The Effect on Parental Buying Habits of Children Exposed to Children's Television Programs," *Journal of Broadcasting,* 2 (Summer), 253-258.

Murray, Henry A. (1938), *Explorations in Personality,* New York: Oxford University Press.

Neelankavil, James P., John V. O'Brien, & Richard Tashjian (1985), "Techniques to Obtain Market-Related Information from Very Young Children," *Journal of Advertising Research,* 25 (June/July), 41-47.

Nelson, J.E. (1978), "Children as Information Sources in the Family Decision to Eat Out," *Advances in Consumer Research,* 6, 419-23.

Nord, Walter R., & J. Paul Peter (1980), "A Behavior Modification Perspective on Marketing," *Journal of Marketing,* 44 (Spring), 36-47.

Norris, Eileen (1984), "Marketers Pack Big Effort into Little Prize," *Advertising Age* (May 10), 26, 37, 38.

Packard, Vance (1959), *The Hidden Persuaders,* New York: McKay.

Paine, Lynda Sharp (1984), "Children as Consumers: An Ethical Evaluation of Children's Television Advertising," *Business and Professional Ethics Journal,* 2 (Spring/Summer), 119-145.

Piaget, Jean (1952), *The Origins of Intelligence in Children,* New York: International University Press.

———— & B. Inhelder (1958), *The Growth of Logical Thinking from Childhood to Adolescence,* A. Parsons & S. Seagrin, translators, New York: Basic Books.

Popper, Edward T. (1979), "Mothers Mediation of Children's Purchase Requests," in Neal Beckwith et al., eds., *Educators Conference and Proceedings,* Chicago: American Marketing Association, 645-648.

President's Committee on Consumer Interests (1970), *Suggested Guidelines for Consumer Education, Grades K-12,* Washington: U.S. Government Printing Office.

Pride, William M., & O.C. Ferrell (1985), *Marketing: Basic Concepts and Decisions,* fourth edition, Boston: Houghton Mifflin Company.

Reading Fun (1981), Racine, WI: Western Publishing Company, Inc.

Reid, Leonard N. (1979), "The Impact of Family Group Interaction on Children's Understanding of Television Advertising," *Journal of Advertising,* 8, 13-19.

———— (1979), "Viewing Rules as Mediating Factors of Children's Responses to Commercials," *Journal of Broadcasting,* 23 (Winter), 15-25.

———— & Charles F. Frazer (1979), "Studying the Child/Television Advertising Interaction: A Symbolic interactionist Approach," *Journal of Advertising,* 8, 13-19.

Reiling, Lynn (1985), "Kids and Collegians Targeted by New Networks," *Advertising Age* (April 12), 14.

Resnik, Alan J., & B.L. Stern (1977), "Children's Television Advertising and Brand Choice: A Laboratory Experiment," *Journal of Advertising,* 6, 11-17.

————, Bruce L. Stern, & Barbara Alberty (1979), "Integrating Results from Children's Television Advertising Research," *Journal of Advertising,* 8, 3-12, 48.

Richardson, Lee (1977), *Consumer Education: A Position on the State of the Art,* Washington: Office of Consumers' Education.

Riecken, Glen, & A.C. Samli (1981), "Measuring Children's Attitudes Toward Television Commercials: Extension & Replication," *Journal of Consumer Research,* 8 (June), 57-61.

Riesman, David, Nathan Glazer & Reuel Denney (1953), *The Lonely Crowd,* New York: Doubleday and Company.

Robertson, Thomas S. (1972), "The Impact of Television Advertising on Children," *Wharton Quarterly* (Fall), 38-41.

———— (1979), "Parental Mediation of Television Advertising Effects," *Journal of Communication,* 29 (Winter), 12-25.

———— & Shel Feldman (1976), "Children as Consumers: The Need for Multitheoretical Perspectives," *Advances in Consumer Research,* 3, 308-312.

———— & J.R. Rossiter (1974), "Children and Commercial Persuasion: An Attribution Theory Analysis," *Journal of Consumer Research,* 1 (June), 13-20.

———— & J.R. Rossiter (1976). "Short-Run Advertising Effects on Children: A Field Study," *Journal of Marketing Research,* 13 (February), 68-70.

———— & J.R. Rossiter (1977), "Children's Responsiveness to Commercials," *Journal of Communication,* 21 (Winter), 101-06.

————, J.R. Rossiter, & T.C. Gleason (1977), "Children's Conceptions of Medicine: The Role of Advertising," *Advances in Consumer Research,* 5, 515-517.

———— J.R. Rossiter, & T.C. Gleason (1979A). "Children's Receptivity to Proprietary Medicine Advertising," *Journal of Consumer Research,* 6 (December), 247-255.

————, J.R. Rossiter, & T.C. Gleason (1979B), *Televised Medicine Advertising and Children,* New York: Praeger.

————, Joan Zielinski, & Scott Ward (1984), *Consumer Behavior,* Glenview, IL: Scott, Foresman and Company.

Roedder, Deborah L. (1981), "Age Differences in Children's Responses to Television Advertising: An Information-Processing Approach," *Journal of Consumer Research,* 8 (September), 144-153.

————, Brian Sternthal, & Bobby J. Calder (1983), "Attitude-Behavior Consistency in Children's Responses to Television Advertising," *Journal of Marketing Research,* 20 (November), 337-349.

Rosen, Larry (1976), "Kids Aren't Easily Fooled by Ads," *Advertising Age* (July 12), 6.

Rossiter, John R. (1976), "Visual and Verbal Memory in Children's Product Information Utilization," *Advertising in Consumer Research,* 3, 523-527.

———— (1977), "Reliability of a Short Test Measuring Children's Attitudes Toward TV Commercials," *Journal of Consumer Research,* 3 (March), 179-184.

———— (1978), "Children's Consumer Research: A Call for Rigor," *Advances in Consumer Research,* 6, 424-426.

———— (1979), "Does TV Advertising Affect Children?" *Journal of Advertising Research,* 19 (February), 49-53.

———— (1980), "Source Effects of Self-Concept Appeals in Children's Television Advertising," in Richard P. Adler et al., *The Effects of Television Advertising on Children,* Lexington, MA: Lexington Books, 61-64.

———— & T.S. Robertson (1974), "Children's TV Commercials: Testing the Defenses," *Journal of Communication,* 24 (Winter), 137-145.

———— & T.S. Robertson (1975), "Children's Television Viewing: An Examination of Parent-Child Consensus," *Sociometry,* 39 (September), 309-326.

Rotbart, Dean (1981), "Allowances Stay Flat, Candy Rises—and Kids Lose Their Innocence," *The Wall Street Journal* (March 2), 1, 13.

Rotfield, Herbert J., & Leonard N. Reid (1979), "Potential Secondary Effects of Regulating Children's Television Advertising," *Journal of Advertising,* 8, 9-14.

Rothschild, Michael L., & William C. Gaidis (1981), "Behavioral Learning Theory: Its Relevance to Marketing and Promotions," *Journal of Marketing,* 45 (Spring), 70-78.

Royer, Gayle, & Nancy Nolf (1980), *Education of the Consumer: A Review of Historical Developments,* Washington: Consumer Education Resource Network.

Rubin, Ronald S. (1974), "The Effects of Cognitive Development on Children's Responses to Television Advertising," *Journal of Business Research,* 2 (October), 409-19.

Ryans, A.B. & T. Deutscher (1975), "Children and Commercial Persuasion: Some Comments," *Journal of Consumer Research,* 2 (December), 237-39.

Scherf, Gerhard W.H. (1974), "Consumer Education as a Means of Alleviating Dissatisfaction," *The Journal of Consumer Affairs,* 8 (Summer), 61-75.

Schiele, George W. (1974), "How to Reach the Young Consumer," *Harvard Business Review,* 52 (March-April), 77-86.

Schleier, Curt (1985), "Reilly Group's Findings Not Child's Play," *Advertising Age* (November 14), 26-29.

Schneider, Kenneth C. (1977), "Prevention of Accidental Poisoning Through Package and Label Design," *Journal of Consumer Research,* 4 (September), 67-74.

Schoenfeld, David (1968), *Consumer Education: Using the Full Team,* Albany, NY: State Education Department.

Seitz, Wesley (1972), "Consumer Education as the Means to Attain Efficient Market Performance," *Journal of Consumer Affairs,* 6 (Winter), 198-208.

Sheikh, Anees A., & L.M. Moleski (1977), "Conflict in the Family Over Commercials," *Journal of Communication,* 27 (Winter), 152-57.

Sheikh, Anees A., V.K. Prasad, & T.R. Rao (1974), "Children's TV Commercials: A Review of Research," *Journal of Communication,* 24 (Autumn), 126-36.

Shimp, Terence A., Robert F. Dyer, & S.F. Divita (1976), "An Experimental Test of the Harmful Effects of Premium-Oriented Commercials on Children," *Journal of Consumer Research,* 3 (June), 1-11.

Sloan, Pat (1982), "Kids' Clothes-Buying Role a Marketer's Dilemma," *Advertising Age* (April 5), 24.

Soldow, Gary F. (1983), "The Ability of Children to Understand the Product Package: A Study of Limitations Imposed by Cognitive Development Stage," *Journal of Public Policy and Marketing,* 4, 55-68.

Spillman, Susan (1984), "Nickelodeon Takes Pitch Direct to Kids," *Advertising Age* (May 21), 3, 91.

Stampfl, Ronald W., G. Moschis, & J.T. Lawton (1978), "Consumer Education and the Preschool Child," *Journal of Consumer Affairs,* 12 (Summer), 12-29.

Stephens, Lowndes F., & Roy L. Moore (1975), "Price Accuracy as a Consumer Skill," *Journal of Advertising Research,* 15 (August), 27-34.

Stephens, Nancy, & Mary Ann Stutts (1982), "Preschoolers' Ability to Distinguish Between Television Programming and Commercials," *Journal of Advertising,* 11, 16-26.

Stone, Gregory P. (1958), "City Shoppers and Urban Identification," *The American Journal of Sociology,* 60 (July), 36-45.

Strauss, Anselm L. (1952), "The Development and Transformation of Monetary Meanings in the Child," *American Sociological Review,* 17 (June), 275-286.

Stupening, Edward (1982), "Detrimental Effects of Television Advertising on Consumer Socialization," *Journal of Business Research,* 10 (March), 75-84.

Stutts, Mary Ann, D. Vance, & S. Hudleson (1981), "Program-Commercial Separators in Children's Television: Do They Help a Child Tell the Difference Between 'Bugs Bunny' and the 'Quik Rabbit'?," *Journal of Advertising,* 10, 16-25.

Szybillo, George J., & A. Sosanie (1976), "Family Decision Making: Husband, Wife & Children," *Advances in Consumer Research,* 4, 46-49.

————, A.K. Sosanie, & A. Tenebein (1977), "Should Children Be Seen but Not Heard?" *Journal of Advertising Research,* 17 (December), 7-13.

Tai, Pauline (1968), "Who Is That Babe in the New Fur Coat? A 3-Year-Old Perhaps," *The Wall Street Journal* (September 23), 1.

Tucker, W.T. (1964), *The Social Context of Economic Behavior,* New York: Holt, Rinehart and Winston Inc.

Turk, Peter (1979), "Children's Television Advertising: An Ethical Morass for Business and Government," *Journal of Advertising,* 8, 4-8.

Turner, Josephine, & Jeanette Brandt (1978), "Development and Validation of a Simulated Market to Test Children for Selected Consumer Skills," *Journal Consumer Affairs,* 12 (Winter), 266-276.

Veblen, Thorstein (1899), *The Theory of the Leisure Class,* New York: The Macmillan Company.

Vogl, A.J. (1964), "The Changing Face of the Children's Market," *Sales Management,* 93 (December 18), 35-38.

Wackman, Daniel, & Scott Ward (1976), "The Development of Consumer Information Skills: Contributions from Cognitive Development Theory," *Advances in Consumer Research,* 3, 531-35.

———— & Ellen Wartella (1977), "A Review of Cognitive Development Theory and Research and the Implication for Research on Children's Responses to Television," *Communication Research,* 4 (April), 203-224.

————, E. Wartella, & S. Ward (1977), "Learning to be Consumers: The Role of the Family," *Journal of Communication,* 27 (Winter), 138-151.

Ward, Scott (1971), *Effects of Television Advertising on Children and Adolescents: An Overview,* Cambridge: Marketing Science Institute.

———— (1972A), "Advertising and Youth: Two Studies," *Sloan Management Review,* 14 (Fall), 63-82.

———— (1972B), "Children's Reactions to Commercials," *Journal of Advertising Research,* 12 (April), 37-45.

———— (1972C), "Kids' TV—Marketers on Hot Seat," *Harvard Business Review,* 50 (July-August), 16-37.

———— (1974), "Consumer Socialization," *Journal of Consumer Research,* 1 (September), 1-13.

———— (1978A), "Compromise in Commercials for Children," *Harvard Business Review,* 56 (November-December), 128-136.

———— (1978B), "Researchers Look at the 'Kid-Vid' Rule: Overview of Session," *Advances in Consumer Research,* 6 (October), 7-11.

———— (1978C), "Research on Marketing and Children: Upside or Downside on the Product Life Cycle?" *Advances in Consumer Research,* 5 (October), 427-30.

———— & J. Ettema (1974), "A Cognitive Developmental Study of Children's Attention to Television Commercials," *Communication Research,* 1 (January), 69-88.

————, E.T. Popper, & D.B. Wackman (1977), *Parents Under Pressure: Mothers' Responses to Children's Purchase Requests,* Cambridge: Marketing Science Institute.

———— & D.B. Wackman (1972), "Children's Purchase Influence Attempts and Parental Yielding," *Journal of Marketing Research,* 9 (August), 316-19.

Wartella, E., D.B. Wackman, & S. Ward (1978), "Children's Consumer Information Processing: Representation of Information from Television Advertisements," *Advances in Consumer Research,* 5, 535-39.

————, D.B. Wackman, & E. Wartella (1975), *Children Learning to Buy: The Development of Consumer Information Processing Skills,* Cambridge: Marketing Science Institute.

————, D. Wackman, & E. Wartella (1977A), *How Children Learn to Buy,* Beverly Hills, CA: Sage Publications.

————, D. Wackman, & E. Wartella (1977B), "The Development of Consumer Information-Processing Skills: Integrating Cognitive Development and Family Interaction Theories," *Advances in Consumer Research,* 4, 166-71.

Weil, Arthur W. (1981), "Preteen Beauty-Aid Sales Near $10 Million," *Product Marketing and Cosmetic and Fragrance Retailing,* 10 (May), 27-28.

Wells, William D. (1965), "Communicating with Children," *Journal of Advertising Research,* 5 (June), 2-14.

—— (1966), "Children as Consumers," in J. Newman (ed.), *On Knowing the Consumer,* New York: John Wiley and Sons, Inc., 138-145.

—— & L.A. Lo Sciuto (1966), "Direct Observation of Purchasing Behavior," *Journal of Marketing Research,* 3 (August), 227-235.

Winick, Charles, L.G. Williamson, S.F. Chuzmir, & M.P. Winick (1973), *Children's Television Commercials: A Content Analysis,* New York: Praeger.

Winn, Marie (1983), *Children Without Childhood,* New York: Pantheon Books.

Index

About the Author

James U. McNeal is Professor of Marketing at Texas A&M University where he specializes in teaching consumer behavior at the graduate and undergraduate levels. Professor McNeal's primary research field is the consumer behavior of children. He is author of *Consumer Behavior: An Integrative Approach,* and co-editor of *Consumer Behavior: Classical and Contemporary Dimensions.* His research has been reported in such major journals as the *Journal of Marketing Research, Journal of Retailing* and the *Journal of Consumer Affairs.* In addition to consulting with a variety of businesses, he has been a consultant in the area of consumer education to both state and national governments.

About the Author

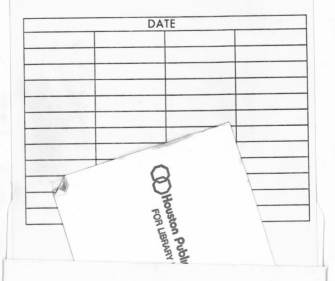